The Prevention of Eating Disorders

STUDIES IN EATING DISORDERS
An International Series

Series Editor
Walter Vandereycken (University of Leuven, Belgium)

Advisers
Janet Treasure (Institute of Psychiatry, London)
Glenn Waller (University of Southampton, UK)

The aim of this Series is to present 'state of the art' information on important issues related to the understanding, treatment and prevention of eating disorders. To this end, the series will contain high-level monographs that provide a comprehensive overview of up-to-date scientific knowledge as well as an in-depth critical analysis of the topic concerned.

The selection of authors and topics reflects both the international scope of the Series and the multidisciplinary interest in eating disorders. The Series is aimed at a wide professional readership concerned with this area.

Treating Eating Disorders: Ethical, Legal and Personal Issues
Walter Vandereycken and Pierre J. V. Beumont (Eds)

The Prevention of Eating Disorders
Walter Vandereycken and Greta Noordenbos (Eds)

The Prevention of Eating Disorders

Edited by
Walter Vandereycken and Greta Noordenbos

NEW YORK UNIVERSITY PRESS
Washington Square, New York

Published by Athlone Press, U.K., in 1998

First published in the U.S.A. in 1998 by
NEW YORK UNIVERSITY PRESS
Washington Square
New York, N.Y. 10003

Library of Congress Cataloguing-in-Publication Data
The prevention of eating disorders / edited by Walter Vandereycken and
   Greta Noordenbos.
       p.   cm.
Includes index.
      ISBN 0–8147–8798–3 (cloth). — ISBN 0–8147–8799–1 (pbk.)
      1. Eating disorders—Prevention.   I. Vandereycken, Walter,
   1949–   .   II. Noordenbos, Greta.
   RC552.E18P74   1998
   616.85′2605—dc21   98–4537
                                                                  CIP

Printed in Great Britain

Contents

Preface

To be effective, primary prevention must reduce risk, either by removing the causes or by rendering invulnerable the individual at risk. In the first chapter, Striegel-Moore and Steiner-Adair discuss the feminist perspective on primary prevention. They criticize the 'specific disease' model for eating disorders problems because these problems are caused, at least in part, by social and cultural factors. According to these authors, the conceptualization of primary prevention as opposite to treatment is conceptually flawed. Rather, they argue that prevention and treatment interventions lie on one continuum of interventions and that theory and research in both areas can benefit from mutual influence.

The chapter by Levine and Smolak explores the literature connecting mass media to the developmental psychology of eating disorders and to classroom-based primary prevention efforts. This review suggests a great need for further etiological research based on an integration of social comparison theory, developmental social learning theory, and vulnerability-stressor models of disordered eating. There is also a need for primary prevention research based on the multidimensional, community-oriented theories which have emerged from fairly successful efforts to equip young adolescents with the skills to resist initiation of cigarette smoking. The authors also argue that people committed to primary prevention should learn how to use mass media for health promotion, political activism, and development of protective factors such as 'media literacy skills'.

Shisslak and colleagues describe a ten-year, four phase, multisite, prospective study of eating disorder risk and protective factors in 4th-12th grade girls in the USA. In phase 1 of the study (which has been completed), an instrument to identify eating disorder risk and protective factors was developed and evaluated. In phase 2 (which began in the Fall of 1996), this instrument is being used in conjunction with individual interviews to evaluate girls yearly for four years to determine how the risk and protective factors relate to the development of problematic eating and weight control behaviors, as well as the occurrence of eating disorder cases. Phase 3 will involve the development and evaluation of school-based interventions to prevent eating disorders and precursors to these disorders, based on the results obtained in phase 2. Phase 4 will focus on the dissemination of the results of these school-based interventions.

Too often, preventive work is highly praised in political speeches, but not carried out in practical actions. For reduced economical resources the 'easy' way out is to focus on treatment and not to wait for the 'silent' and long-term effects of prevention. By influencing the political system, this situation can be changed. The chapter by Gresko and Rosenvinge demonstrates the effects of such influence by showing how the prevention of eating disorders is converted into nationwide practical actions within the Norwegian public school system.

The chapter by Stewart describes the experience of designing and carrying out an eating disorder prevention program with young adolescent school girls in England. First of all the challenges of designing prevention programs are discussed followed by a brief review of previous school-based prevention programs. After a discussion of the theoretical basis of this program, the content of the six-session program is described in detail. Practical aspects of carrying out the program, including the difficulties encountered, are reported on. The methodology of a research evaluation of the program is described and finally there is a discussion of the implications for further work in this area.

Smolak, Levine and Schermer present an elementary school prevention program in Ohio (USA). First, the authors discuss the risk factors and protective factors which might be addressed in a school prevention program. Next, they review research data on behavior, attitudes, and knowledge concerning body image, weight and shape among elementary school children. Finally, they describe the content and detailed evaluation of their prevention program aimed at fourth-grade children.

In contrast to a predetermined curriculum, the participatory approach to prevention relies on interaction with the participants to determine the course of intervention. Piran describes the professional path that has led her to choose this approach in the prevention of eating disorders in schools. As an illustration of this approach she presents a participatory program which was implemented in a high risk setting: a Canadian ballet school.

Moving from primary to secondary prevention, Schoemaker discusses the effectiveness and efficiency of early recognition of eating disorders with special reference to screening. Using a theoretical framework for the evaluation of the principles of screening for diseases, the relevant knowledge with regard to eating disorders is presented in a systematic manner. The evaluation of screening for eating disorders proves to be problematic. Therefore, this overview compels to modesty. As long as it is not known whether there exists a suitable screening system for eating disorder, and whether there is a suitable treatment for those screened, there seems to be no valid reason to start large-scale screening programs. Much more research is necessary, which allows for a valid evaluation of the benefits as well as the costs. Some recommendations for future research are presented.

The final chapter by Noordenbos is about improving the general practitioners' contribution to secondary prevention (early identification and intervention) of eating disorders. First the most important problems in the interaction between anorectic and bulimic patients and their physicians are described: patient delay, doctor delay, inadequate communication between patient and physician, gender differences, negative attitude towards eating-disordered patients, and inadequate treatment by general practitioners. In the second part of this chapter several suggestions are given for general practitioners to improve their possibilities for secondary prevention of eating disorders. An educational program for general practitioners in the Netherlands has shown that better information can lead to better prevention. We hope that this book will contribute to that goal.

Contributors

Susan Bryson is a Programmer/Statistician in the Department of Psychiatry and Behavioral Sciences at Stanford University School of Medicine, USA.

Marjorie Crago, Ph.D., is a Research Specialist in the Department of Family and Community Medicine, Arizona Prevention Center at the University of Arizona College of Medicine, USA.

Linda S. Estes, Ph.D., is a staff clinical psychologist at David Grant Medical Center, Travis Air Force Base, California, USA.

Norma Gray, Ph.D., is a Clinical Psychologist and Assistant Professor in the Department of Family and Community Medicine, Arizona Prevention Center at the University of Arizona College of Medicine, USA.

Runi Børresen Gresko, B.A., was the manager of the Norwegian prevention programme "Eating Disorders 1993–1995" and is currently affiliated with the National Board of Health and with the Norwegian Ministry of Health and Social Affairs, Drammen, Norway.

Joel D. Killen, Ph.D., is an Associate Professor (Research) in the Department of Medicine, Stanford University School of Medicine, USA.

Michael P. Levine, Ph.D., is Professor at the Department of Psychology, Kenyon College, Gambier (Ohio), USA

Kathy McKnight, M.A., is a graduate student majoring in Clinical Psychology and minoring in Research Methodology at the University of Arizona, USA.

Greta Noordenbos, Ph.D., is Associate Professor at the Department of Women's Studies, Leiden University, and at the Department of Women and Health, University of Maastricht, The Netherlands.

Ori Parnaby is a Research Technician in the Department of Family and Community Medicine, Arizona Prevention Center at the University of Arizona College of Medicine, USA.

Niva Piran, Ph.D., is Professor at the Faculty of Education, University of Toronto, Canada. She is also a practising feminist clinical psychologist and a consultant to the National Ballet School and other schools.

Jan H. Rosenvinge, Ph.D., is Associate Professor at the Department of Psychology, University of Tromsø, and Consultant Psychologist at the Asgard University Psychiatric Hospital, Tromsø, Norway.

Florence Schermer is Consulting Dietitian to Kenyon College, Gambier (Ohio), USA

Casper Schoemaker, Ph.D., is a Research Associate at the Trimbos Institute, Netherlands Institute of Mental Health and Addiction, Utrecht, The Netherlands.

Tamara Sharpe is a researcher in the Department of Psychiatry and Behavioral Sciences at Stanford University School of Medicine, USA.

Catherine M. Shisslak, Ph.D., is an Associate Professor of Family and Community Medicine, Arizona Prevention Center at the University of Arizona College of Medicine, USA.

Linda Smolak, Ph.D., is Professor at the Department of Psychology, Kenyon College, Gambier (Ohio), USA

Catherine Steiner-Adair, Ph.D., is Director of Education and Outreach, Harvard Center for Eating Disorders, Boston (Massachusetts), USA.

Anne Stewart, M.D., is a Consultant child and adolescent psychiatrist at the Highfield Family and Adolescent Unit, Warneford Hospital, Oxford, UK.

Ruth H. Striegel-Moore, Ph.D., is Professor and Chair of Psychology, Wesleyan University, Middletown (Connecticut), USA.

C. Barr Taylor, M.D., is a Professor of Psychiatry in the Department of Psychiatry and Behavioral Sciences at Stanford University School of Medicine, USA.

Walter Vandereycken, M.D., Ph.D., is Professor of Psychiatry at the University of Leuven, Belgium

Primary prevention of eating disorders: Further considerations from a feminist perspective

Ruth H. Striegel-Moore and Catherine Steiner-Adair

In a report on the state of the art of prevention research, commissioned by the Congress of the United States of America, the Committee on Prevention of Mental Disorders of the Institute of Medicine prefaced its recommendations as follows: 'There could be no wiser investment in our country then a commitment to foster the prevention of mental disorders and the promotion of mental health through rigorous research with the highest of methodological standards' (Mrazek and Haggerty, 1994, p. xvii). More recently, Munoz, Mrazek and Haggerty (1996) wrote: 'Prevention is intended to avert suffering. The disruption in people's lives, the considerable emotional pain involved, and the sometimes irreparable impact on the lives of the families and communities of those afflicted by mental disorders make it imperative for us as a society to devote substantial resources to prevention' (p. 1121). In light of these quotes it may come as a surprise to hear that few topics in the field of eating disorders engender as much emotional debate as the topic of prevention. There is profound disagreement about the importance of prevention in the landscape of interventions in our field.

Proponents of prevention argue that treatment, no matter how successful, does not reduce the incidence of a disorder and that it makes good sense morally and financially to engage in efforts to reduce the incidence. Proponents of prevention give urgency to their advocacy by pointing to the significance of these disorders from a public health standpoint. Eating disorders and disordered eating have become more prevalent during the past few decades, and these disorders are associated with significant physical, psychological, and social impairment. Proponents of prevention recognize research of treatment outcome studies which has shown that early intervention is the strongest predictive factor of recovery, as well as the most economical curb on potentially very costly treatment. Proponents further point to a rich theoretical literature that provides ample guidance for both the content and the strategies for prevention efforts.

Opponents of prevention argue that prevention is not cost-effective because the prevalence of eating disorders is low. Indeed some go so far as to say that prevention efforts are irresponsible because they are costly and to suggest that the money spent on prevention would be better spent on treatment. Moreover, opponents justify their stance by pointing out that the etiology of eating disorders is either insufficiently known, too complex to isolate effectively risk factors amenable to elimination or modification, or involves risk factors that fundamentally are not amenable to change. Lastly, and perhaps most damningly, opponents point out that, to date, prevention efforts have produced very disappointing results. Just how problematic it is that prevention studies have produced negative findings is illustrated in this quote: 'Prevention proponents will lose the battle for funding without good data which is capable of documenting the effectiveness and social utility of prevention programs' (Heller et al., 1980, p. 288).

Historically, prevention efforts in eating disorders have been advocated most vocally by self-help organizations. There are now self-help groups for eating disorders in many countries, and we suspect that wherever those self-help groups are, the call for prevention is being heard. In many cases, these are grass-roots groups formed and supported by individuals who themselves have suffered from an eating disorder, or who have a close relative or friend with an eating disorder. To resist efforts to develop prevention programs means to enter an adversarial relationship with the very population we serve and thus creates enormous tension. In the USA, researchers in eating disorders differ from their colleagues focusing on other serious mental disorders in that we have not yet established a coherent, close working relationship with 'consumer groups.' This is to the detriment of both the consumers and the professionals, because self-help groups are often quite effective at teaching the professionals about the nature and course of the illness and advocating for more compassionate and effective treatment. Moreover, self-help groups are often quite successful at obtaining the financial support of private foundations and, in some cases, have exerted considerable political influence in the absence of appreciable input from scientific advisory boards.

Opposition to prevention is being expressed primarily by researchers who work from a traditional, medical 'hard' science model. These opponents, in turn, are also effective at marshaling support for their view point. They have scientific data to support their view: based on research so far, prevention programs appear to be ineffective at best. Researchers also control the review process of governmental funding bodies and thus can stop efforts to generate the research needed to prove that there is cause to support developing prevention programs. The fact that there is considerable support for prevention among the lay public, support that may translate into funding of programs of undetermined scientific validity, combined with the fact that many in the research community oppose prevention efforts, reinforces the unfortunate view of prevention as 'unprofessional' or 'unscientific.'

In this chapter, we ask what the feminist perspective can contribute to this debate (for important feminist contributions, see: Graber and Brooks-Gunn, 1996; Killen, 1996; Levine, 1994; Paxton, 1996; Piran, 1996; Shisslak, Crago, Neal and Swain, 1987; 1994; Shisslak, Crago, Estes and Gray, 1996; Steiner-Adair and Purcell, 1996; Striegel-Moore, 1992). In our opinion research of eating disorders has reached a critical stage; in many ways it is at an impasse and we need a new paradigm. We wish to suggest that underlying these arguments for and against prevention lie a number of artificial dichotomies and conceptual incongruities that plague our scholarship not only in the area of primary prevention, but also in research of the etiology and treatment of eating disorders.

After a brief review of key terms used in this chapter, we will propose three ways in which the field can move forward constructively on the question of whether prevention should be an important goal. Specifically, we hope to illustrate that there are definite limitations inherent in adopting a 'specific disease' model for problems that are caused, at least in part, by social and cultural factors. To be effective, primary prevention must reduce risk, either by removing the causes or by rendering invulnerable the individual at risk. The conceptualization of primary prevention as opposite to or in conflict with treatment is conceptually flawed in that it invokes an artificial dichotomy; rather, we will argue that prevention and treatment interventions lie on one continuum of interventions and theory and research in both areas benefit from mutual influence. We hope that our observations about prevention will stimulate a dialogue that may generate fresh ideas and approaches not only to primary prevention but also to our understanding of etiology and treatment of eating disorders.

DEFINITION OF KEY CONCEPTS

Three terms need to be defined before we can address the main subject matters of this chapter, namely primary prevention, eating disorders, and feminism. As there is an extensive literature concerning each of these concepts, we will keep this section brief.

PRIMARY PREVENTION

Primary prevention refers to efforts at reducing the incidence of eating disorders in individuals who have not yet developed any clinically significant symptoms of the disorder. As will be discussed later on, this definition is not without its problems, because the demarcation between 'normative concerns' about body weight and eating disorders is far from clear (Rodin, Silberstein and Striegel-Moore, 1985). Prevention efforts are based on the assumption that causal factors involved in the development of eating disorders can be identified. Moreover, prevention requires the further assumption that the particular causal factors can be either eliminated or rendered ineffective. This distinction is important when evaluating the success or failure of a articular intervention program.

The various approaches to primary prevention that have been proposed for reducing the incidence of eating disorders fall into one of two major categories: efforts to eliminate or render ineffective factors involved in the causation of the disorder, and efforts to 'strengthen the host' against the impact of the noxious influences (reviews: Levine and Smolak, 1996; Steiner-Adair, 1995; Steiner-Adair and Purcell, 1996; Striegel-Moore and Silberstein, 1989). A further dimension for categorization of prevention efforts involves the level of the intervention. Theoretically speaking, prevention may be attempted at varying levels of breadth ranging from the individual level (e.g. sheltering a particular child from exposure to the noxious stimulus such as television or fashion magazines, or providing strategies that minimize the potency of the noxious factor) to the societal level (e.g. removing a certain causal factor from an entire society, or 'inoculating' an entire population in an attempt to make it resilient to the noxious stimulus). In practice, such clear distinctions among levels of intervention are difficult to maintain; however, for heuristic purposes, it is useful to maintain this distinction. To date, the majority of interventions of eating disorders have involved 'strengthening the host' by targeting young girls, typically in school based interventions.

DEFINITION OF EATING DISORDERS

In this chapter, we adopt the definition of eating disorders as provided in DSM-IV (American Psychiatric Association, 1994). We focus on anorexia nervosa, bulimia nervosa, and 'eating disorders not otherwise specified'. We wish to point out, however, that future prevention efforts may well be directed toward reducing not only the incidence of full-syndrome eating disorders (i.e. anorexia nervosa, bulimia nervosa, eating disorders not otherwise specified), but also at reducing clinically significant symptoms of eating disorders (e.g. inappropriate compensatory behaviors such as vomiting or excessive exercise).

FEMINISM

Many definitions of feminism have been offered (see Peplau and Conrad, 1989). The various feminist approaches to scholarship share in common that they consider gender a core variable of relevance in understanding human behavior, affirm a positive view of women, take a contextual approach, value a broad spectrum of research methods, and consider the implications of research findings for social change (Striegel-Moore, 1993a). The feminist stance requires that we consider behavior in its broader cultural content; we will take up this issue in the section on the disease model of eating disorders. The feminist perspective focuses our attention to issues of social equality and to the question of how power imbalances between men and women may contribute to the development of eating disorders. Feminist approaches to prevention include the following foundations (Steiner-Adair, 1993; Steiner-Adair and Purcell, 1996):

(1) 'The personal is political', i.e. it is necessary to offer an understanding of eating disorders that includes as central a critique of socio-cultural values and norms that create a cultural context in which eating disorders exist (for example, teaching skills of media literacy recasting eating disorders as a diversity or social justice issue).

(2) Gender differences in the epidemiology of eating disorders need to be considered from a political perspective.

(3) Prevention should include an opportunity to actively resist and speak out against perceived sources of the problem (for example, write a letter to a teen magazine or start a 'no diet' campaign at school).

(4) Teach the history of other times when cultural values about female beauty and worth led to different forms of illness in women (for example hysteria in the Victorian era, see Ehrenreich and English, 1989).

(5) Eating disorders are identified as a means of coping and alternative healthier ways of coping are offered.

(6) Feminist approaches to prevention examine the systems in which girls live-school and home, and require the system to change in ways that support the individual girls' health.

Feminist approaches to prevention strategies suggest that curricula design should be based on the literature on girls psychological development and girls' ways of learning (for example: girls are the experts on their own experience; collaborative, interactive and relational approaches to learning should be used; inter-generational mentoring would be useful). Girls learn all subjects best when a relational models is used for teaching (AAUW, 1992; Jordan, 1991; Sadker and Sadker, 1994) and prevention programs should incorporate a relational or connected learning approach. A consistent finding of the research on girls' healthy development is that they need confiding relationships in order to be healthy; they need someone (preferably a female) who will be there, listen, teach and model alternative healthy choices. Also, research of curricula development and evaluation suggests that programs designed with methodologies which are interactive, utilize reflection techniques, interactive performances, and self-assessment are particularly effective (Gardner, 1991). Also, feminist approaches to prevention take into account the role and responsibility of adults in children's lives and therefore include parent education and staff education, and systemic prevention strategies for home and school.

While space does not permit a full consideration of the feminist etiologic model of eating disorders (see, for example, Steiner-Adair, 1984; Striegel-Moore, Silberstein and Rodin, 1986; Striegel-Moore, 1993b), we touch upon this issue in the section on etiology of eating disorders. The feminist stance requires a critical exploration of how scientific knowledge is generated with questions ranging broadly from what research methodology is being used to whose interest in being served by certain research findings. For example, we are intrigued by the fact that enormous financial resources continue to be expended in efforts to identify successful weight loss therapies despite hundreds of studies with very discouraging empirical results (Garner and Wooley, 1995). On the other hand, efforts to achieve a reduction in the incidence of eating disorders have been met with serious criticisms which, to date, have focused largely on the fact that primary prevention interventions have not been shown to be effective. It is important to note, however, that funding of prevention studies on eating disorders has been limited and, to date, less than ten empirical studies have been published. With very few exceptions, the existing studies were conducted on 'shoe-string' budgets, and this line of research is still in a very early stage. Rather than attempting to reconcile that seemingly different standards are being applied to the evaluation of obesity treatments versus primary prevention of eating disorders, we chose to focus constructively on the question of how treatment approaches and primary prevention interventions share similarities which, if uncovered, may enhance both treatment studies and prevention studies.

THE SPECIFIC DISEASE CONCEPT

The disease model of eating disorders has considerable heuristic and clinical value. However, the understanding of eating disorders as a specific disease has clear limitations when it comes to primary prevention. We focus here on three aspects: the notion that a clear demarcation would be possible between 'normal' and 'abnormal' states; the difficulty encountered in defining a distinct onset of eating disorders; and the high rates of comorbidity observed among individuals with an eating disorder.

CONTINUUM

The key symptoms of eating disorders occur on a continuum of severity, yet the disease model of eating disorders requires that we designate a threshold beyond which a given symptom constellation differs fundamentally from the milder forms of eating and weight concerns. How eating disorders are defined affects quite dramatically the incidence rates of the disorder. Major epidemiologic studies of eating disorders have shown that by adopting subthreshold criteria, defined as meeting all but one diagnostic criteria for anorexia nervosa or bulimia nervosa, the number of cases more than doubled (Garfinkel et al., 1995, 1996; Kendler et al., 1991; Walters and Kendler, 1995). For example, a comparison of women who met full-syndrome criteria for anorexia nervosa and women who met all criteria except amenorrhea found few statistically significant differences in terms of demographic characteristics, psychiatric comorbidity, family history, or early childhood experiences (Garfinkel et al., 1996). Walters and Kendler (1995) found that only three of seventeen proposed risk factors differentiated among full-syndrome and partial syndrome anorexia nervosa, namely dieting, parental occupation, and college education. These authors concluded that there exists an etiologic continuum of impact for the risk factors across the spectrum of anorexic-like behaviors. Similarly, studies suggest that the same factors that influence risk for full-syndrome bulimia nervosa also apply to less severe bulimia-like syndromes (Garfinkel et al., 1995; Kendler et al., 1991).

The DSM-IV category of 'eating disorders not otherwise specified' has been ignored almost entirely in the literature on primary prevention of eating disorders. A number of recent studies have shown that more women with this type of eating disorder present for treatment than women with anorexia nervosa or bulimia nervosa (Striegel-Moore and Marcus, 1995). In the USA, binge eating disorder, has been studied extensively in recent years. Prevalence rates of approximately 2 per cent have been reported (Spitzer et al., 1992; Striegel-Moore et al., 1996). A recent risk factor study found that women with binge eating disorder and women with bulimia nervosa share certain risk factors such as childhood obesity and social pressure about weight (Fairburn, 1997).

Taken together, these studies suggest that the current diagnostic criteria for anorexia nervosa and bulimia nervosa are unnecessarily narrow and that certain syndromes now defined as 'eating disorder not otherwise specified' may be more suitably defined under revised, broader definitions of anorexia nervosa and bulimia nervosa. Such redefinitions will affect the incidence rates and prevalence rates of eating disorders. Hence, whether there are many cases to be prevented or just a few depends in large part on how wide we cast the 'definitional net' when defining eating disorders.

AGE OF ONSET

The disease model implies a distinct, identifiable onset of the eating disorders. Information about age of onset is critical for deciding when to initiate preventive intervention which, by definition, must occur before the disease has been developed. Such a demarcation, however, is difficult to achieve in eating disorders. Different investigators use different criteria for determining age of onset and, not surprisingly, as a result the mean age of onset reported in the literature vary accordingly. For example, Kendler et al. (1991) and Garfinkel et al. (1995) define age of onset as the age when the person first met criteria for full syndrome anorexia nervosa or bulimia nervosa. In contrast, Fairburn et al. (1997) define onset as the age at which the first clinically significant symptom (e.g. severely restrictive dieting, or recurrent binge eating, or recurrent purging) emerges.

The decision regarding what definition of age of onset to apply has important consequences for primary prevention. Age of onset of symptoms is significantly earlier than age of onset of full syndromes. This is particularly true for eating disorders which are culturally mediated disorders. Ubiquitous exposure to our culture's extremely thin ideal of female beauty, its construction of femininity as defined by beauty and a relational self, and its profound intolerance of overweight, contributes to the develop-ment of body image disturbance (e.g. fears of fatness, body dissatisfaction, and over-valuation of weight and shape) and disordered eating (e.g. restrictive dieting) (Steiner-Adair, 1986; Striegel-Moore, 1993b). It is not uncommon that girls as young as six years old equate thinness with 'goodness,' worry about being too fat, and initiate dieting for self-improvement. What may be primary prevention by the onset definition of one researcher may be actually secondary prevention by another researcher's defini-tion of age of onset.

COMORBIDITY

After some twenty years of research of bulimia nervosa, debate still continues whether bulimia nervosa is a 'variant of anorexia nervosa' (Russell, 1979) or a disorder distinct from anorexia nervosa, and/or whether eating disorders should be subsumed under some other form of psychopathology such as mood disorder, anxiety disorder, or substance use disorder (Striegel-Moore and Marcus, 1995). Epidemiologic studies of comorbidity have import-ant implications for theory and research of primary prevention. For example, a prospective epidemiological study of some 2,000 children in New Zealand found that an astonishing 40 per cent had experienced at least one mental disorder by the time they reached age 21 (Newman et al., 1996). Even more remarkably, nearly half of those diagnosed with one psychiatric disorder were also diagnosed with a second disorder. Comorbidity rates for anorexia nervosa and bulimia nervosa exceeded 75 per cent in this study. Similar comorbidity rates for anorexia nervosa with bulimia nervosa have been reported in North American studies (Garfinkel et al., 1995; Kendler et al., 1991). Moreover, similar rates of high comorbidity of eating disorders and various other mental disorders have been found in several studies conducted among representa-tive samples of adolescents or adults in the USA (Lewinsohn, Hops, Roberts, Seeley, and Andrews, 1993; Kessler et al., 1994).

These high rates of comorbidity raise questions about the utility and validity of differential diagnosis in general and their usefulness for primary prevention of eating disorders in particular. By sorting the various emotional difficulties women experience into distinct categories (depression, anxiety, eating disorders), the extent of these problems is minimized because the number of individuals affected in any given, narrowly defined, category is smaller than if one were to apply broader categories. Moreover, efforts to understand the causes of these disorders become *unduly* focused on understanding the *unique* causes for each specific disease, rather than on understanding the most *potent* causal factors that contribute to psychopathology. For the purpose of primary prevention, ignoring comorbidity may result in competition and costly duplication of effort. One can easily imagine, for example, how eating disorder prevention advocates compete with prevention advocates for other disorders not only for resources to design and carry out their prevention projects but also for access to the individuals for whom they develop their programs.

THE ETIOLOGY OF EATING DISORDERS

Numerous theoretical models have been proposed to explain the etiology of eating disorders. These models suggest several risk domains including the cultural context, the familial context, constitutional vulnerability, and adverse life events (for review, see Striegel-Moore, 1993b, 1997). Even though the theoretical models differ in the emphasis placed on given risk domains, there is considerable agreement that the etiology of eating disorders is *multifactorial*, that risk derives from a combination of *specific risk factors* (i.e. risk factors unique to the specific disease) and *general risk factors* (i.e. risk factors that are associated with a number of different disorders), that exposure to risk occurs in *diverse settings* (e.g. family, school, peer groups, etc), that the salience or potency of risk factors derives in part from *when in development* they occur, and that risk is *cumulative* (i.e. the greater the number of risk factors experienced, the greater the chance of developing an eating disorder). For example, figure 1 summarizes, in greatly simplified form, what has been shown empirically regarding the risk for eating disorders involving binge eating. Because it summarizes empirical studies, this figure does not delineate comprehensively the many risk factors that have been theorized to contribute to risk for developing an eating disorder but for which there is no conclusive empirical evidence.

Risk factor studies have identified several specific risk factors

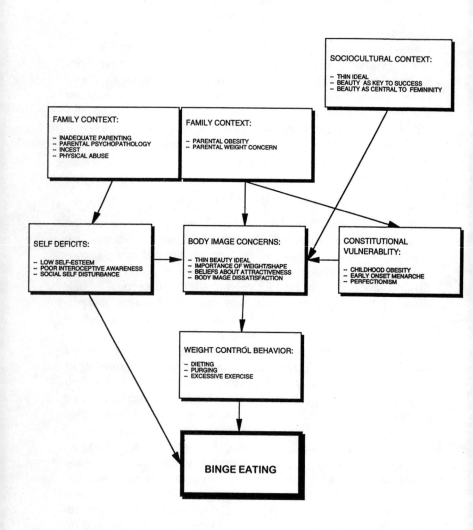

FIGURE 1: Risk factors for binge eating

for eating disorders (see Table 1 and 2). For example, childhood obesity, negative attitudes about weight and shape, irrational beliefs about the benefits of dieting, social pressure to control one's weight, and dieting itself all have been implicated as specific risk factors (Fairburn et al., 1997). A major focus of prevention efforts to date has been to develop better body image and to reduce risk by trying to help girls resist the pressure to diet (Shisslak et al., 1996). Such efforts are attempted within a social context that glorifies thinness and villifies failure to achieve thinness. Paradoxically, the socio-cultural context facilitates the development of obesity by the overabundance of highly palatable, high-fat, highly sweet, and easily-accessible food and the support of an increasingly sedentary life-style.

To date, prevention efforts may have failed not only because of their neglect of the social context in which messages such as 'a waist is a terrible thing to mind' and 'you cannot be too rich or too thin' are disseminated. Perhaps as important, or even more important, is the neglect of entire classes of risk factors that contribute to the development of eating disorders but are not addressed by prevention programs. Prevention programs aimed at eliminating disordered eating behaviors may miss the fact that disordered eating may be used as coping mechanisms in response to a wide range of difficulties and stresses.

As shown in Figure 1 and Table 1 and 2, the following factors have been found to be associated with risk for developing an eating disorder: having parents who themselves experience significant psychopathology, being brought up in a physically or sexually abusive household, and experiencing deficiencies in parental attachment (Fairburn et al., 1997; Garfinkel et al., 1995; 1996; Kendler et al., 191; Walters and Kendler, 1995). Interventions aimed at reducing risk for eating disorders rarely include efforts to eliminate or render less potent these risk factors. This omission may, in part, be due to the over-emphasis on specificity of risk factors. For example, childhood physical and/or sexual abuse has been established to increase risk for eating disorders *and* for other forms of psychopathology among women, including depression, anxiety disorders, post-traumatic stress disorder, and substance use disorders (Duncan et al., 1996; Garfinkel et al., 1995; Welch and Fairburn, 1994). An unintended consequence of the research focus on specific risk factors may be that prevention programs do

Table 1. Risk Factors for Anorexia Nervosa.

* High parental education and income (Walters and Kendler, 1996)
* Early feeding problems (Marchi and Cohen, 1990; Rastam, 1992)
* Low self-esteem (Walters and Kendler, 1996)
* High neuroticism (Walters and Kendler, 1996)
* Maternal overprotectiveness (Walters and Kendler, 1996)
* Having a female relative with anorexia nervosa or bulimia nervosa
  (Strober et al., 1990; Walters and Kendler, 1996)
* Parental psychopathology (Garfinkel et al., 1996)
* Childhood sexual abuse (Garfinkel et al., 1996)

Table 2. Risk Factors for Bulimia Nervosa.

* Early timing of menarche (Fairburn et al., 1997)
* External locus of control (Kendler et al., 1991)
* Low self-esteem (Fairburn et al., 1997; Kendler et al., 1991)
* Childhood obesity (Fairburn et al., 1997)
* Weight concern (Killen et al., 1994)
* Social pressure about weight and/or eating (Fairburn et al., 1997)
* Family dieting (Fairburn et al., 1997)
* Eating disorders among family members (Fairburn et al., 1997; Kendler
  et al., 1991)
* Parental psychopathology (Fairburn et al., 1997; Kendler et al., 1991;
  Garfinkel et al., 1995)
* Inadequate parenting (Fairburn et al., 1997; Kendler et al., 1991)
* Parental discord (Fairburn et al., 1997)
* Childhood sexual abuse (Fairburn et al., 1997; Garfinkel et al., 1995)

not encompass efforts to reduce non-specific risk factors such as physical or sexual abuse. Hence, an important question remains whether efficacy of prevention programs could be improved by interventions that focus on eliminating the most *potent* risk factors, regardless of whether these are specific or non-specific to eating disorders.

THE CONTINUUM OF INTERVENTIONS

While many researchers have been reluctant to engage in prevention research, recently there has been an upsurge in interest in research of self-help and other forms of minimal intervention (Garvin and Striegel-Moore, 1997). A lot can be learned about how to enhance the effectiveness of prevention programs from these new research efforts. Rather than conceptualizing prevention and treatment as dichotomous, it is useful to think of interventions as falling along a continuum ranging from prevention to case identification to minimal intervention to 'gold standard' treatment to relapse prevention to rehabilitation (see also Munoz et al., 1996). Next, we will illustrate the ways in which prevention research and research of minimal interventions face similar challenges. We will show that prevention research involves concepts from traditional therapy such as motivation to change, therapeutic alliance, treatment matching, risk assessment and management, and outcome criteria. To design effective interventions all along this continuum will require cross-fertilization of research of those who do clinical research and those who do research in the area of prevention.

SIMILARITIES BETWEEN MINIMAL INTERVENTION AND PRIMARY PREVENTION

Both types of interventions share the underlying assumption that increase in knowledge and behavioral skills will result in attitudinal and/or behavioral change. Identifying what particular educational approaches work in minimal interventions should help us improve interventions aimed at prevention. For example, preliminary research of minimal interventions suggests that recognizing and enhancing the interpersonal aspects of the intervention may result in improved outcomes (Garvin, Striegel-Moore and Wells, 1997). To date, the prevention literature rarely considers the importance of the relational context of the intervention. As Levine (1996) has shown, a pedagogical approach that is didactic, leader-focused, non-interactive, and non-experiential is less effective than a more interactive approach involving peer leaders. Quite likely, the success of minimal and preventive interventions depends in part of the degree to which relational needs of the participants are recognized and addressed, and in part on the relational skills of the person providing the intervention.

MOTIVATION TO CHANGE

Both types of interventions essentially require voluntary participation. Treasure (1997) is exploring this important, yet so far
overlooked, aspect of minimal intervention, namely motivation to
change. To date, research of prevention has neglected the question
of how we are to expect good outcome when we pay no attention
to the possibility that participants in the prevention programs may
see little reason to change. Finding ways to increase motivation to
change is clearly a challenge in eating disorders. Given the cultural
'myth of transformation' associated with dieting (i.e. to achieve
thinness means to achieve popularity and success) it is very
difficult, for example, to convince girls or women that they should
not engage in excessively restrictive eating. Treasure's (1997) data
may be informative as to how to increase motivation of participants in prevention programs.

Most primary prevention programs in the field of eating disorders assume that participation in these programs is voluntary. It
is interesting to note that many of the successful public health
initiatives in other areas (e.g. personal safety; dental health) have
involved involuntary interventions (e.g. seat belt laws, fluoride
administration to drinking water). The literature on prevention of
eating disorders does not include a discussion of the fact that some
of the potent risk factors for eating disorders are unlikely to be
amenable to change by interventions that require *voluntary* participation. As the literature on interventions to reduce physical
violence against women shows, legal and punitive interventions
are more effective at reducing subsequent abusive incidents than
educational interventions aimed at the abuser. We may feel more
comfortable educating young girls about the perils of dieting than
we are about trying to achieve social change necessary to reduce
physical and sexual victimization perpetrated against young girls,
yet perhaps the latter will be more effective than the former in
reducing the incidence of eating disorders (and, of course, other
forms of female psychopathology).

MATCHING OF PROGRAMS TO CONSUMER NEEDS

Both prevention programs and minimal intervention programs are
economical because they represent low-level interventions that

can be disseminated to large numbers of individuals. Beyond the concerns about motivation, we need to understand better what type of interventions appeals to what type of participant. The consumers of these interventions will be able to tell us what motivates them to work with a particular program. Moreover, we need to tailor programs to different individuals' needs. Paradoxically, even though these programs are thought to be appropriate for large numbers of individuals, very likely the success of either a minimal intervention or a preventive intervention depends in part on the extent to which they can be individualized. For example, participants in guided minimal intervention report that an attractive feature of this type of intervention is the self-pacing of the material – the consumer is in charge of her progress (Garvin et al., 1997). It is plausible that preventive intervention may similarly benefit from giving participants some control over the pacing of the intervention.

DIAGNOSTIC ASSESSMENT AND RISK MANAGEMENT

Both minimal interventions and prevention programs face certain challenges in terms of diagnostic assessment and on-going risk assessment. Entry criteria should be developed that help guide the decision regarding who may be admitted to a program; these could range from simple criteria such as a certain level of reading ability (for example, in the USA illiteracy rates are high), or clinical criteria such as current level of functioning. Guidelines are needed for ongoing risk assessment; minimal interventions or even prevention programs may have unintended adverse effects and research is needed both on how to screen out individuals who may not be suitable for these interventions and how to detect participants who are experiencing iatrogenic effects.

DEFINITION AND MEASUREMENT OF OUTCOME

Both types of interventions face the paradox that the more they are geared toward broad dissemination, the less intensive they will be, yet the less intensive programs may be less successful at effecting major behavior changes. For both types of intervention programs, the expected outcome needs to be carefully specified and measurement of outcome should be planned accordingly. The field has yet to begin a discussion of what constitutes reasonable outcome expectations for either minimal interventions or prevention programs. We suggest that outcome measures for minimal interventions should go beyond measures typically included in treatment outcome studies (improvement of clinical symptoms and of role functioning). For example, willingness to enter treatment should be considered a positive outcome in participants who fail to show behavior change as a result of a minimal intervention program. Similarly, failure of a certain number of participants to show improvement or behavioral change in response to a prevention program may suggest the need for a subsequent, more intensive (or different) intervention in some participants. Clearly, however, this raises the question of what the minimal level of change is that we can still accept as good outcome, or what the minimal number of participants is that need to improve in order for us to find a program to be of acceptable effectiveness.

CONCLUSION

We hope to have shown that arguments about the lack of cost-effectiveness of prevention programs due to the low incidence of the eating disorder need to be challenged. The potential impact of these interventions is much broader than one would assume from a specific disease perspective. A considerable wealth of information is accumulating about the etiology of eating disorders. Efforts need to be focused toward a better understanding of risk factors that are most potent and that are amenable to change, and a broad range of levels of intervention needs to be considered for preventive interventions to make a difference. Lastly, the dichotomy of treatment versus prevention is problematic. By conceptualizing prevention and treatment along a continuum, research will progress more rapidly as cross-fertilization among prevention and treatment studies becomes viable.

REFERENCES

AAUW (American Association of University Women) Educational Foundation (1992) *Shortchanging girls, shortchanging America*, Washington, D.C.: AAUW Educational Foundation.
American Psychiatric Association (1994) *Diagnostic and Statistical*

Manual of Mental Disorders (fourth edition). Washington, D.C.: American Psychiatric Association.

Duncan, R.D., Saunders, B.E., Kilpatrick, D.G., Hanson, R.F. and Resnick, H.S. (1996) 'Childhood physical assault as a risk factor for PTSD, depression, and substance abuse: Findings from a national survey'. *American Journal of Orthopsychiatry*, 66: 437–48.

Ehrenreich, B. and English, D. (1989) *For her own good: 150 years of experts advice to women*, New York: Doubleday.

Fairburn, C.G. (1997) *Risk factors for eating disorders: Two integrated case control studies*. Paper presented at the Third International Conference on Eating Disorders, London.

Fairburn, C.G., Welch, S.L., Doll, H.A., Davies, B.A. and O'Connor, M.E. (1997) 'Risk factors for bulimia nervosa: A community-based case control study'. *Archives of General Psychiatry*, 54: 509–17.

Gardner H. (1991) *The unschooled mind*, New York: Basic Books.

Garfinkel, P.E., Lin, E., Goering, P., Spegg, C., Goldbloom, D., Kennedy, S., Kaplan, A.S. and Woodside, B. (1995) 'Bulimia nervosa in a Canadian community sample: Prevalence and comparison of subgroups'. *American Journal of Psychiatry*, 152: 1052–8.

——(1996) 'Should amenorrhoea be necessary for the diagnosis of anorexia nervosa?' *British Journal of Psychiatry*, 168: 500–6.

Garner, D.M. and Wooley, S.C. (1991) 'Confronting the failure of behavioral and dietary treatments of obesity'. *Clinical Psychology Review*, 11: 729–80.

Garvin, V., Striegel-Moore, R.H., Kaplan, A. and Wonderlich, S. (1998) The potential of self-help interventions: Lessons learned from eating disorders research. Middletown (CT): Wesleyan University.

Garvin, V., Wells, A. and Striegel-Moore, R.H. (1998) 'Participant reactions to a cognitive behavioral guided self-help program for binge eating: Developing criteria for program evaluation'. *Journal of Psychosomatic Research*, 44: 407–412.

Gilbert, S. and Thompson, K. (1996) 'Feminist explanations of the development of eating disorders: Common themes, research findings, and methodological issues'. *Clinical Psychology: Science and Practice*, 3: 183–202.

Graber, J.A. and Brooks-Gunn, J. (1996) 'Prevention of eating disorders: Including parents'. *Eating Disorders: The Journal of Treatment and Prevention*, 4: 348–63.

Jordan, J. (1991) *Women's growth in connection: Writings from the Stone Center*, New York: Guilford Press.

Kendler, K.S., MacLean, C., Neale, M. Kessler, R., Heath, A. and Eaves,

L. (1991) 'The genetic epidemiology of bulimia nervosa'. *International Journal of Eating Disorders*, 10: 679–87.

Kessler, R.C., McGonogle, K.A., Zhao, S., Nelson, C.B., Hughes, M., Eshleman, S., Wittchen, H.V. and Kendler, K.S. (1994) 'Lifetime and 12-month prevalence of DSM-III-R psychiatric disorders in the United States'. *Archives of General Psychiatry*, 51: 8–19.

Killen, J.D. (1996) 'Development and evaluation of a school-based eating disorders symptoms prevention program'. In Smolak, L., Levine, M. and Striegel-Moore, R.H. (eds) *The developmental psychopathology of eating disorders* (pp. 313–40), Mahwah, N.J.: Lawrence Erlbaum.

Levine, M.P. (1994) '"Beauty myth" and the beast: What men can do and be to help prevent eating disorders'. *Eating Disorders: The Journal of Treatment and Prevention*, 2: 101–13.

Levine, M.P. and Smolak, L. (1996) 'Media as a context for the development of eating problems'. In Smolak, L., Levine, M. and Striegel-Moore, R.H. (eds) *The developmental psychopathology of eating disorders* (pp. 235–58), Mahwah, N.J.: Lawrence Erlbaum.

Lewinsohn, P.M., Hops, H. Roberts, R.E., Seeley, J.R. and Andrews, J.A. (1993) 'Adolescent psychopathology: I. Prevalence and incidence of depression and other DSM-III-R disorders in high school students'. *Journal of Abnormal Psychology*, 102: 133–44.

Mrazek, P.J. and Haggerty, R.J. Eds. (1994) *Reducing risks for mental disorders: Frontiers for prevention intervention research*, Washington, D.C.: National Academy Press.

Munoz, R.F., Mrazek, P.J. and Haggerty, R.J. (1996) 'Institute of medicine report on prevention of mental disorders'. *American Psychologist*, 51: 1116–22.

Newman, D.L. Moffitt, T.E., Caspi, A. Magdol, L., Silva, P.A. and Stanton, W.R. (1996) 'Psychiatric disorder in a birth cohort of young adults: Prevalence, comorbidity, clinical significance, and new case incidence from ages 11 to 21'. *Journal of Consulting and Clinical Psychology*, 64: 552–62.

Paxton, S. (1996) 'Prevention implications of peer influences on body image dissatisfaction and disturbed eating in adolescent girls'. *Eating Disorders: The Journal of Treatment and Prevention*, 4: 334–47.

Peplau, I.A. and Conrad, E. (1989) 'Beyond nonsexist research: The perils of feminist methods in psychology'. *Psychology of Women Quarterly*, 13: 379–400.

Piran, N. (1996) 'The reduction of preoccupation with body weight and shape in schools: A feminist approach'. *Eating Disorders: The Journal of Treatment and Prevention*, 4: 323–33.

Rodin, J., Silberstein, L.R. and Striegel-Moore, R.H. (1985) 'Women and weight: A normative discontent'. In Sonderegger, T.B. (ed) *Nebraska Symposium on Motivation* (pp. 267–308), Lincoln: University of Nebraska Press.

Sadker J.M. and Sadker D. (1994) *Failing at fairness: How America's schools cheat girls*, New York: Guilford Press.

Shisslak, C.M. and Crago, M. (1994) 'Toward a new model for the prevention of eating disorders'. In Fallon, P., Katzman, M.A. and Wooley, S.C. (eds) *Feminist perspectives on eating disorders* (pp. 419–37), New York: Guilford Press.

Shisslak, C.M., Crago, M., Estes, L.S. and Gray N. (1996) 'Content and method of developmentally appropriate prevention programs'. In Smolak, L., Levine, M. and Striegel-Moore, R.H. (eds) *The developmental psychopathology of eating disorders* (pp. 341–64), Mahwah, N.J.: Lawrence Erlbaum.

Shisslak, C.M., Crago, M., Neal, M.E. and Swain, B. (1987) 'Primary prevention of eating disorders'. *Journal of Consulting and Clinical Psychology*, 55: 660–67.

Smolak, L. and Levine, M.P. (1994) 'Toward an empirical basis for primary prevention of eating problems with elementary school children'. *Eating Disorders: The Journal of Treatment and Prevention*, 2: 293–307.

Spitzer, R.L. Devlin, M., Walsh, B.T., Hasin, D., Wing, R., Marcus, M., Stunkard, A., Wadden, T., Yanovski, S., Agras, S., Mitchell, J. and Nonas, C. (1992) 'Binge eating disorder: A multisite field trial of the diagnostic criteria'. *International Journal of Eating Disorders*, 11: 191–204.

Steiner-Adair, C. (1986) 'The body politic: Normal female adolescent development and the development of eating disorders'. *Journal of the American Academy of Psychoanalysis*, 14: 95–114.

——(1993) 'The politics of prevention'. In Fallon, P., Katzman, M.A. and Wooley, S.C. (eds) *Feminist perspectives on eating disorders* (pp. 381–94), New York: Guilford Press.

Steiner-Adair, C. and Purcell, A. (1996) 'Approaches to mainstreaming eating disorders'. *Eating Disorders: The Journal of Treatment and Prevention*, 4: 294–309.

Striegel-Moore, R.H. (1992) 'Prevention of bulimia nervosa: Questions and challenges'. In Crowther, J.H., Tennebaum, D.L., Hobfoll, S.E. and Stephens, M.A. (eds) *The etiology of bulimia nervosa* (pp. 203–23), Washington, D.C.: Hemisphere.

——(1993a) 'A feminist agenda for psychological research one eating disorders'. In Fallon, P., Katzman, M.A. and Wooley, S.C. (eds) *Feminist perspectives on eating disorders* (pp 438–54). New York: Guilford Press.

——(1993b) 'Etiology of binge eating: A developmental perspective'. In Fairburn, C.G. and Wilson, G.T. (eds) *Binge eating: Nature, assessment, and treatment* (pp. 144–72), New York: Guilford Press.

——(1997) 'Risk factors for eating disorders'. In Jacobson, M.S., Golden, N.H., Irwin, E.E. and Reese, J.M. (eds) *Adolescent nutritional disorders: Prevention and treatment*, New York: New York Academy of Sciences.

Striegel-Moore, R.H. and Marcus M. (1995) 'Eating disorders in women: Current issues and debates'. In Stanton, A. and Gallant, S. (eds) *Psychology of women's health* (pp. 445–87), Washington, D.C.: American Psychological Association.

Striegel-Moore, R.H., Pike, K.M., Wilfley, D.E., Dohm, F.A. and Fairburn, C.G. (1996) *Eating disorder symptoms in black American women: The New England Women's Health Project.* Paper presented at the annual meeting of the Research Society for Eating Disorders, Pittsburgh (PA).

Striegel-Moore, R.H. and Silberstein, L.R. (1989) 'Early identification of bulimia nervosa'. In Johnson, W. (ed) *Advances in eating disorders, Volume II. Bulimia nervosa: Conceptualization, assessment, and treatment* (pp. 267–81), Greenwich (CT): JAI Press.

Striegel-Moore, R.H., Silberstein, L.R. and Rodin, J. (1986) 'Toward an understanding of risk factors for bulimia'. *American Psychologist*, 41: 246–63.

Welch, S.L. and Fairburn, C.G. (1994) 'Sexual abuse and bulimia nervosa: Three integrated case control comparisons'. *American Journal of Psychiatry*, 151: 402–7.

Walters, E.E. and Kendler, K.S. (1995) 'Anorexia nervosa and anorectic-like syndromes in a population-based female twin sample'. *American Journal of Psychiatry*, 152: 64–71.

CHAPTER TWO

The mass media and disordered eating: Implications for primary prevention

Michael P. Levine and Linda Smolak

INTRODUCTION

Theorists in the fields of eating disorders and women's studies have for many years been criticizing fashion magazines, television, and other mass media for their promotion of the thin-ideal body and of dieting, both of which are risk factors for disordered eating (see, e.g. Garfinkel and Garner, 1982; Kilbourne, 1994). This 'sociocultural perspective' informs the media-analysis and media-resistance lessons which are a part of most school-based and community-based educational programs for the primary prevention of eating disorders (e.g. Levine and Hill, 1991; Piran, Bear and Jasper, 1993). The curricular prevention programs have been only modestly successful at best (Shisslak, Crago, Estes and Gray, 1996), particularly when compared to the primary prevention of cigarette smoking and alcohol use by students ages 11–14 (see, e.g. Schinke, Botvin and Orlandi, 1991). Consequently, we believe it is time for the eating disorder field's own 'media literacy' to be enlarged in order to create more effective primary prevention programs.

This chapter is an update and extension of our recent review of the literature on mass media, developmental psychology, and eating disorders (Levine and Smolak, 1996). Our goal is to explore the implications of that knowledge base for the prevention of eating problems, and to consider ways in which mass media might be transformed from monolithic obstacle to collaborator in primary prevention.

SOME IMPORTANT ELEMENTS OF MASS MEDIA

A 'mass medium' is a form of communication generated by shifting networks of individuals (e.g. writers, photographers, computer specialists, actors) and financial organizations (e.g. communications conglomerates, production companies, banks), all of whom are motivated in part to maximize profits by attracting and holding very large, anonymous audiences (Harris, 1994). Types of mass media which may be especially relevant to the etiology or prevention of eating disorders include fashion magazines, television, and self-help weight-loss books. Radio, billboards, the opinion-editorial section of newspapers, and computer networks may also be relevant for health promotion (Rice and Atkin, 1989).

Messages emanating from mass media can be usefully, if not always convincingly, divided into those intended by their 'authors' (e.g. tracking down a mass murderer is exciting to watch and reveals something interesting about aggression and human nature) and those incidental or 'cultivated' (e.g. women are 'natural' victims of essentially uncontrollable male aggression). Regardless of intent, media messages serve multiple purposes such as entertainment, socialization, information management, social organization, education, government, and – lest we forget – frequent opportunities for businesses to sell many different things to an extraordinarily large number of potential consumers (McCracken, 1993; Murray and Ozanne, 1991). Although the intended 'audience' of a television program or a fashion magazine may be 'segmented' for marketing purposes (e.g. 20–45-years old, educated, and middle-to-upper-middle class), the actual audience is often much larger and more heterogeneous. For example, naturally curious children and adolescents often have ready access to media ostensibly produced for adults (Harris, 1994).

It is our impression that some eating disorders professionals base some of their prevention work on the following assumption: Simplistic but pleasurable media stimuli, which are cleverly designed to have broad and immediate appeal for children and adolescents, somehow 'brainwash' this audience of naturally uncritical and hedonistic innocents into assimilating the media's pernicious messages about beauty, dieting, indulgence, and success. This belief is well-intentioned and certainly understandable in the face of omnipresent and salient messages that objectify women, glorify slenderenss, etc. (Kilbourne, 1994). However, research from developmental psychology (Austin, 1995), media studies and semiotics (Buckingham, 1990), and women's studies (Budgeon and Currie, 1995; McCracken, 1993) converges to leave no doubt that mass media do not 'brainwash' people. Rather, media provoke a complex process of attention and interpretation by individuals who, depending on their developmental stage, their personality, their immediate situation, and other sociocultural contexts, bring various motives and information processing strategies to the task.

THEORIES OF MASS MEDIA AND DISORDERED EATING:
CONTENT ANALYSES

There are numerous reviews of the available content analyses concerning the nature and frequency of TV and fashion magazine messages about ideal shape, dieting, exercising, and nutrition (see, e.g. Gordon, 1990; Levine and Smolak, 1996; Stice, 1994). This scholarship documents that for the past 20 years – a period in which there appears to have been a significant increase in the incidence of anorexia nervosa and bulimia nervosa among females ages 15–24 (Kendler et al., 1991; Lucas, Beard, O'Fallon and Kurland, 1991; see also Gordon, 1990) – the mass media have been filled with 'images' of fashion models and actresses who are young, tall, long-legged, and very slender. In fashion magazines these ubiquitous and homogeneous pictures co-exist with a truly bulimic assortment of the following: advertisements for diets; articles on weight loss (some of which contain undisguised endorsements of specific products); articles and advertisements presenting sumptuous amounts of low- and high-calorie food; advertisements featuring body parts, submissive postures, and other forms of sexual objectification; and exhortations to be a voracious 'consumer' (Budgeon and Currie, 1995; Kilbourne, 1994; Levine and Smolak, 1996).

Two other more abstract points are also important in thinking about the relationship between mass media and disordered eating. First, media images and stories revolving around body shape and fashion are inextricably linked to persuasive communications about race and class, gender roles and feminine identity, desire (fantasy) and its limits, power and danger, and indulgence and self-control (Budgeon and Currie, 1995; Gordon, 1990; McCracken, 1993). Second, the symbolic world of mass media significantly distorts the diversity of female body shapes and weights. Fat women are obliterated (Jasper, 1993), and the culture's few definitions of great beauty are portrayed as frequent occurrences instead of romantic fantasies (Heinberg, Thompson and Stormer, 1995).

The 'editorial' content and advertisements of those American fashion magazines and television programs favored by adolescent girls drive home the message that a beautiful, slender appearance is much more important than intelligence, careers, social causes, and even health (Budgeon and Currie, 1995; Peirce, 1990; Dietz and Strasburger, 1991). For example, although the high growth rate of adolescent girls necessitates increased amounts of energy, calcium, and iron, Guillen and Barr's (1994) review of 132 issues of *Seventeen* magazine published in even years from 1970 to 1990 found only 24 major articles on nutrition. Half of those promoted weight-loss through calorie-counting or categorization of foods into 'good versus bad,' and in three instances consumption of less than 1200 kcal per day was recommended. The 35 major fitness articles published during the study period emphasized attractiveness and calorie-burning more frequently than health.

The images and content just described combine to constitute a set of messages which can be easily organized and expressed, by young girls and authors alike, as a schematic set of beliefs (see Chapter by Smolak, Levine and Schermer in this volume): 'Beauty is the principal project of a woman's life'; 'Image is substance'; 'A slender appearance is a crucial aspect of beauty, fitness, success, and goodness'; 'Women are naturally anxious, self-conscious, and ashamed about their bodies'; 'Women can transform and renew themselves through the technology of fashion, dieting, and exercise'; and 'Fat is a sign of personal loss of control and failure.' These beliefs are abhorrent from a humanistic or feminist perspective, and maladaptive when taken to the extremes seen in disordered eating. However, they are practical from a sociocultural perspective, given the undeniable links in industrialized societies between slenderness and female beauty, and between beauty and various forms of success. The image(s) *and* substantial power generated and represented by Madonna remind us that our prevention programs will miss connection with their young audiences if we illuminate these schematic principles only to dismiss them imperiously as patently 'irrational' or 'distorted' or 'false' (Buckingham, 1990; Worsnop, 1994).

EXPOSURE AND APPEAL

Mass media are an important component of the daily lives of most children and adolescents, regardless of age, race, gender, or socioeconomic status (Arnett, 1995; Harris, 1994). A vast majority of White adolescent girls in the USA frequently read fashion or self-improvement magazines (Levine and Smolak, 1996). For example, *Seventeen* magazine currently claims a total readership of over 11,000,000 (Ms. Foundation, 1996). In the typical American household, the television is on for more than seven hours per day, providing, among other things, potential exposure to over 35,000 commercials per year. The awesome significance of the 'mass' in front of 'medium' is seen in the finding that during the 8:00 p.m. to 9:00 p.m. 'prime time' slot, more than half of all American children are watching television (Comstock and Paik, 1991).

Adolescents select and use various media for entertainment, sensation-seeking, emotion-focused coping, identification with subcultures, and exploration of identity and sexuality issues such as gender roles (Arnett, 1995). In regard to gender role exploration and socialization, several studies suggest that female adolescents and college students consider fashion ('women's') magazines and television at least a moderately important source of information about beauty, nutrition, weight management, and fitness (Herzler and Grun, 1990; Levine, Smolak and Hayden, 1994).

EARLY ADOLESCENCE AND MEDIA INVOLVEMENT

Between ages 8 and 12 the amount of time spent watching TV programs, most of which are intended for adults, increases from 2.5 to 4 hours per day (Harris, 1994). There is evidence that adolescents pay closer attention to television than do children or (for some types of programs) adults (Comstock and Paik, 1991).

In this regard, Greenberg (1974, cited in Austin and Johnson, 1996) reported that the most common reason given by children ages 9–15 for watching TV is learning about things and themselves.

Girls' intense interest in fashion magazines also emerges in early adolescence, and some preliminary evidence indicates that younger adolescent girls may be more interested than older adolescents in the magazines' beauty and style messages (Levine and Smolak, 1996). If this apparent shift toward a special intensity of media involvement during early adolescence is borne out by further research, it has clear implications for the primary prevention of eating disorders. A full understanding of those implications, however, will require a careful exploration of at least two other developmental factors in the lives of girls. These are (1) the intensification during late childhood of social comparison for the purpose of self-evaluation (Ruble, 1983); and (2) the heightening during early adolescence of the experience of one's female body as a 'site of struggle and control' in the face of harassment and objectification (Larkin, Rice and Russell, 1996).

THEORIES OF MASS MEDIA AND DISORDERED EATING: PROCESS

In a recent study by Murray, Touyz and Beumont (1996) 60–80 per cent of 80 eating-disordered patients reported that mass media had influenced the way they felt about their bodies, in part because they wanted to look like the media ideals of beauty. One 25-year-old woman with anorexia nervosa stated:

> Every magazine that you open has an article somewhere in it about different food, or diet and exercise, and when it's there constantly bombarding you – as in ads on television – you can't help but take it in. (Murray et al., 1996, p. 44)

This study emphasizes three key questions for an understanding of the relationship between mass media and disordered eating:
(1) What is the status of the evidence for the generally accepted proposition that girls and women judge themselves negatively on the basis of comparisons to the slender women portrayed so frequently and gloriously in the mass media?
(2) Is there evidence, beyond personal testimonies, for a relationship between disordered eating and exposure to glorified images of slenderness and other unhealthy media messages?

(3) Are some women more sensitive (vulnerable) to unhealthy media influences?

SOCIAL COMPARISON TO MEDIA CONTENT

Martin and Kennedy (1993, 1994) used self-report questionnaires and a projective story-telling technique to study what girls ages 8 through 18 think about as they read magazines and look at the models in advertisements and fashion layouts. For a majority of girls, even at the younger ages, there is a process of social comparison involving noticing how pretty the models are and then feeling badly about one's own appearance. Moreover, the more physically unattractive the girl perceived herself to be, the greater was her tendency to compare herself with models in advertise-ments ($r = .48$). With respect to the incentive function of pretty girls and women portrayed in the media, a 1995 Louis Harris and Associates survey commissioned by Girls Incorporated (1996) found that a significant minority of girls ages 8–11 (15 per cent) and girls ages 12–18 (16 per cent) reported that they 'diet or exercise to look like a character I've seen on TV.'

These findings, along with others reviewed elsewhere (Levine and Smolak, 1996) are fairly straightforward in supporting the relevance of social comparison for an understanding of media effects. What is not well understood are the processes linking activation of various social comparison motives to media exposure and to media influences on body image, dieting behavior, etc. For example, why would a 14-year-old working class girl from Kansas 'choose' a 25-year-old, successful New York fashion model as a standard for self-evaluation and self-improvement? Is such upward social comparison linked to the novelty, complexity, and emotional intensity of the early adolescent transition, coupled with emerging abilities for abstract thinking? Is the probability of attending to, assimilating, and comparing oneself to this standard of beauty greater for the subset of girls who enter adolescence already feeling very badly about their bodies and their selves as a result of critical messages from peers, family, coaches, etc. (Smolak and Levine, 1994; Stice, 1994)?

Heinberg, Thompson and Stormer (1995) reported the devel-opment of a Sociocultural Attitudes Towards Appearance Ques-tionnaire (SATAQ). One 8-item factor analytic subscale, which

nominally reflects 'internalization' of the cultural ideal of slenderness (cf. Stice, 1994), consists of 7 items pertaining to media
images and social comparison (e.g. 'I wish I looked like a swimsuit
model'). The SATAQ responses of children and younger adolescents have not yet been studied, but in the university sample
surveyed by the investigators there are significant relationships
(beyond self-esteem and BMI) between the internalization subscale and the drive for thinness, body dissatisfaction, and bulimia
subscales of the Eating Disorders Inventory (Heinberg et al.,
1995). Other research with college students conducted by these
investigators supports the proposition that dispositional differences in motives for social comparison concerning physical appearance are important for understanding the impact of mass media
and other cultural influences (see, e.g. Stormer and Thompson,
1996). Such findings are quite consistent with our model's conten-
tion that childhood weight- and shape-consciousness increases
both the motivation for media use in early adolescence *and* the
probability that this sociocultural influence will generate or reinforce the beliefs, anxieties, and motives at the roots of disordered
eating (Smolak and Levine, 1994, 1996).

CONTROLLED EVALUATIONS OF MEDIA EXPOSURE AND BODY
IMAGE

Currently, our understanding of the relationship between media,
social comparison, body image, and disordered eating is beset by
ambiguities and contradictions. The research reviewed above,
coupled with numerous anecdotal testimonies, strongly suggests
that (often against their better judgment) some girls and young
women ages 8–25 compare themselves unfavorably to the slender
models in fashion layouts and other advertisements. However, our
review (Levine and Smolak, 1996) of ten controlled studies (a
total of 13 experiments) clearly demonstrates that exposure to
magazine images of slender models does *not* have an immediate
negative effect on the body image of adolescent girls or young
women – *unless* they come to the laboratory already sensitive or
anxious about their body shape because of eating disordered
attitudes or pregnancy (see also Shaw and Waller, 1995). A recent
study by Shaw (1995), published after that review, is the only one
to date which has varied the type of photograph (neutral, slender

adolescent, and slender adult) and age of participants. There was a tendency for adolescent girls (mean age = 14.5) to report more body dissatisfaction than did adults (mean age = 27.3), particularly in response to pictures of slender *adult* women. In addition, as predicted by both Stice's (1994) model and our transitions model (see the next section), heavier adolescent girls reported greater body dissatisfaction in response to pictures of either slender adolescent girls or slender adult women.

The immediate effect of televised images of slender 'beauty' on body image has received far less research attention, but apparently there is still room for perplexing ambiguity. Shaw and Waller (1995) reported that 6 to 7 minutes of viewing television images of 'ideal women's bodies' did not affect the body images of either eating-disordered or non-eating-disordered women. In contrast, Heinberg and Thompson (1995) found that female university students who had high scores on a measure of bulimic cognitions and who saw 20 consecutive commercials (10 minutes) featuring attractive, slender women reported significant increases in depression and body dissatisfaction. It is ironic, given the negative results reported by Shaw and Waller (1995), that the interaction reported by Heinberg and Thompson (1995) replicates Waller and Shaw's previous findings that photographs of slender, beautiful women do indeed have a negative effect on the body image of women who already have a high drive for thiness, a fear of fat, and a belief that (slender) body shape is a central component of self-concept.

GENERAL THEORIES

The literature on media content, social comparison, and disordered eating indicates that the relationships between media and eating problems are complex and poorly understood. Unfortunately, strong suspicions or convictions (e.g. Kilbourne, 1994) about mass media as a sociocultural 'risk factor' have rarely been elaborated into theories of etiology which provide clear guidance for either studies of media effects or efforts at primary prevention (Berel and Irving, 1996). We turn now to two attempts to move beyond cumulative risk factor models (e.g. Garfinkel and Garner, 1982) to theorize about and investigate the *processes* by which mass media contribute to disordered eating in a subset of women.

The dual-pathway model. According to Stice and colleagues (1994; Stice, Nemeroff and Shaw, 1996), unhealthy messages in the mass media become a basis for bulimia nervosa when those messages are reinforced by family and peers, and when the recipient has low self-esteem, a disorganized, unstable self-concept, and a perception of herself as overweight. The disparity between this perception and the internalized ideal of slenderness generates body dissatisfaction, which then leads to restrained eating and/or negative affect. These two outcomes constitute 'dual pathways,' which operate independently or synergistically to increase the probability of binge-eating and purging. Media influences may play a secondary role in the path(s) to bulimia nervosa by providing guidance concerning extreme dietary restriction, excessive exercising, and even purging. Portions of the dual-pathway model have enough research support that this perspective should be considered a promising development for our understanding of the relationship between mass media and disordered eating (Stice, 1994; Stice et al., 1994, 1996).

The developmental transitions model. We have proposed, and provided some data in support of, a developmental model of disordered eating (see, e.g. Levine et al., 1994; Smolak and Levine, 1994, 1996; Chapter by Smolak et al. in this volume). This model concurs with Stice (1994) in emphasizing that childhood 'predispositions' are developed and maintained by teasing about weight and shape and by family and peer modeling of weight concerns. However, our model also proposes that the meaning, organization, and behavioral implications of individual and social risk factors will *change* during the early adolescent transition, as the young girl copes with transformations in her body, feelings (including sexuality), cognitive abilities, gender role expectations, relationships with girls and boys, and relationships with mother and/or father. Specifically, our model predicts that, for approximately 10–15 per cent of young girls, subthreshold and full-blown eating disorders will be a likely adaptation to the *normative* demands of the early adolescent transition. The disordered eating of this significant minority is seen as the outcome of a transaction between vulnerabilities (e.g. schematic beliefs about the importance of thinness) and *simultaneous* adolescent changes (e.g. weight gain plus dating plus increased academic demands). These transactional pathways to disordered eating are formed and reinforced within a context characterized by powerful, consistent messages from family, peers, media, educators, and the medical profession. Examples of these culturally normative but pathogenic messages are: (1) 'slenderness is very desirable and important'; (2) 'calorie-restrictive dieting is a viable path to slenderness and a testament to self-control'; and (3) 'weight and shape of the female body are legitimate targets of public scrutiny and public harassment, such as teasing about body fat' (Smolak and Levine, 1994, 1996).

The transitions model proposes that mass media may be an influential factor at several points in this process. Exposure to television programs and commercials could possibly contribute directly to a ten-year-old girl's schematic beliefs that 'fat is very bad.' Later, fashion magazines might directly trigger a 12-year-old girl's re-evaluation of the importance of attractiveness-as-slenderness in the definition of femininity. Or mass media might contribute more indirectly by serving as a socially approved source of knowledge ('There are diets that really work!') and inspiration ('*You* can use this exercise machine to transform yourself into a winner with a flat abdomen!') for an already weight-conscious 13-year-old girl as she struggles to make sense of pubertal weight gain and a budding interest in boys.

IMPLICATIONS FOR PREVENTION

Both our model and Stice's (1994) imply an opportunity for primary and secondary prevention. Although not all girls and women affected by media develop disordered eating, virtually everyone, male and female alike, is a strand of the cultural fabric which sustains anorexia nervosa, bulimia nervosa, etc. (Maine, 1991). Further, it appears that the lives of large percentages of females ages 10–40 who live in industrialized societies are adversely affected by negative body image, calorie-restrictive dieting, and binge-eating (Gordon, 1990). Thus, there is a general need to focus concurrently on reducing pressures for slenderness emanating from media *and* from family and peers, while somehow enhancing the desire and skills to resist those influences. In terms of primary prevention, both models also emphasize the need for parents, teachers, coaches, etc., to help redefine and reinforce female self-concept so that avenues for achievement, 'success', and self-acceptance include various healthy alternatives to a 'successful appearance' (see also Neumark-Sztainer, 1996; Shisslak et al., 1996). Our transitions model also predicts that primary prevention of disordered eating will be facilitated by helping girls 8–11 become critical 'readers' of media, and by providing girls 10–14 with various forms of social support (Maine, 1991; Piran, 1995; Shisslak et al., 1996), with healthier media images and narratives (Jasper, 1993; Wolf, 1991), and with special attention to their adolescent development as individuals with a 'voice' and a 'presence,' not just a body (Piran, 1995; Steiner-Adair, 1994).

Secondary prevention is indicated by the emphasis of both models on the interaction or transaction between vulnerabilities and negative sociocultural influences, including mass media (see also Killen, 1996). High risk youth from the general school population, or from certain groups (e.g. gymnastics teams), could be identified with brief screening instruments and then, with the consent of their parents, presented with a multifaceted prevention program that includes skills to resist various social pressures for slenderness, irrational fear of fat, etc. (see next sections). A good deal of work remains to be done in working out the ethics, finances, and practicality of this approach (Ponton, 1996; Shisslak et al., 1996).

MEDIA AND CURRICULUM-BASED PREVENTION

Primary prevention tries to reduce or eliminate those factors which increase the probability of disorder, while increasing those personal 'strengths' and environmental supports which decrease the probability of disorder (Albee and Gullotta, 1986). Most curricula for the primary prevention of eating disorders (e.g. Killen, 1996; Levine and Hill, 1991) try to accomplish these twin goals by offering several lessons which (1) deconstruct mass media to dilute its influence; and (2) encourage development and expression of healthier attitudes and behaviors through small-scale media production by students (see Shisslak et al., 1996). These prevention programs try to illuminate how the form (e.g. advertising techniques) and content (e.g. long-legged, slender models) of media messages combine with unhealthy messages from various sociocultural sources (e.g. teasing by peers) to glorify slenderness, denigrate fat women, delimit gender roles, promote dietary restraint,

etc. Drawing from theories which guide the prevention of substance use (e.g. Schinke et al., 1991), it is hoped that analysis of
unrealistic, unhealthy media messages, coupled with the teaching
of generalizable skills in critical thinking and decision-making, will
create and reinforce resistance to the various sociocultural influences which sustain disordered eating. In addition, students are
encouraged to create their own 'counter-media' public service
announcements, collages of pictures culled from magazines, or rap
songs. These quasi-media productions are designed to facilitate
social learning and public expression of healthy statements and
feelings about, for example, acceptance of diversity in size/shape,
or development of inner strength as opposed to a rock hard poste-
rior. Thus, the mass media component of current curriculum-based
primary prevention programs concentrates primarily on increasing
knowledge, 'improving' beliefs and attitudes, teaching critical
thinking and self-expressive 'life skills', and reinforcing public
commitment to healthier behavior.

As emphasized by Smolak and colleagues (see Chapter in this
volume), the research conducted to date does not permit us to say
whether or not multi-component curriculum-based programs sub-
sequently prevent the emergence of eating disorder symptoms in
the long run. However, the short-term effectiveness of the available programs for children and adolescents, beyond modest
increases in knowledge, is open to dispute, and we are concerned
because the programs most rigorous in their design and evaluation
(e.g. Killen, 1996) have produced only modest increases in knowledge and very little or no change in attitudes and behaviors that
increase the risk for disordered eating. Further research and
program development is clearly needed, and there are several
potentially productive directions for future investigations (see
Piran, 1995; Shisslak et al., 1996; Smolak and Levine, 1994). We
believe one of the good places to begin is a careful evaluation of
the primary prevention of cigarette smoking. As will be seen, mass
media play several important and interesting roles in effective
prevention programs in this area of health promotion.

LESSONS FROM THE PREVENTION OF CIGARETTE SMOKING

The art and science of preventing the initiation of cigarette-
smoking by adolescents ages 10–14 is far more advanced than the

prevention of eating disorders. There is compelling evidence that programs featuring certain components can retard the initiation of smoking by some students, and prevent smoking completely for other students (Pentz et al., 1989; Schinke et al., 1991). These components include: (1) provision of information about the immediate negative physical and psychological consequences of smoking cigarettes; (2) training and practice in assertive resistance of media (and other social) encouragement to smoke; (3) training and practice in 'life-skills' which improve self-esteem, communication, and coping with stress; (4) modification of prevalence estimates so as to reduce both the belief that smoking is normative and the perception of peer approval; and (5) creation of a school and community climate which does not support smoking by people in general and youth in particular. It appears that programs with a focus on changing norms and increasing life-skills, coupled with one or two of the other components, reduce the rate of experimental smoking in adolescents 12–14 by 40–75 per cent over the course of a year, and longer if booster sessions are used (Schinke et al., 1991).

The primary prevention program reported by Killen (1996) – who has worked with many leading practitioners of the primary prevention of substance abuse and cardiovascular illness – was carefully designed to incorporate the first three components listed above, but it did not address important sources of influence within the school or community. The findings of Killen's (1996) well-crafted and thoroughly evaluated project were very disappointing. In this regard researchers in Australia reported that the otherwise positive effects on girls of a norms-plus-resistance skills smoking prevention program were significantly reduced by a host of social factors, such as having a father or sister or best friend who smoked (Armstrong et al., 1990).

Such studies point to the importance of 'comprehensive community programming' for primary prevention (Murray, Prokhorov and Harty, 1994; Neumark-Sztainer, 1996). Within this approach to multidimensional social change, mass media may play a key role in increasing knowledge and motivation for change, and in helping create school/community norms which do not 'reinforce' unhealthy attitudes and behaviors. Flynn and colleagues (1994) have shown that a *combination* of school-based resistance skill training plus radio and television 'spots' pertaining to the social

learning components listed above resulted in more effective prevention of cigarette smoking by 9–12-year-olds at two-year follow-
up than did the school intervention alone.

For purposes of illustration, two more detailed examples of
multidimensional, community interventions incoporating mass
media are presented here. One is the Midwestern Prevention
Project (MPP), which has been in operation in 50 American
middle and junior high schools since 1984. It has been fairly
successful in preventing or delaying initiation (for several years)
of cigarette smoking by 11–14-year-old boys and girls from both
high and low-risk categories (see, e.g. Pentz et al., 1989). The MPP
combines classroom prevention lessons (which emphasize resistance skills and changing perceived norms), mobilization of parents
for review and support of relevant school policies, and organization and training of community leaders (including representatives
of the mass media). An important part of this community effort is
fairly extensive news coverage of the project, as well as numerous
educational 'events' on television, radio, and in the newspapers.

A second example is a project for Black elementary and middle
school children in Chicago (Kaufman, Jason, Sawlski and Halpert,
1994) in which classroom lessons (e.g. life skills, social resistance,
public commitment not to smoke) were synchronized with various
presentations by the mass media. A newspaper having a predominantly Black readership printed a 5-week curriculum. A radio
station with a weekly audience of more than 1,000,000 Black
listeners presented public service announcements, a call-in talk
show for parents, and a smoking prevention rap contest. A very
interesting feature of this moderately successful program was a
poster contest in which the five student winners had their creations
displayed on billboards throughout the community.

IMPLICATIONS

This brief review of advances in the prevention of cigarette
smoking in early adolescence points to the importance of integrat-
ing classroom lessons with changes in school policy, education of
and collaboration with various school personnel, and community
programming for parents and professionals, including frequent
mass media reinforcement of healthy knowledge, attitudes, and
behaviors (Murray et al., 1994; Neumark-Sztainer, 1996; Piran,

1995). Indeed, one reason why the prevention of cigarette smoking seems to be more effective than the prevention of alcohol use is that community norms regarding the former have changed more dramatically in the past 25 years. It is worth noting, however, that current curricular programs for the primary prevention of disordered eating are in one respect more ambitious than programs designed to prevent cigarette smoking in early adolescence. This is due to the fact that even those prevention programs which are designed for girls and boys ages 9–11 aim to reduce those weight concerns and weight management behaviors which already exist in a significant minority of the children (see Chapter by Smolak et al. in this volume).

As the experience of various non-profit eating disorder organizations has demonstrated, changing community norms about the value of slenderness, the morality of calorie-restrictive dieting, and prejudice against fat people will not be easy. Yet recent historical and sociological changes in attitudes and laws pertaining to drunk driving, cigarette smoking, and domestic violence are cause for optimism. Moreover, currently there are numerous 'pockets of resistance' on which to build sociocultural prevention efforts, including the National Association for the Advancement of Fat Acceptance, prominent actress and talk show host Rosie O'Donnell, media literacy associations, media advocacy groups (e.g. About Face/Stop Starvation Imagery), and many national and regional organizations addressing disordered eating (e.g. Eating Disorders Awareness and Prevention, Inc.; the Body Image Task Force). A full discussion of specific theories and strategies by which mental health professionals, eating disorders organizations, and other concerned citizens can change community norms is beyond the scope of this chapter (see, e.g. Piran et al., 1993). However, the next sections introduce various ways in which learning about and using the mass media can contribute to this goal.

MEDIA LITERACY

Stormer and Thompson (1995) randomly assigned young American university women to receive either no contact, a placebo health presentation, or a 30-minute psychoeducational program designed to help them resist the glorification of slenderness in magazines. This program briefly discussed the nature and impact of the slender beauty ideal, and then considered in detail how fashion models and magazines use plastic surgery, airbrushing, computer graphics, and other technology to fabricate the idealized images. The contrast between such unreal images and the average American woman was emphasized. The last 5–7 minutes of the media analysis presentation were devoted to cognitive techniques for reducing the negative effects of social comparisons by focusing on the unreality of the images. This brief instruction in 'media literacy' had no significant between-group effect on dispositional measures of body image or disordered eating. However, it did produce significant pre-to-post-program reductions in appearance- and weight-related anxiety, and in idealization of the slenderness embodied by fashion models and actresses.

GENERAL ISSUES

Stormer and Thompson's (1995) study reinforces the sense that many prevention specialists have about the importance of helping children and adolescents learn how to 'read' and 'study' media (Berel and Irving, 1996; Shisslak et al., 1996). The National Telemedia Council (1992, p. 12) offers a useful, albeit very broad, working definition of 'media literacy':

> The ability to choose, to understand – within the context of the content, form/style, impact, [media] industry and production [of media] – to question, to evaluate, to create and/or produce and to respond thoughtfully to the media we produce. It is mindful viewing, reflective judgement.

The field of media literacy is vast, rocky, and prone to the problem of colonization by an increasingly wide variety of disciplines (Buckingham, 1990). Yet, in general, practitioners of media literacy try to help students understand, among other things, that (1) all media are 'constructed,' despite their immediate and seamless appearance as reflected reality; (2) all media are linked to commercialism; (3) all media have social and political implications; and (4) at least some of the time mass media are skillfully produced and pleasurable (Worsnop, 1994).

LESSONS IN THE CLASSROOM AND AT HOME

A critical and more appreciative 'attitude' concerning media can be developed in the classroom and at home. For example, Brockie (1992) described a very clever and effective exercise in which 13-year-old boys and girls were asked to sniff unmarked scents (perfumes) and guess whether they were intended for males or females. The large number of errors students made were then contrasted with the techniques which advertisers of the scents used to establish 'obvious' gender distinctions in the marketing of their products. More so than content analysis, this engaging experience of cognitive dissonance brought about a very personal understanding of media manipulation and 'construction' or 'reality.'

Erica Austin and colleagues at Washington State University have skillfully blended developmental psychology and prevention research in the field of media literacy (see, e.g. Austin, 1993, and Austin and Johnson, 1996, for explication of their cognitive social learning approach and for data in support of the model). Austin's 'Message Interpretation Process' (MIP) model postulates two partially independent paths through which concrete operational children (ages 7–11) internalize televised messages concerning the positive effects of alcohol use. The first path is a logical sequence of questions: Is this a *realistic* or 'normative' portrayal? If so, am I (or is my experience) *similar* to this person("s)? If so, then do I want to act or be like (*identify* with) this person? Consider, for example, a 9-year-old boy who sees a commercial for beer which features young adult males playing football on a beach littered with admiring, attractive females. According to the MIP model, if the boy decides that the portrayal is realistic and that he is similar to those athletic, fun-loving males, then he will be more likely to want to 'identify with' them, which in and of itself will be translated into positive expectancies and intentions concerning the drinking of beer. The vicarious reinforcements for beer drinking – and other emotional appeals (e.g. rock music) – contained in the commercial constitutes a second, less logical path to the desire to act or be like the televised portrayal.

Using the MIP model, Austin and Johnson (1996) conducted a well-designed, well-controlled study to test the effects on children ages 7–8 of a media literacy program emphasizing the persuasive intent of commercials, the unreality of the portrayals, and the undesirability of the behavior in terms of good and bad, right and wrong. Prior to age 7 children have a good deal of difficulty understanding 'intent to sell' as a key feature of commercials and advertisements (Comstock and Paik, 1991). In Austin and Johnson's (1996) study understanding of persuasive intent (including emotional appeals) was facilitated by a 28-minute video tape (*Buy Me That!*) developed by Consumer Reports to teach children about advertising techniques. Then the children viewed and discussed a series of soda pop and beer ads, identifying the techniques they had learned about. This discussion also served as a focus for the 3 *R*'s of critical viewing (Messaris, 1982, as applied by Austin, 1993): *R*ealism, *R*ight and Wrong, and *R*elation of the information source to what other sources of information say.

Austin and Johnson (1996) found that MIP treatment vs. control differences in expectancies (e.g. 'drinking makes your happier/ more grown-up') and desirability (e.g. 'people in beer and wine ads have lots of fun') were not statistically significant. However, their brief media literacy program was effective (relative to a control group) in increasing the children's understanding of persuasive intent, in reducing how realistic they perceived the commercials to be, and in reducing the choice of an alcohol-theme toy versus a soda-pop-theme toy. Moreover, analysis of changes between the post-test and three-month follow-up revealed some evidence of a truly 'preventative' dampening effect in that control groups significantly increased their desirability ratings, whereas the experimental groups held steady.

Based on Austin's work, Berel and Irving (1996) have proposed that teachers and parents alike can, in the course of 'lessons' or more casual interactions with media, ask children a set of questions based on Austin's model: Does this advertisement present a realistic image? Do real women look like models in advertising? Will buying this product make me look like this model? Does this model look like this because of this product? In this regard Austin's model is consistent not only with the encouraging preliminary work of Stormer and Thompson (1996) described earlier, but also with developmental research suggesting that active parental interpretation and discussion of television programming can reduce its potentially negative effects (Comstock and Paik, 1991). This does not mean a blanket condemnation of 'watching the boob tube' for pleasure. Rather, parents can facilitate media literacy by 'talking back' to disturbing TV content, by actively protesting or praising content through letters to the media, and by advocating coordination between the schools and parents in the teaching of literacy skills (Osborn, 1993).

AN IMPORTANT CAVEAT

A scholarly examination of the role of mass media in the phenomenon of eating disorders, coupled with the promise of both programs like Austin's and the media literacy movement in general, emphasizes the importance of helping adults and children develop a critical resistance to destructive media messages about gender, body shape, weight, and so forth. However, we must be sensitive to the possibility of doing this in an overzealous, authoritarian fashion which simplistically condemns sources of people's pleasure (i.e. magazines and television) and thereby turns off their willingness to engage in thoughtful analysis of those messages (Buckingham, 1990; Worsnop, 1994). We should not lose sight of the fact that media literacy is a set of goals and techniques designed in part to reduce vulnerability to various negative outcomes of media exposure (e.g. sexual objectification, violence, the glorification of slenderness) by strengthening independent, informed decision-making (Osborn, 1993; Worsnop, 1994).

MASS MEDIA AND HEALTH PROMOTION

HEALTH COMMUNICATION AND PROMOTION

Theories of etiology (e.g. Stice, 1994), studies of media content (Levine and Smolak, 1996), and analysis-as-resistance prevention lessons (Killen, 1996) demonstrate that at present, for those committed to the primary prevention of eating disorders, the mass media serve primarily as a many-headed monster to be engaged in battle. This perspective is understandable, but it diverts attention from the fact that television, radio, and print media are capable of delivering messages which clearly promote size acceptance, positive body image, etc. A good example is journalist Linda Ellerbee's one-hour television program (Nick News Special Edition, 1996) showing a variety of adolescents discussing (and promoting) these messages with plus-size and popular comedian Rosie O'Donnell and with noted eating disorder expert Dr. James Rosen of the University of Vermont. As the host of a very popular daytime talk show, Ms. O'Donnell is currently using her position to model and otherwise promote size acceptance to a very large audience of women and men. All in all, however, American television has presented very little information which might help undermine drive for thinness, fear of fat, looksism as sexism, etc. (Levine and Smolak, 1996). And even though television news specials and magazines marketed for women have devoted considerable attention to eating disorders, the theme is usually an individual's descent into hell followed by a remarkable recovery/salvation. This drama could be helpful in secondary and tertiary prevention, but it maintains a medical model of individual disease which ignores primary prevention by deflecting attention away from unhealthy sociocultural contexts (Wallack et al., 1993).

Television shows, whether they are dramas or documentaries, do carry a special risk. It is impossible to monitor who views these shows. It is likely, for example, that elementary school-age children will see programs intended for adolescents and even adults (Harris, 1994). Young children might easily misinterpret information, especially concerning eating disorders. Indeed, we have argued elsewhere (Smolak and Levine, 1994) that inclusion of such material is inappropriate in elementary school primary prevention curricula. Producers of these programs need to keep in mind that children will probably not be watching the shows together with adults trained to help them process frightening or confusing material. Similarly, girls who are on the brink of an eating disorder might view the iron determination of some of the featured women to lose weight as admirable and even inspirational. Again, such girls have no one there to help them reinterpret these messages.

We suggest, then, that producers avoid the admittedly dramatic images of women suffering from anorexia nervosa and bulimia nervosa, and instead emphasize positive images of body esteem and acceptance. Should a program focus on the actual eating disorders, warnings should be provided to parents and the program should be scheduled at a time or in a context when it is less likely to be viewed by young children. Finally, as is true of all prevention efforts, evaluation research can help us to understand both the intended effects and the unentional consequences of such programs.

Given the media's status as and dependency on big business, it is reasonable to contend that media self-scrutiny and media involvement in promoting good health are complete oxymorons. It has long been known that women's magazines provide inadequate coverage of lung cancer as a health risk because to do so effectively would jeopardize millions of dollars in revenue from cigarette advertising (Strasburger, 1993). The 3 June 1996 issue of *People* magazine, whose cover story focused on media and disordered eating, could well be said to have accomplished little more than providing a tidy opportunity to accentuate more of the slender, 'beautiful' bodies it was ostensibly analyzing.

Less cynical but well-informed readers would be correct in adding that media 'health campaigns' are very difficult for even experts to do effectively (Brown and Walsh-Childers, 1994). American mass media and much of its audience prefer 'controversy and high drama' over clear and informative messages (Comstock, 1983), and the relationship between mass media and consulting scholars committed to health promotion is an uneasy one (Johnson and Ettema, 1982). Moreover, some attitudes (e.g. drinking alcohol is fun, desirable, and essentially harmless for teenagers; predatory sexual behavior is 'cool') are notoriously resistant to curricular or media counterarguments (Austin and Meili, 1994), if for no other reason than these attitudes are continually reinforced by the frequent exposure of adolescents to adult and peer modeling of the behavior. It is also very challenging to produce health promotion messages in a manner that combines good theory, artistic merit, and solid research. And even if high-quality messages result, there is still the imposing tasks of attracting and holding the attention of the desired audiences, getting them to discuss and elaborate the material, and developing the summative research necessary to document changes, if any, in attitudes and behavior (Flay and Burton, 1990).

Yet none of these important methodological concerns should dissuade those of us devoted to a full exploration of the ideal of primary prevention of eating disorders from discussing ways in which the mass media might help that cause. Americans who were born between 1945 and 1967 need only remind ourselves how the relationships between big business, media, cultural attitudes, scholarly activism, and both cigarette smoking and women's roles have changed in the past 25 years (Comstock, 1983). One reason the cigarette industry acceded to the 1971 ban on use of American television for advertising is that the 1967 Fairness Doctrine of the US Federal Communications Commission compelling (relatively limited) opportunities for anti-cigarette advertising was having an extremely negative impact on sales (Altman, 1990). It is worth keeping in mind that by law in the USA the mass media serve the public interest, and that the public has a great interest in health issues (Wallack et al., 1993).

There is also a fairly substantial research basis for optimism about the role of mass media *as one factor* in setting health agendas, communicating good information about health, and promoting health in various, creative ways (Comstock, 1983; Rice and Atkin, 1989). Several research projects conducted in the United States have demonstrated conclusively that a well-planned combination of mass media campaigns, public education and school curricula based on social learning theory, and organizing to affect the business and medical communities can reduce the initiation of cigarette smoking by middle school children (Pentz et al., 1989), increase nutritional knowledge and healthy eating behavior in that same population (Kelder, Perry, Lytle and Klepp, 1995), and improve cardiovascular health in adults (Flora, Maccoby and Farquhar, 1989). In some of these multi-dimensional programs particular attention was paid to 'social marketing' issues, such as the segmentation of audiences based on differential needs, and analysis of which 'channels' (e.g. TV, radio, newspapers) are most likely to be used by those audiences (Wallack et al., 1993).

'Prosocial' television programs designed to promote health and to be entertaining are also a promising possibility. In the mid-1980s the Indian soap opera *Hum Log* (We People), broadcast twice per week in Hindi to 50–80 million viewers, accomplished one of its major priorities by changing viewer attitudes towards equal status for women and small family size (Singhal and Rogers, 1989). In the same vein, Johnston and Ettema (1982) described efforts by government agencies, academic researchers, curriculum experts, and members of the TV industry to blend story-telling and social learning theory in the production of the 1977–1978 dramatic series *Freestyle* and accompanying curricular materials. The 13 episodes were designed to promote healthier sex-role concepts in 9-to-12-year-old boys and girls by emphasizing 'nurturant activities for boys, and mechanics, science, and athletics for girls' (Johnston and Ettema, 1982, p. 142). The thorough summative evaluation indicated that, when supplemented by classroom discussion and elaboration, exposure to the series was successful in increasing positive attitudes towards men and women who engage in various nontraditional roles and pursuits.

This brief consideration of mass media and health promotion is intended to raise two key points. First, primary prevention programs for schools and communities will probably be more effective if they are buttressed and extended by some type of mass media campaign. Second, if mass media are as potent a negative force as many prevention specialists seem to think, then those and other media need to be explored more fully as potential avenues for positive change. Although production costs may be high, there are potential public and private funding sources, and the cost of the messages per receiver is quite low because so many people of all ages are engaged with media so frequently (Schilling and McAlister, 1990). If projected costs are too high, then collaboration with a good public relations firm could result in a limited campaign which targets a small percentage of the audience, e.g. physicians or coaches, who are opinion leaders and agents of change (Alcalay and Taplin, 1989).

At this point we are not prepared to offer specific, detailed proposals for the 'five Ps' – Product, Price, Promotion, Place, Positioning (Solomon, 1989) – of social marketing campaigns or for prosocial dramatic productions designed to help prevent eating disorders. In the interest of stimulating further discussion, we suggest that, for example, popular music, public service announcements on MTV, and engaging sites on the World Wide Web may be potentially effective ways of communicating health promotion messages to various segmented groups of adolescents. The content of such messages could address one's right to be safe from harassment (Larkin et al., 1996), the need for non-body-related avenues of success for women (Wolf, 1991), and the relationship between dieting and binge-eating (Garner and Wooley, 1991). Promising themes for dramatic presentations on television and in magazines might well include the tragedy of discrimination against fat people, the dangers presented by an unregulated diet industry (Garner and Wooley, 1991), a father's recognition of his real priorities through a commitment to being physically and emotionally present during his daughter's development in early adolescence (Maine, 1991), and the ability of women to provide each other with social support toward the goal of abandoning vicious cycles of negative body image, dieting, and weight-gain.

ACTIVISM AND PROTEST

It is very unlikely that even a large improvement in the amount of health promotion through the mass media will eclipse the many unhealthy messages concerning weight, shape, eating, gender roles, etc. Thus, we believe that primary prevention will require more of the type of political and economic activism shown by such groups as Boycott Anorexic Marketing (Miller, 1994), About-Face (1996; formerly, the Stop Starvation Imagery Campaign), the National Association for the Advancement of Fat Acceptance (NAAFA), and the National Association of Anorexia Nervosa and Associated Disorders (ANAD, 1989). In late September of 1988 ANAD, led by Dr Vivian Meehan, mounted a petitions and letter-writing campaign to protest the Hershey Foods Corporation's advertising campaign (for a thin chocolate bar) which proclaimed that 'You can never be too rich or too thin.' The company withdrew the ad on October 17, 1988. Similarly, in the summer of 1996, Dr Cynthia Whitehead-Laboo of the Emory University Counseling Center and Dr Michael Levine of Kenyon College mobilized a group of eating disorder professionals (who had formed an electronic mail discussion group following attendance at a Pennsylvania State University conference) to protest a Hormel Meat Company commercial in which a five-year-old girl refuses a piece of birthday cake because 'it will go straight to my hips.' The company later suspended this advertising campaign.

Stephens, Hill and Hanson (1994) suggest that prevention activists in the United States direct their attention to claims by diet centers, cosmetic surgeons, and others who might well be in violation of Federal Trade Commission guidelines for fair advertising. In this regard the Academy of Eating Disorders and other professional organizations whose mission encompasses primary prevention might follow the lead of the American Academy of Pediatricians in developing a subcommittee devoted to the study and positive transformation of mass media (Dietz and Strasburger,

1991). This sort of activism serves the cause of prevention in two ways: It highlights the possibility of educating businesses about the social and economic implications of unhealthy promotional messages, and it models for children and adolescents the power of collaboration between passionately committed women and respectful men.

MEDIA ADVOCACY

Another compelling possibility for the role of mass media in the prevention of disordered eating is media advocacy. This is a set of tactics 'for community groups to communicate their own story in their own words. It [combines] community advocacy approaches with the strategic and innovative use of media to better pressure decision makers to change policy' (Wallack et al., 1993, p. xi). This type of activism draws on an understanding of how media in general and news reporting in particular work to determine agendas and delimit dialogue. As such, media advocacy techniques could aid prevention groups such as the Association of Anorexia Nervosa and Associated Disorders (ANAD) and the National Eating Disorder Organization (NED0) in helping the public and its leaders to construe eating disorders, not just as individual cases of disease, but in terms of social policy issues pertaining to public safety, public health, and gender equity. We recommend that those committed to primary prevention of eating disorders consult with, and perhaps join forces with, advocacy organizations such as Children Now or Girls Incorporated (1996).

CONCLUSIONS AND FUTURE DIRECTIONS

At present, future directions clearly outnumber solid conclusions in the study of the relationship between mass media and disordered eating (Levine and Smolak, 1996). The content of fashion magazines and television, a vast amount of data from clinical interactions with eating disordered clients, and a growing body of correlational data strongly implicate mass media in the development and maintenance of disordered eating (Kilbourne, 1994; Levine and Smolak, 1996; Stice, 1994). The nature of those influences remains a tantalizing mystery, and there is a need for more research guided by multidimensional theoretical models such as that of Stice (1994) and by incorporation of findings from the developmental psychology of both media effects and health promotion (Austin, 1995; Brooks-Gunn, 1993; Van Ezra, 1990).

This said, it is a stultifying fallacy to believe that effective primary prevention requires a complete understanding of developmental pathways (Albee and Gullotta, 1986), or that primary prevention research is fundamentally incompatible with studies of etiology. Lack of clarity in the developmental pathways to disordered eating need not deter us from moving forward with comprehensive school-plus-community efforts to: (1) use mass media to frame the phenomenon of eating disorders in terms of important social issues (Wallack et al., 1993); (2) promote personal and systemic changes which reduce risk factors (Neumark-Sztainer, 1996); and (3) enhance protective factors such as a sense of competency apart from weight and shape management (Smolak and Levine, 1994), media literacy (Berel and Irving, 1996), and safety from harassment and objectification (Larkin et al., 1996).

We close by emphasizing what we hope is now obvious. To realize the dream of transforming mass media from 'major risk factor' to 'advocacy tool and significant source of health promotion' will require a new, 'bolder' model of the prevention specialist as scientist, researcher, activist, collaborator, artist, cultural critic and even business associate (Murray and Ozanne, 1991). The challenges are enormous, but so, we believe, is the potential for the type of personal-professional-social transformation that may well be necessary to buffer and eventually reverse the weightism and sexism embodied in today's mass media.

REFERENCES

About-Face (1996) *About-face: About time*, San Francisco: About-Face.

Albee, G.W. and Gullotta, T.P. (1986) 'Facts and fallacies about primary prevention'. *Journal of Primary Prevention*, 6: 207–18.

Alcalay, R. and Taplin, S. (1989) 'Community health campaigns: From theory to action'. In Rice, R.E. and Atkin, C.K. (eds) *Public communication campaigns* (2nd ed., pp. 105–29), Newbury Park, CA: Sage.

Altman, D.G. (1990) 'The social context and health behavior: The case of tobacco'. In Shumaker, S.A., Schron, E.B. and Ockene, J.K. (eds) *The handbook of health behavior change* (pp. 241–69), New York: Springer.

Armstrong, B.K., de Klerk, N.H., Shean, R.E., Dunn, D.A. and Dolin,

P.J. (1990) 'Influence of education and advertising on the uptake of smoking by children'. *Medical Journal of Australia*, 152: 117–24.

Arnett, J.J. (1995) 'Adolescents' use of media for self-socialization'. *Journal of Youth and Adolescence*, 24: 519–33.

Austin, E.W. (1993) 'Exploring the effects of active parental mediation of television content'. *Journal of Broadcasting and Electronic Media,*, 37: 147–58.

——(1995) 'Reaching young audiences: Developmental considerations in designing health messages'. In Parrott, R. and Maibach, E. (eds) *Designing health messages: Approaches from communication theory and public health practice* (pp. 114–43), Thousand Oaks, CA: Sage.

Austin, E.W. and Johnson, K.K. (1996) *Immediate and delayed effects of media literacy training on third graders' decision-making for alcohol,* Seattle: Washington State University.

Austin, E.W. and Meili, H.K. (1994) 'Effects of interpretation of televised alcohol portrayal on children's alcohol beliefs'. *Journal of Broadcasting and Electronic Media*, 38: 417–35.

Berel, S. and Irving, L. (1996, March) *Media and disturbed eating: An analysis of media influence and implications for prevention*, Paper presented at the Association for Women in Psychology Conference, Portland, OR.

Brockie, D. (1992) 'Sniffing out stereotypes: Using fragrances to explore gender images in advertising'. In Alvarado, M. and Boyd-Barrett, O. (eds) *Media education: An introduction* (pp. 350–8), London: British Film Institute.

Brooks-Gunn, J. (1993) 'Why do adolescents have difficulty adhering to health regimes?' In Krasnegor, N.A., Epstein, L., Johnson, S.B. and Yaffe, S.J. (eds) *Developmental aspects of health compliance behavior* (pp. 125–52), Hillsdale, NJ: Lawrence Erlbaum Associates.

Brown, J.D. and Walsh-Childers, K. (1994) 'Effects of media on personal and public health'. In Bryant, J. and Zillman, D. (eds) *Media effects: Advances in theory* (pp. 389–415). Hillsdale, NJ: Lawrence Erlbaum Associates.

Buckingham, D. (Ed.) (1990) *Watching media learning: Making sense of media education,* London: Falmer Press.

Budgeon, S. and Currie, D.H. (1995) 'From feminism to postfeminism: Women's liberation in fashion magazines'. *Women's Studies International Forum*, 18: 173–86.

Comstock, G. (1983) 'The mass media and social change'. In Seidman, E. (ed) *Handbook of social intervention* (pp. 268–88), Beverly Hills, CA: Sage.

Comstock, G. and Paik, H. (1991) *Television and the American child,* San Diego: Academic Press.

Debold, E. (1994) *Body politic: Transforming adolescent girls' health. A report of the 1994 proceedings of Healthy Girls/Health Women Research Roundtable,* New York: Ms. Foundation for Women.

Dietz, W.H. and Strasburger, V.C. (1991) 'Children, adolescents, and television'. *Current Problems in Pediatrics,* 21: 8–31.

Flay, B.R. and Burton, D. (1990) 'Effective mass media communication strategies for health campaigns'. In Atkin, C. and Wallack, L. (eds) *Mass communication and public health: Complexities and conflicts* (pp. 129–46), Newbury Park, CA: Sage.

Flora, J.A., Maccoby, N. and Farquhar, J.W. (1989) 'Communication campaigns to prevent cardiovascular disease: The Stanford community studies'. In Rice, R.E. and Atkin, C.K. (eds) *Public communication campaigns* (2nd ed., pp. 233–52), Newbury Park, CA: Sage.

Flynn, B.S., Worden, J.K., Scker-Walker, R.H., Pirie, P.L., Badger, G.J., Carpenter, J.H. and Geller, B.M. (1994) 'Mass media and school interventions for cigarette smoking: Effects 2 years after completion'. *American Journal of Public Health,* 84(7): 1148–50.

Garfinkel, P.E. and Garner, D.M. (1982) *Anorexia nervosa: A multidimensional approach,* New York: Brunner/Mazel.

Garner, D.M. and Wooley, S.C. (1991) 'Confronting the failure of behavioral and dietary treatments for obesity'. *Clinical Psychology Review,* 11: 729–80.

Girls Incorporated (1996) *Re-casting TV: Girls' views. A nationwide survey of school-age children (by Louis Harris and Associates),* New York: Girls Inc.

Gordon, R.A. (1990) *Anorexia and bulimia: Anatomy of a social epidemic,* Cambridge, MA: Basil Blackwell.

Guillen, E.O and Barr, S.I. (1994) 'Nutrition, dieting, and fitness messages in a magazine for adolescent women, 1970–1990'. *Journal of Adolescent Health,* 15: 464–72.

Harris, R.J. (1994) *A cognitive psychology of mass communication* (2nd ed.). Hillsdale, NJ: Erlbaum.

Heinberg, L.J. and Thompson, J.K. (1995) 'Body image and televised images of thinness and attractiveness: A controlled laboratory investigation'. *Journal of Social and Clinical Psychology,* 14: 325–38.

Heinberg, L.J., Thompson, J.K. and Stormer, S. (1995) 'Development and validation of the Sociocultural Attitudes Towards Appearance Questionnaire'. *International Journal of Eating Disorders,* 17: 81–9.

Herzler, A.A. and Grun, I. (1990) 'Potential nutrition messages in magazines read by college students'. *Adolescence*, 25: 717–24.

Jasper, K. (1993) 'Monitoring and responding to media messages'. *Eating Disorders: The Journal of Treatment and Prevention*, 1: 109–14.

Johnston, J. and Ettema, J.S. (1982) *Positive images: Breaking stereotypes with children's television,* Beverly Hills, CA: Sage.

Kaufman, J.S., Jason, L.A., Sawlski, L.M. and Halpert, J.A. (1994) 'A comprehensive multi-media program to prevent smoking among black students'. *Journal of Drug Education*, 24: 95–108.

Kelder, S.H., Perry, C.L., Lytle L.A. and Klepp, K.-I. (1995) 'Community-wide youth nutrition education: Long-term outcomes of the Minnesota Heart Health Program'. *Health Education Research*, 10: 119–31.

Kendler, K.S., MacLean, C., Neale, M., Kessler, R., Heath, A. and Eaves, L. (1991) 'The genetic epidemiology of bulimia nervosa'. *American Journal of Psychiatry*, 148: 267–72.

Kilbourne, J. (1994) 'Still killing us softly: Advertising and the obsession with thinness'. In Fallon, P.A., Katzman, M.A. and Wooley, S.C. (eds) *Feminist perspectives on eating disorders* (pp. 395–418), New York: Guilford.

Killen, J.D. (1996) 'Development and evaluation of a school-based eating disorder symptoms prevention program'. In Smolak, L., Levine, M.P. and Striegel-Moore, R. (eds) *The developmental psychopathology of eating disorders* (pp. 313–39), Mahwah, NJ: Lawrence Erlbaum Associates.

Larkin, J., Rice, C. and Russell, V. (1996) 'Slipping through the cracks: Sexual harassment, eating problems, and the problem of embodiment'. *Eating Disorders: The Journal of Treatment and Prevention*, 4: 5–26.

Levine, M.P. and Hill, L. (1991) *A 5 day lesson plan book on eating disorders: Grades 7–12,* Tulsa, OK: National Eating Disorder Organization.

Levine, M.P. and Smolak, L. (1996) 'Media as a context for the development of disordered eating'. In Smolak, L., Levine, M.P. and Striegel-Moore, R. (eds) *The developmental psychopathology of eating disorders* (pp. 235–57), Mahwah, NJ: Lawrence Erlbaum Associates.

Levine, M.P., Smolak, L. and Hayden, H. (1994) 'The relation of sociocultural factors to eating attitudes and behaviors among middle school girls'. *Journal of Early Adolescence*, 14: 472–91.

Lucas, A.R., Beard, C.M., O'Fallon, W.M. and Kurland, L.T. (1991) '50-year trends in the incidence of anorexia nervosa in Rochester, Minn: A population-based study'. *American Journal of Psychiatry*, 148: 917–22.

Maine, M. (1991) *Father hunger: Fathers, daughters and food.* Carlsbad, CA: Gürze Books.

Martin, M.C. and Kennedy, P.F. (1993) 'Advertising and social comparison: Consequences for female preadolescents and adolescents'. *Psychology and Marketing*, 10: 513–30.

Martin, M.C. and Kennedy, P.F. (1994) 'Social comparison and the beauty of advertising models: The role of motives for comparison'. *Advances in Consumer Research*, 21: 365–71.

McCracken, E. (1993) *Decoding women's magazines: From Mademoiselle to Ms,* New York: St. Martin's Press.

Miller, C. (1994) '"Give them a cheeseburger": Critics assail waif look in Sprite, Calvin Klein ads'. *Marketing News*, 28(12): 1, 6.

Ms. Foundation (1996) *Teenagers under pressure: A report commissioned by Seventeen and the Ms. Foundation*, New York: Ms. Foundation for Women.

Murray, D.M., Prokhorov, A.V. and Harty, K.C. (1994) 'Effects of statewide antismoking campaign on mass media messages and smoking beliefs'. *Preventive Medicine*, 23: 54–60.

Murray, J.B. and Ozanne, J.L. (1991) 'The critical imagination: Emancipatory interests in consumer research'. *Journal of Consumer Research*, 18: 129–44.

Murray, S.H., Touyz, S.W. and Beumont, P.J.V. (1996) 'Awareness and perceived influence of body ideals in the media: A comparison of eating disorder patients and the general community'. *Eating Disorders: The Journal of Treatment and Prevention*, 4(1): 33–46.

National Association of Anorexia Nervosa and Associated Disorders (ANAD) (1989) *Hershey Foods Corporation agrees to discontinue ad,* Highland Park, IL: ANAD.

National Telemedium Council (1992) 'Media literacy'. *Telemedium: The Newsletter of the National Telemedia Council*, 38: 12.

Neumark-Sztainer, D. (1996) 'School-based programs for preventing eating disturbances'. *Journal of School Health*, 66(2): 64–71.

Nick News Special Edition (1996) *The Body Trap*, New York: Nickelodeon. [On-line information available at http://www.metropolis-studios]

Osborn, J. (1993) *TV alert: A wakeup guide for television literacy (Leader's guide and handout master*. Los Angeles: Center for Media and Values.

Peirce, K. (1990) 'A feminist theoretical perspective on the socialization of teenage girls through *Seventeen* magazine'. *Sex Roles*, 23: 491–500.

Pentz, M. A., Dwyer, J., MacKinnon, D.P., Flay, B.R., Hansen, W.B., Wang, E.Y. and Johnson, C.A. (1989) 'A multicommunity trial for primary prevention of adolescent drug abuse: Effects on drug use prevalence'. *Journal of the American Medical Association*, 261: 3259–66.

Piran, N. (1995) 'Prevention: Can early lessons lead to a delineation of an alternative model? A critical look at prevention with schoolchildren', *Eating Disorders: The Journal of Treatment and Prevention*, 3: 28–36.

Piran, N., Bear, M. and Jasper, K. (1993) 'Prevention of eating disorders'. In Kennedy, S. (ed) *Handbook of the treatment of eating disorders* (pp. 55–65), Toronto: University of Toronto Press.

Ponton, L.E. (1996) 'Disordered eating'. In DiClemente, R.J., Hansen, W.B. and Ponton, L.E. (eds) *Handbook of adolescent health risk behavior* (pp. 83–113), New York: Plenum.

Rice, R.E, and Atkin, C.A. (Eds.) (1989) *Public communication campaigns* (2nd ed.), Newbury Park, CA: Sage.

Ruble, D.N. (1983) 'The development of social-comparison processes and their role in achievement-related self-socialization'. In Higgins, E.T., Ruble, D.N. and Hartup, W.W. (eds) *Social cognition and social development: A sociocultural perspective* (pp. 134–57), Cambridge: Cambridge University Press.

Schilling, R.F. and McAlister, A.L. (1990) 'Preventing drug use in adolescents through media interventions'. *Journal of Consulting and Clinical Psychology*, 58: 416–24.

Schinke, S.P., Botvin, G.J. and Orlandi, M.A. (1991) *Substance abuse in children and adolescents: Evaluation and interventions,* Newbury Park, CA: Sage.

Shaw, J. (1995) 'Effects on fashion magazines on body dissatisfaction and eating psychopathology in adolescent and adult females'. *European Eating Disorders Review*, 3: 15–23.

Shaw, J. and Waller, G. (1995) 'The media's impact on body image: Implications for prevention and treatment'. *Eating Disorders: The Journal of Treatment and Prevention*, 3: 115–23.

Shisslak, C.M., Crago, M., Estes, L.S. and Gray, N. (1996) 'Content and method of developmentally appropriate prevention programs'. In Smolak, L., Levine, M.P. and Striegel-Moore, R. (eds) *The developmental psychopathology of eating disorders: Implications for research, prevention, and treatment* (pp. 341–63), Mahwah, NJ: Lawrence Erlbaum Associates.

Singhal, A. and Rogers, E.M. (1989) 'Prosocial television for development in India'. In Rice, R.E. and Atkin, C.K. (eds) *Public communication campaigns* (2nd ed., pp. 331–50), Newbury Park, CA: Sage.

Smolak, L. and Levine, M.P. (1994) 'Critical issues in the developmental psychopathology of eating disorders'. In Alexander, L. and Lumsden, D.B. (eds) *Understanding eating disorders* (pp. 37–60), Washington, D.C.: Taylor and Francis.

——(1996) 'Adolescent transitions and the development of eating problems'. In Smolak, L., Levine, M.P. and Striegel-Moore, R. (eds) *The developmental psychopathology of eating disorders* (pp. 207–33), Mahwah, NJ: Lawrence Erlbaum Associates.

Solomon, D.S. (1989) 'A social marketing perspective on communication campaigns'. In Rice, R.E. and Atkin, C.K. (eds) *Public communication campaigns* (2nd ed., pp. 87–104), Newbury Park, CA: Sage.

Steiner-Adair, C. (1994) 'The politics of prevention'. In Fallon, P., Katzman, M. and Wooley, S.C. (eds) *Feminist perspectives on eating disorders* (pp. 381–94). New York: Guilford Press.

Stephens, D.L., Hill, R.P. and Hanson, C. (1994) 'The beauty myth and female consumers: The controversial role of advertising'. *Journal of Consumer Affairs*, 28: 137–53.

Stice, E. (1994) 'Review of the evidence for a sociocultural model of bulimia nervosa and an exploration of the mechanisms of action'. *Clinical Psychology Review*, 14: 633–61.

Stice, E., Nemeroff, C. and Shaw, H. (1996) 'A test of the dual pathway model of bulimia nervosa: Evidence for restrained-eating and affect-regulation mechanisms'. *Journal of Social and Clinical Psychology,* 15: 340–63.

Stice, E., Schupak-Neuberg, E., Shaw, H.E. and Stein, R.I. (1994) 'Relation of media exposure to eating disorder symptomatology: An examination of mediating mechanisms'. *Journal of Abnormal Psychology,* 103: 836–40.

Stormer, S.M. and Thompson, J.K. (1995) *The effect of media images and sociocultural beauty ideals on college-age women: A proposed psycho-educational program.* Paper presented at the annual meeting of the Association for the Advancement of Behavior Therapy, Washington, D.C.

——(1996) 'Explanations of body image disturbance: A test of maturational status, negative verbal commentary, social comparison, and sociocultural hypotheses'. *International Journal of Eating Disorders*, 19: 193–202.

Strasburger, V.C. (1993) 'Adolescents, drugs, and the media'. *Adolescent Medicine: State of the Art Reviews*, 4: 391–415.

Van Ezra, J. (1990) *Television and child development.* Hillsdale, NJ: Lawrence Erlbaum Associates.

Wallack, L., Dorfman L., Jernigan, D. and Themba, M. (1993) *Media advocacy and public health: Power for prevention,* Newbury Park, CA: Sage.

Wolf, N. (1991) *The beauty myth: How images of beauty are used against women,* New York: William Morrow.

Worsnop, C.M. (1994) *Screening images: Ideas for media education,* Mississauga, Ontario: Wright Communications.

ACKNOWLEDGEMENT

The supportive efforts of Ms Cynthia Wallace and her staff at the Interlibrary Loan Office of the Kenyon College Library are gratefully acknowledged.

CHAPTER THREE

The McKnight Foundation prospective study of risk factors for the development of eating disorders

Catherine M. Shisslak, Marjorie Crago, Norma Gray, Linda S. Estes, Katherine McKnight, Ori G. Parnaby, Tamara Sharpe, Susan Bryson, Joel Killen and C. Barr Taylor

INTRODUCTION

Eating disorders are the third most common chronic condition among adolescent girls in the United States (Fisher et al., 1995). Full syndrome eating disorder cases occur in approximately 1–3 per cent of the adolescent population, but many more adolescents suffer from partial syndrome eating disorders, meeting many, but not all, of the criteria for full syndrome disorder. Individuals with a partial syndrome disorder often engage in the same disturbed eating behaviors as those with full syndrome eating disorders, but at a somewhat lower level of frequency or severity. Partial syndrome eating disorders are estimated to occur in 5–10 per cent of the adolescent population (Shisslak, Crago and Estes, 1995; Killen et al., 1997).

In addition, a number of adolescent girls are engaging in unhealthy eating and weight-related behaviors that could lead to eating disorders in the future. Approximately two-thirds of adolescent girls in the United States report that they feel too fat and have engaged in dieting to lose weight (Shisslak, Crago and Estes, 1995). Even prepubertal girls report dieting to lose weight. In one study, 28 per cent of second grade girls reported that they had been on a diet (Thelen, Lawrence and Powell, 1992). There is evidence that girls who begin dieting in elementary school increase the frequency of their dieting behavior by middle school and have poorer body esteem than non-dieting girls (Smolak and Levine, 1996). Many of the girls who are dieting are not overweight, and some are even underweight (Killen et al., 1987; Koff and Rierdan, 1991). In addition to dieting, 5–15 per cent of adolescent girls are using unhealthy weight control methods such as self-induced vomiting, laxatives, and diuretics (Killen et al., 1986; Phelps et al., 1993).

Dieting in prepubertal girls can have serious health consequences since excessive weight loss at this age can lead to retarded growth and delayed puberty (Mallick, 1983). In addition, children who diet may show the same hyperemotionality, fatigue, impaired concentration, low self-esteem, and depression that adult dieters do (Polivy and Thomasen, 1988; Rosen, Gross and Vara, 1987). Moreover, eating disorders are serious and life threatening illnesses with various medical complications (Kaplan and Garfinkel, 1993) and have the highest mortality rates of any psychiatric disorder (Herzog and Copeland, 1985).

Because of the subsequent health problems and the increased likelihood of death associated with the unhealthy eating and weight-regulation practices characteristic of both partial- and full-syndrome eating disorders, successful prevention is vitally important to the health and well-being of developing girls. Therefore we need a strong knowledge base on which to build successful prevention programs. This includes a clear understanding of which factors are associated with the onset of partial- and full-syndrome eating disorders (i.e. risk factors and risk markers), which factors are associated with the reduction of risk (i.e. protective factors) and the mechanism(s) by which these factors work. It is important to design studies that not only identify risk and protective factors, but that assess the trajectories of these factors over time. Specification of risk and protective factors as well as their trajectories can best be accomplished through longitudinal studies. The correct identification of factors and their trajectories also highlights the importance of carefully considering at what developmental level one should begin measuring. Finally, developing sound risk models emphasizes the importance of taking into account multiple factors in the etiology of eating disorders.

In this chapter we describe an ongoing, multi-site, longitudinal study for the identification of risk and protective factors for the onset of partial- and full-syndrome eating disorders, as well as the measurement of their trajectories over a four year period. We will describe the design of this study taking into consideration the above points for improving the knowledge base on which to build successful prevention programs for eating disorders.

RISK AND PROTECTIVE FACTORS

As previously stated, to correctly model the trajectories of risk and protective factors over time, it is important to consider at what developmental level to begin the longitudinal study. Because body image and dieting behaviors begin to emerge in girls between the ages of 9 and 11 (Koff and Rierdan, 1991; Mellin, Irwin and Scully, 1992) and increase dramatically during the transition to middle/junior high school (Richards, Casper and Larson, 1990), it is important to focus on elementary and middle school girls. Therefore, our longitudinal study begins with 6 cohorts of girls (grades 4–9), the youngest starting at age 9, and follows each of these cohorts for 4 years. In addition, because risk factors of a biological, psychological, familial, and sociocultural nature are hypothesized to contribute to the development of eating disorders (Striegel-Moore, Silberstein and Rodin, 1986; Levine and Smolak, 1992), we designed a survey to measure both risk and protective factors from multiple domains. Some of these domains are described in detail below.

PUBERTY/MATURATIONAL DEVELOPMENT

Several studies have found that early maturation and pubertal development are risk factors for eating disorders (Graber et al., 1994; Killen et al., 1992). Such a finding is not surprising, since puberty is associated with a considerable increase in fat tissue for girls and the avoidance of weight/fat gain is a major risk factor for developing eating disorders. However, the role of puberty remains controversial and needs further clarification. It is not known if early maturation, per se, is important or if the increased risk for developing eating disorders reflects some other factor associated with early maturation such as early dating.

BINGE-PURGE BEHAVIORS

Although behaviors such as self-induced vomiting and laxative or diuretic use are symptoms of an eating disorder, they can occur in the absence of other necessary symptoms for a diagnosis of partial- or full-syndrome eating disorders. However, these behaviors have been found to contribute to the later development of an eating disorder. Five to 15 per cent of adolescent girls use these unhealthy weight control methods (Killen et al., 1986; Phelps et al., 1993; Mellin, Irwin and Scully, 1992).

WEIGHT REGULATION/OVERCONCERN WITH WEIGHT AND SHAPE

By age 13, 80 per cent of girls (compared with 10 per cent of boys) have already been on a weight-loss diet (Mellin, Scully and Irving, 1986). In a study of 61 London school girls drawn from an epidemiological sample, 41 per cent were no longer dieting 12 months later and a similar sized group (38 per cent) were still classified as dieters. However, about 20 per cent of this dieting group had progressed to an eating disorder after 12 months. By contrast, only 3 per cent of non-dieters were diagnosed as having such a disorder after 12 months (Patton et al., 1990). In a study of 4th, 6th, and 8th grade girls, diet history was the only consistent predictor of abnormal eating attitudes and behaviors at all three grade levels (Rhyne-Winkler, 1994). Smolak and Levine (1996) found that children who were dieters in elementary school had poorer body esteem and more abnormal eating attitudes and behaviors when re-tested two years later than did non-dieting children. Clearly, an instrument designed to assess risk for dis-ordered eating must include items that determine whether a girl is dieting and concerned with weight loss.

Related to weight-regulation, excessive weight/shape concerns play an important mediating role in the development of eating disorders. Killen et al. (1994a) and Taylor et al. (1997) showed that a measure of weight concerns (combined scores of fear of weight gain, worry over weight, body shape, importance of weight, diet history and perceived fatness) was the best predictor of high risk status for eating disorder symptoms in an elementary and middle school population. This measure was significantly associated with onset of eating disorder symptoms in several longitudinal studies (Killen et al., 1994b, 1997).

BODY IMAGE/DISSATISFACTION

Body dissatisfaction reflects the belief that specific parts of one's body, related to shape, are unacceptable because they are 'too large' or 'too fat' (i.e. thighs, hips, buttocks). Body dissatisfaction led to restrictive eating in a three-year study (Cattarin and Thompson, 1994). Killen et al. (1994b) also found this variable to be significantly related to onset of eating disorder symptoms over a three-year period.

GENERAL PSYCHOLOGICAL FUNCTIONING

Difficulties with *affect regulation or affective instability* have been proposed as risk factors for bulimia (Johnson, Lewis and Hagman, 1984; Leon et al., 1993). Several family studies have revealed a high incidence of affective disorders among first-degree relatives of bulimic patients. Killen et al. (1987) has found comorbidity between depression symptoms and eating disorders. And negative emotionality has been posited as a risk factor for eating disorders (Leon et al., 1993).

As to *personality*, bulimic women appear to have a strong desire for social approval, a tendency to avoid conflict, and difficulties in identifying and asserting their own needs (Boskind-White and White, 1983). The personality of the restricting anorectic has been described as obsessional, socially inhibited, compliant, and emotionally restrained (Wonderlich, 1995). Although these factors are associated with eating disorders, they may or may not precede eating disorders and have a causal role. Therefore, their roles in the onset of eating disorders must be investigated.

Perfectionism is the tendency to set unrealistic performance standards, and is characteristic of individuals with anorexia nervosa. Personal expectation of high performance, perhaps in combination with a high-pressure environment, may also be a risk factor. For instance, Herzog et al. (1985) have reported that 15 per cent of female medical students, a group that is likely to be perfectionistic, have an eating disorder. In addition, anorexia nervosa was twice as great among dancers in a higher pressure versus lower pressure setting (Garfinkel, Garner and Goldbloom, 1987).

Low self-esteem in women has been shown to be correlated with negative attitudes toward the body (Grant and Fodor, 1986; Mintz and Betz, 1986), and these negative attitudes are more common in females than in males (Rosen, Gross and Vara, 1987). Furthermore, adolescents with higher scores on an eating disorder screening test had lower self-esteem (Killen et al., 1987). Fisher et al. (1994) also found an association between lower self-esteem and eating disturbances in high school students.

PEERS

Peers can be influential, particularly as children reach adolescence. The perception of what one's friends are doing and what they value exercises a pervasive role in adolescence. This has been demonstrated with alcohol, drug and tobacco use (Watts and Ellis, 1992) as well as eating disorder risk (Killen et al., 1986). Women who reported having more friends who dieted also had more eating disorder symptoms themselves (Crandall, 1988). In addition, Cattarin and Thompson (1994) found that teasing by peers led to body dissatisfaction which then led to restrictive eating in a three-year study of adolescent girls.

CULTURE AND MEDIA

A primary cultural influence on the development of eating disorders is thought to be society's glamorization of thinness. The cultural desire for thinness may interact with career goals to increase risk. For instance, girls who wanted to have career, family and beauty (i.e. to achieve the 'superwoman' ideal) had elevated scores for eating pathology, whereas the non-eating disordered girls had more modest goals for themselves (Steiner-Adair, 1986). In a review of the effects of the media on the development of eating disorders, Levine and Smolak (1996) conclude that media portrayals of feminine beauty and success are an important aspect of the context within which disordered eating develops.

THE MCKNIGHT RISK FACTOR PROJECT

The first step in the development of early intervention/prevention programs for eating disorders involves the identification of risk factors across the developmental span from elementary school through high school. Once these factors have been empirically determined, they can be used for the early identification of girls at high risk for the development of varying degrees of eating and weight-related problems. These girls can then be followed over a period of time to observe the progression of healthy and unhealthy eating and weight regulation practices. Most risk factor studies of eating disorders published thus far have not included elementary school girls in their samples. Also, no instrument currently exists which is appropriate for use with younger girls. Therefore, it was important to develop an instrument that could be used with younger girls to assess factors that are hypothesized to contribute to the development of eating disorders and to study how these factors evolve or change over time.

The McKnight Risk Factor Project described in this chapter is a ten-year, multi-site (University of Arizona and Stanford University, USA), longitudinal research study that aims to identify both risk and protective factors for unhealthy eating and weight regulation practices, as well as eating disorders, in pre-adolescent and adolescent girls. Only girls are included in the study because eating disorders occur predominantly among females. A further aim of this study is to promote healthy eating and weight regulation and to reduce the onset of eating disorders through the development of school-based prevention programs. At present, little research has been devoted to the development of prevention programs for eating disorders. Only a few prevention programs have been evaluated, and most have been geared toward middle or high school students (Killen et al., 1994b; Levine, Smolak and Striegel-Moore, 1996; Shisslak et al., 1996a). In general, these programs have not been very successful in changing disturbed eating attitudes and behaviors, perhaps because they have not targeted high risk girls or specific risk factors (Killen, 1996). The McKnight Risk Factor Project was designed to address these limitations of past research on the prevention of eating disorders.

The McKnight Risk Factor Project, funded by the McKnight Foundation, is divided into four phases. The first phase, completed in the spring of 1996, was aimed at developing an instrument to identify potential risk and protective factors for problematic eating and weight control behaviors in elementary, middle, and high school girls.

The two-year process of developing the instrument began with an extensive review of the eating disorder literature. This then formed the basis for focus groups with elementary, middle, and high school girls to ensure that the list of potential risk and protective factors was complete. The instrument called the *McKnight Risk Factor Survey-Version 1* (MRFS-I) was then pilot tested for the first time. Following the administration of the pilot instrument, interviews were conducted with the test sample of girls to determine if there were any items that were difficult to comprehend. Changes to the instrument were again made based on feedback from the interviewees and interviewers. The revised instrument (i.e. MRFS-II) was then pilot tested for a second time. A combination of clinical (i.e. eating disorder experts) and actuarial (e.g. factor analyses) analyses was then used to make additional modifications to the instrument. The psychometric properties of the third version of the instrument (i.e. MRFS-III) were then established. Test-retest reliability was assessed by administering the questionnaire to the same sample of elementary, middle, and high school girls after a one-week interval. In addition, several other measures were administered to assess the convergent validity of the instrument. These included the Weight Concerns Scale (Killen et al., 1997), Rosenberg Self-Esteem Scale (Rosenberg, 1965), Child Depression Inventory (Kovacs, 1985), and the Center for Epidemiological Studies Depression Scale (Roberts et al., 1990). Internal consistency was determined by calculating Cronbach Alphas for items hypothesized to assess similar risk factors.

A detailed report of the results of the statistical analyses is beyond the scope of this chapter and has been reported elsewhere (Shisslak et al., 1996b). To summarize, the results of the analyses indicated that the MRFS-III possessed high test-retest reliability and internal consistency and low to high convergent validity, depending on the construct of interest. The fact that: (a) about 90 per cent of the parents gave permission for their daughters to participate in the study, (b) data was collected from two geographically disparate sites, and (c) the survey was completed by students from diverse ethnic backgrounds suggests that the MRFS-III possesses good generalizability.

The final list of potential risk and protective factors that the MRFS-III assesses includes many of those described in detail in the introduction to this chapter. There are, however, additional potential risk factors that have not been discussed in detail here, but can be found elsewhere (Shisslak et al., 1996b).

PHASE 2 OF THE MCKNIGHT RISK FACTOR PROJECT

Phase 2 of the project began in the fall of 1996 and involves four assessments (baseline plus three follow-up) of girls in grades 4 through 9 over a four-year period. Approximately 150 girls per grade, per site (Arizona and California) will be enrolled in the study for a total of about 1,800 girls.

Each year girls in each grade will be asked to complete the MRFS-III. Height and weight, will also be collected at the same time so that Body Mass Index can be calculated. Within one week of completing the MRFS-III, individual *Eating Behavior Interviews* (EBI) will be conducted with each girl by a trained research assistant. The purpose of the EBI, which takes about 15 minutes to complete, is to diagnose full or partial cases of eating disorders. Within two weeks of completing the EBI, the girls' parents are contacted for a 20–30 minute telephone interview (Arizona Site only). One purpose of the parent interview is to gather relevant medical and family history information on factors that may predispose a girl to an eating disorder.

For the younger girls (grades 4–6), the emphasis of Phase 2 will be on determining the factors that promote and protect against excessive weight concerns (one of the empirically established precursors to eating disorders), since actual cases of eating disorders are rare in children this young. For the middle and high school girls with excessive weight concerns, the emphasis will be on the factors that promote and protect against eating disorders. Overall, the aims of Phase 2 are to:

(1) identify both risk factors and protective factors for eating disorders,

(2) assess how these factors interact and change over time,

(3) determine how well the MRFS-III is able to predict new cases of both partial and full syndrome eating disorders,

(4) establish guidelines to target students for preventive interventions,

(5) establish the optimal timing of specific preventive interventions.

The beginning of Phase 2 has presented many challenges. First, it was necessary to obtain information about the 'feeder' system within the school district. That is, we needed to identify the middle schools that elementary students would be likely to attend. Similarly, we needed to identify which high schools the middle school girls would be likely to attend. Understanding this flow of students was critical in minimizing the level of attrition.

The next challenge was obtaining approval for the study from: (a) the local school board, (b) the Principals at each of the individual schools, (c) the teachers/administrators within each school, (d) the parents, and (e) the children. This was a formidable administrative task that took numerous meetings and several months to complete.

As Phase 2 of the project will be ongoing for another three years, the issue of attrition and how it can be minimized is important. As mentioned above, understanding the school feeder system should help reduce the drop-out rate. We anticipate that the parent interviews conducted at the Arizona site will also help to reduce attrition in at least two ways. First, by involving the parents in the project they are more likely to become interested in the study and allow their daughter to continue to participate in the project. Second, the parent interviews serve a useful tracking function. Parents are usually more aware than their children as to where they may be living next year and what school their daughter might be attending.

Another method of minimizing attrition is to have a well conceived tracking system. The tracking system must be able to integrate data provided by schools and include error checking components. We have been unable to find any single computer software package capable of managing this task. Consequently several software packages are used in conjunction with each other to help track student movement. It is our experience that a comparison of the databases created by different software packages also serves as a useful error checking mechanism. Finally, attrition can be minimized by keeping the students aware and interested in the project. Methods that we are exploring include the use of newsletters and small gifts for participation.

PHASES 3 AND 4 OF THE MCKNIGHT RISK FACTOR PROJECT

Phase 3 of the study, which is expected to last three years, will involve the development and evaluation of school-based interventions to prevent the occurrence of problematic eating and weight control practices in preadolescent and adolescent girls. To date, many of the models devoted to changing health outcomes focus on changing attitudes and knowledge, but these have met with limited success. A significant challenge in designing the Phase 3 intervention will be to focus on changing malleable risk factors. The results of the longitudinal risk factor study conducted in Phase 2 will be critical in helping identify the potential risk and protective factors that are (a) specific to eating disorders, (b) common to other illnesses, and (c) not prevalent in the general population. Being able to categorize potential risk and protective factors in this manner will allow subsequent interventions to be focused more meaningfully.

Phase 4, which is expected to last one year, will involve the dissemination of these school-based interventions. There are numerous methods for disseminating information, some of which are ideally tailored to professionals and some for the layperson (Renger, Grava-Gubins and Orr, 1996). The challenge will be to determine the means of dissemination that strikes a balance between costs and effective communication of findings to the target audience.

CONCLUSIONS

The McKnight Risk Factor Project is one of only a few longitudinal studies aimed at assessing potential risk and protective factors for eating disturbances in preadolescent and adolescent girls. A further goal of the project is to promote healthy eating and weight regulation and to reduce the onset of eating disorders through the development of school-based prevention programs. These programs will be developed based on the results of the longitudinal risk factor study conducted in Phase 2 of the project. This will enable us to focus specifically on those factors found to be associated with the development of eating disturbances during the baseline data collection and three-year, follow-up study in Phase 2 of the project. It is expected that these factors will be somewhat different in the three groups being studied (elementary, middle, and high school girls) since previous research has indicated that there are developmental differences in dieting and disordered eating in early and middle adolescence (Gralen et al., 1990). Levine, Smolak, and Striegel-Moore (1996) have emphasized the need to design developmentally sensitive measures that tap self-representation of appearance, weight, and shape unique to age-related cognitions. For example, the 'thinness schema' thought to be inherent in unhealthy eating practices in adolescent girls may be poorly developed as such in elementary school girls. However, precursors that begin to develop in the younger age girls can be assessed.

Some of the strengths and limitations of the McKnight Risk Factor Project should be mentioned. The strengths of the project include:

(1) the evaluation of a large number of subjects (approximately 1,800 girls),

(2) the use of a longitudinal rather than cross-sectional design,

(3) data collection at two sites rather than one,

(4) use of interviews as well as self-report measures,

(5) on a more practical level, utilizing the information obtained about risk factors to develop preventive interventions for eating disorders and other problematic eating behaviors which can then be implemented in the schools.

The primary limitation of the project is the reliance on a self-report measure (the MRFS-III) to assess risk factors for disordered eating. Since most of the risk factors to be assessed are subjective in nature (i.e. attitudes, feelings, beliefs, and motivations) it is assumed that the individual is in a better position to report their own beliefs, feelings, and motivations than is anyone else. Traditionally, assessment methods have included self-report, ratings by others (e.g. parents, teachers, peers), behavioral observations, physiological measures, interviews, and statistical records (e.g. grade point average, hospital admissions). In addition to the self-report measures used in this project, interviews with each girl and a parent (or guardian), at the Arizona site, will be conducted.

All of the traditional methods of assessment have their weaknesses and limitations (Kidder, 1981; Osberg and Shrauger, 1990). Self-report measures, for example, are vulnerable to distortion due to faking (good or bad), inaccurate recall of events, and/or response sets. Interviews, though often considered the gold standard of assessment techniques, are subject to distortion as well. Interviews can yield inaccurate information due to interviewer bias or the lack of a feeling of confidentiality or anonymity which can lead a subject to lie about sensitive issues such as substance use or sexual behavior. Ratings by others can also be biased, sometimes by the halo effect (carrying over a generalized impression of the person from the rating of one characteristic to the next) and the generosity error (a tendency to rate more favorably those subjects whom the rater likes). Given that all assessment procedures have their weaknesses, it is important to institute as many safeguards as possible against bias and distortion. It is generally agreed, therefore, that it is important to: use several methods of assessment rather than one, use trained raters or interviewers, use a structured interview format, and develop self-report measures that consist of questions that are clearly written and easy to understand. It is also important to pilot test new measures before they are used, assess the reliability and validity of each of the measures, and assure all subjects that their responses to the measures will be confidential. Many of these safeguards have been instituted in the McKnight Risk Factor Project.

Another limitation of the study may be that assessment on a yearly basis is not sensitive enough to establish the critical time at which malleable risk factors could be affected. Given the enormity of the task (i.e. assessing about 1,800 girls) and the risk of alienating schools because of added disruptions, it was simply impractical to make additional assessments.

It has been the aim of this project to design a survey that teases out both precursors as well as more cogent patterns of attitudes and behaviors associated with disordered eating. Phase 3 of the project involving the development and evaluation of school-based prevention programs will begin in the year 2000, followed by the dissemination of these programs. At that time, we hope to have a better understanding of the presence, nature, and pathways of risk factors and the complex interactions among these factors over time. Ultimately, the goal is to determine relevant risk and protective factors, and to develop effective preventive interventions that change the onset and course of eating disorders in school girls.

REFERENCES

Boskind-White, M. and White, W.C. (1983). *Bulimarexia: The binge/ purge cycle,* New York: Norton.

Cattarin, J.A. and Thompson, J.K. (1994) 'A three-year longitudinal study of body image, eating disturbances, and general psychological functioning in adolescent females'. *Eating Disorders: The Journal of Treatment and Prevention,* 2: 114–25.

Crandall, C. (1988) 'The social contagion of binge eating'. *Journal of Personality and Social Psychology,,* 55: 589–99.

Fisher, M., Golden, N.H., Katzman, D.K., Kriepe, R.E., Rees, J., Schebendach, J., Sigman, G., Ammerman, S. and Hoberman, H.M. (1995) 'Eating disorders in adolescents: A background paper'. *Journal of Adolescent Health,,* 16: 420–37.

Fisher, M., Pastore, D., Schneider, M., Pegler, C. and Napolitano, B. (1994) 'Eating attitudes in urban and suburban adolescents'. *International Journal of Eating Disorders,* 16: 67–74.

Garfinkel, P.E., Garner, D.M. and Goldbloom, D.S. (1987) 'Eating disorders: Implications for the 1990s'. *Canadian Journal of Psychiatry,,* 32: 624–31.

Graber, J.A., Brooks-Gunn, J., Paikoff, R.L. and Warren, M.P. (1994) 'Prediction of eating problems: An 8-year study of adolescent girls'. *Developmental Psychology,,* 30: 823–34.

Gralen, S.J., Levine, M.P., Smolak, L. and Murnen, S. (1990) 'Dieting and disordered eating during early and middle adolescence: Do the influences remain the same?' *International Journal of Eating Disorders,,* 9: 501–12.

Grant, C.L. and Fodor, I.G. (1986) 'Adolescent attitudes toward body image and anorexic behavior'. *Adolescence,,* 21: 269–81.

Herzog, D.B. and Copeland, P.M. (1985) 'Eating disorders'. *New England Journal of Medicine,,* 313: 295–303.

Herzog, D.B., Pepose, M., Norman, D.K. and Rigotti, N.A. (1985) 'Eating disorders and social maladjustment in female medical students'. *Journal of Nervous and Mental Disease,* 173: 734–40.

Johnson, C., Lewis, C. and Hagman, J. (1984) 'The syndrome of bulimia'. *Psychiatric Clinics of North America,* 7: 247–74.

Kaplan, A.S. and Garfinkel, P.E. (1993) *Medical issues and the eating disorders,* New York: Brunner/Mazel.

Kidder, L.H. (1981) *Research methods in social relations.* New York: Holt, Rinehart and Winston.

Killen, J.D. (1996) 'Development and evaluation of a school-based eating disorder symptoms prevention program'. In Smolak, L., Levine, M.P. and Striegel-Moore, R. (eds) *The developmental psychopathology of eating disorders* (pp. 313–39), Mahwah, NJ: Lawrence Erlbaum.

Killen, J.D., Hayward, C., Litt, I., Hammer, L.D., Wilson, D.M., Miner, B., Taylor, C.B., Varady, A. and Shisslak, C.M. (1992). 'Is puberty a risk factor for eating disorders?' *American Journal of Diseases of Children,* 146: 323–5.

Killen, J.D., Hayward, C., Wilson, D.M., Taylor, C.B., Hammer, L.D., Litt, I., Simmonds, B. and Haydel, F. (1994a) 'Factors associated with eating disorder symptoms in a community sample of 6th and 7th grade girls'. *International Journal of Eating Disorders,* 15: 357–67.

Killen, J.D., Taylor, C.B., Hayward, C., Wilson, D.M., Haydel, K.F., Hammer, L.D., Simmonds, B., Robinson, T.N., Litt, I., Varady, A. and Kraemer, H. (1994b) 'Pursuit of thinness and onset of eating disorder symptoms in a community sample of adolescent girls: A three-year prospective analysis'. *International Journal of Eating Disorders,* 16: 227–38.

Killen, J.D., Taylor, C.B., Hayward, C., Haydel, K.F., Wilson, D.M., Hammer, L.D., Kraemer, H.C., Blair-Greiner, A. and Strachowski, D. (1997) 'Weight concerns influence the development of eating disorders: A four-year prospective study'. *Journal of Consulting and Clinical Psychology,* in press.

Killen, J.D., Taylor, C.B., Telch, M.J., Saylor, K.E., Maron, D.J. and Robinson, T.N. (1986) 'Self-induced vomiting and laxative and diuretic use among teenagers'. *Journal of the American Medical Association,* 255: 1447–9.

Killen, J.D., Taylor, C.B., Telch, M.J., Robinson, T.N., Maron, D.J. and Saylor, K.E. (1987) 'Depressive symptoms and substance use among adolescent binge eaters and purgers: A defined population study'. *American Journal of Public Health,* 77: 1539–41.

Koff, E. and Rierdan, J. (1991) 'Perceptions of weight and attitudes toward eating in early adolescent girls'. *Journal of Adolescent Health,* 12: 307–12.

Kovacs, M. (1985) 'The Children's Depression Inventory'. *Psychopharmacological Bulletin,* 21: 995–8.

Leon, G.R., Fulkerson, J.A., Perry, C.L. and Cudeck, R. (1993) 'Personality and behavioral vulnerabilities associated with risk status for eating disorders in adolescent girls'. *Journal of Abnormal Psychology,* 102: 438–44.

Levine, M. and Smolak, L. (1992) 'Toward a model of the developmental psychopathology of eating disorders: The example of early adolescence'. In Crowther, J.H., Tennenbaum, D.L., Hobfoll, S.E. and Stevens, M.A.P. (eds) *The etiology of bulimia nervosa: The individual and familial context* (pp. 59–80), Washington, DC: Hemisphere.

——(1996) 'Media as a context for the development of disordered eating'. In Smolak, L., Levine, M.P. and Striegel-Moore, R. (eds) *The developmental psychopathology of eating disorders* (pp. 235–57), Mahwah, NJ: Lawrence Erlbaum.

Levine, M., Smolak, L. and Striegel-Moore, R. (1996) 'Conclusions, implications, and future directions'. In Smolak, L., Levine, M.P. and Striegel-Moore, R. (eds) *The developmental psychopathology of eating disorders* (pp. 399–416) Mahwah, NJ: Lawrence Erlbaum.

Mallick, M.J. (1983) 'Health hazards of obesity and weight control in children: A review of the literature'. *American Journal of Public Health,* 73: 78–82.

Mellin, L.M., Irwin, C.E. and Scully, S. (1992) 'Prevalence of disordered eating in girls: A survey of middle-class children'. *Journal of the American Dietetic Association,* 92: 851–3.

Mellin, L.M., Scully, S. and Irving, C.E. (1986) *Disordered eating characteristics in preadolescent girls.* Paper presented at the annual meeting of the American Dietetic Association. Las Vegas.

Mintz, L.B. and Betz, N.E. (1986) 'Sex differences in the nature, realism, and correlates of body image'. *Sex Roles,* 15: 185–95.

Osberg, T.M. and Shrauger, J.S. (1990) 'The role of self-prediction in psychological assessment'. In Butcher, J.N. and Spielberger, C.D. (eds) *Advances in personality assessment: Volume 8,* Hillsdale, NJ: Lawrence Erlbaum.

Patton, G.C., Johnson-Sabine, E., Wood, K., Mann, A.H. and Wakeling, A. (1990) 'Abnormal eating attitudes in London schoolgirls: A prospective epidemiological study, outcome at 12 months'. *Psychological Medicine,,* 20: 383–94.

Phelps, L., Andrea, R., Rizzo, F.G., Johnston, L. and Main, C.M. (1993) 'Prevalence of self-induced vomiting and laxative/medication abuse among female adolescents: A longitudinal study'. *International Journal of Eating Disorders,* 14: 375–8.

Polivy, J. and Thomasen, L. (1988) 'Dieting and other eating disorders'.

In Blechman, E.A. and Brownell, K.D. (eds) *Handbook of behavioral medicine for women* (pp. 345–55) New York: Pergamon.

Renger, R., Grava-Gubins, I. and Orr, V. (1996) 'Dissemination of research findings in family medicine'. *Canadian Family Physician,*, 42: 1783–9.

Rhyne-Winkler, M.C. (1994) 'Eating attitudes in fourth-, sixth-, and eighth-grade girls'. *Elementary School Guidance and Counseling,* 28: 285–94.

Richards, M.H., Casper, R.C. and Larson, R. (1990) 'Weight and eating concerns among pre- and young adolescent boys and girls'. *Journal of Adolescent Health Care,* 11: 203–9.

Roberts, R.E., Andrews, J.A., Lewinsohn, P.M. and Hops, H. (1990) 'Assessment of depression in adolescents using the Center for Epidemiologic Studies Depression Scale'. *Psychological Assessment,* 2: 122–8.

Rosen, J.C., Gross, J. and Vara, L. (1987) 'Psychological adjustment of adolescents attempting to lose or gain weight'. *Journal of Consulting and Clinical Psychology,* 55: 742–7.

Rosenberg, M. (1965) *Society and the adolescent self-image,* Princeton, NJ: Princeton University Press.

Shisslak, C.M., Renger, R., Crago, M., McKnight, K.M., Gray, N., Bryson, S., Sharpe, T., Estes, L.S., Parnaby, O., Killen, J. and Taylor, C.B. (1996b) *Development and evaluation of the McKnight Risk Factor Survey (MRFS-III) for assessing potential risk and protective factors for disordered eating in preadolescent and adolescent girls.* Manuscript in preparation.

Shisslak, C.M., Crago, M. and Estes, L.S. (1995) 'The spectrum of eating disturbances'. *International Journal of Eating Disorders,* 18: 209–19.

Shisslak, C.M., Crago, M., Estes, L.S. and Gray, N. (1996a) 'Content and method of developmentally appropriate prevention programs'. In Smolak, L., Levine, M. and Striegel-Moore, R. (eds) *The developmental psychopathology of eating disorders* (pp. 341–63). Mahwah, NJ: Lawrence Erlbaum.

Smolak, L. and Levine, M. (1996) *Childhood attitudes and behaviors as predictors of early adolescent eating attitudes, behaviors, and problems.* Paper presented at the Society for Research in Adolescence. Boston, MA.

Steiner-Adair, C. (1986) 'The body politic: Normal female adolescent development and the development of eating disorders'. *Journal of the American Academy of Psychoanalysis,*, 14: 95–114.

Striegel-Moore, R.H., Silberstein, L.R. and Rodin, J. (1986) 'Toward an understanding of risk factors for bulimia'. *American Psychologist,*, 41: 246–63.

Taylor, C., Sharpe, T., Shisslak, C., Bryson, S., Estes, L., Gray, N., McKnight, K. Crago, M., Kraemer, H. and Killen, J. (1997) 'Factors associated with weight concerns in adolescent girls'. *International Journal of Eating Disorders: in press.*

Thelen, M.H., Lawrence, C.M. and Powell, A.L. (1992) 'Body image, weight control, and eating disorders among children'. In Crowther, J.H., Tennenbaum, D.L., Hobfoll, S.E. and Stevens, M.A.P. (eds) *The etiology of bulimia nervosa: The individual and familial context* (pp. 81–101), Washington, DC: Hemisphere.

Watts, W.D. and Ellis, A.M. (1992) 'Drug abuse and eating disorders: Prevention implications'. *Journal of Drug Education,* 22: 223–40.

Wonderlich, S.A. (1995) 'Personality and eating disorders'. In Brownell, K.D. and Fairburn, C.G. (eds) *Eating disorders and obesity* (pp. 171–6), New York: Guilford.

CHAPTER FOUR

The Norwegian school-based prevention model: Development and evaluation

Runi Børresen Gresko and Jan H. Rosenvinge

INTRODUCTION

Too often, preventive work is highly praised in political speeches, but not carried out in practical actions. Prevention appears to be the wish of everybody and the priority of nobody. In the world of limited economical resourses and a lot of human suffering, the 'easy' way is to spend money on curative work and not to wait for the 'silent' and long term effects of prevention. This chapter describes how this situation can be changed by influencing the political system and how the increased priority of prevention of eating disorders is converted into practical actions.

Recent reviews of epidemiological studies (Fombonne, 1995; 1996) suggest that the notion of an increase in the prevalence of eating disorders, during the past 10–20 years is a fiction. However, behind the suggested prevalence figures of about 1–2 per cent, many young people suffer from 'subclinical' eating disorders. This term may seem to denote rather harmless psychological problems, but this is true only to a small extent. Mostly, both eating disorders and conditions not qualifying for a clinical diagnosis affect the quality of life of the sufferers and their families. We are faced here with a major public health problem particularly affecting females. A moral and professional commitment to prevent human suffering forces us to believe that it is possible to prevent the development of both subclinical and clinical eating disorders.

Hopefully, in the future it will be possible to identify causes and individuals at risk accurately enough to do prevention work at an individual level. We cannot, however, await such knowledge to appear. Lack of knowledge is a poor excuse to ignore the obligation to work and act according to the knowledge we do have at any time. So, what do we know? At least we know a lot about sociocultural risk factors. They may increase the risk for developing subclinical eating disorders and possibly anorexia nervosa and bulimia nervosa as well. Today's children and youngsters are exposed to a superficial culture and artificial standards about happiness. Many young people suffer from the illusion that happiness, popularity and well-being depend on slimness, dieting and general physical appearance. This reflects deeply-rooted unspoken cultural ideals which are distorted and magnified by, for instance, the mass media. Then it is understandable that body and food preoccupations act as an attempt to cope with the situation in the hope of feeling more successful and accepted.

Preventing eating disorders by counteracting the negative impact of sociocultural factors means, for instance, to limit the amount of positive reinforcement of leanness in society and the punishment of the failure to comply with dietary restrictions or weight standards. We need general preventive actions toward attitudinal changes. Also, we need to teach young people to 'decode' negative cultural messages and to promote mental health in general.

Our contact with young people have made us very surprised about their lack of knowledge for example of pubertal development, both physically and emotionally. Unfortunately, too many teachers seem to lack this kind of knowledge as well. The important thing is to 'demystify' body fat by explaining its link to pubertal development. However, it seems like worthlessness and insecurity are increasing with the body weight. This may be a problem for early maturing girls who develop secondary sex characteristics earlier than their friends. To provide knowledge is then another important part of preventive strategies. This includes the education of parents and teachers with respect to early signs of eating disorders (Rosenvinge, 1994).

Attitudinal change and the providing of information were then the key terms in our way of thinking about prevention. It is essential to keep in mind that they are intrinsically linked together. Information without attitude change is worthless, and attitudinal change is a prerequisite to be able to make use of information. This chapter describes how we accomplish these goals. First, we discuss the choice of prevention strategy and some basic ideas for our work. Secondly, we describe the development, content and practical implementation of the educational materials developed in our prevention programme. We end this chapter by showing how experiences during the accomplishment of the goals also paved the way for new goals in prevention.

BASIC IDEAS OF PREVENTION

In 1989 the Norwegian Minister of Health and Social Affairs formed an interdisciplinary group to report on the different aspects of eating disorders. This report showed that the Norwegian public health services had too little to offer as far as treatment were concerned. Prevention was also mentioned in this report. An important 'white spot' was, however, that no one actually knew the size of the problem, neither in the Norwegian patient population, nor in the general adolescent population. This lack of knowledge was mentioned in particular, thus strongly recommending epidemiological studies to be carried out. Obviously, such data could act as an empirical argument for further actions to improve treatment services as well as prevention.

During the same year, we carried (with the financial support from the Ministry of Health and Social Affairs) out the first Norwegian study on the prevalence of eating problems in the general adolescent population. The study comprised 2,017 pupils aged 12 to 16 years (7–9th grade) in two Norwegian semirural municipalities. The school teachers administered a questionnaire including questions about height, present and desired weight, dieting and pressures toward thinness. Weight was given as Body Mass Index (BMI). The form also included the Eating Attitudes Test (EAT-40; Garner and Garfinkel, 1979), the Bulimic Investigatory Test, Edinburgh (BITE; Henderson and Freeman, 1987) and the General Health Questionnaire (GHQ-30; Goldberg and Hillier, 1979). To reduce drop out, all subjects were told in advance that the aim of the study was to survey nutritional habits.

At the moment of the study 146 pupils were absent and 178 questionnaire forms were rejected due to grossly incomplete or obviously meaningless responses on most of the questions. Thus, 1,693 subjects (84 per cent of the total sample) were included consisting of 819 (48 per cent) boys and 874 (52 per cent) girls.

Table 1: Scores on the Eating Attitudes Test (EAT), the Bulimic Investigatory Test Edinburgh (BITE) and the General Health Questionnaire (GHQ).

		Boys			Girls		
Age (N)		15 (282)	14 (266)	13 (236)	15 (324)	14 (297)	13 (229)
EAT	mean	12.6	13.2	13.7	16.0	15.3	14.3
	SD	7.0	8.5	9.0	9.6	9.6	8.9
BITE	mean	4.1	4.7	4.1	6.8	5.7	4.6
	SD	3.0	3.7	3.6	4.8	4.0	3.9
GHQ	mean	21.3	21.9	21.9	23.5	23.8	22.2
	SD	9.4	8.5	8.5	10.4	10.4	9.4

About 96 per cent of the final sample were in the age rage 13–15 years. Here, the mean BMI value for both boys and girls was 19. Mean questionnaire scores in Table 1 refer to these age groups.

These figures seem quite 'normal'. However, means can be deceptive. Within the limits of the one-stage design, four different methods were applied to identify subjects with unhealthy eating attitudes or serious eating problems:

1) *Straight forward above EAT cut-off scores.* Using the cut-off score of 30 (Garner and Garfinkel, 1979), 4.6 per cent of the boys and 7.0 per cent of the girls were identified. These sex differences were not statistically significant.

2) *Above EAT cut-off scores plus depressive mood state indicators.* Previous findings (Steiger, Leung, Ross and Gulko, 1992) suggest that adolescents at risk may be identified by combining elevated EAT-scores and depressive mood states. Using the most affirmative GHQ-responses to the items 'depressed and unhappy', 'loss of self-confidence', 'think of oneself as worthless', 'life is without hope', 'less positive outlook on the future', and 'life is not worth living' and the EAT scores >30, no boys and 0.3 per cent girls were identified.

3) *Adding to the EAT cut-off scores a reported low weight (BMI <16) and still a desire to become thinner.* With this method, 0.5 per cent boys and 1.3 per cent girls were identified.

4) *Most affirmative responses on clear-cut symptoms of a serious eating disorder.* Here, 1.2 per cent boys and 0.9 per cent girls

reported a persistent anxiety prior to eating and 0.8 per cent of the boys and 1.3 per cent of the girls reported feelings of guilt after eating. Regular vomiting was reported by 0.9 per cente boys and 0.4 per cent of the girls.

In general, girls reported more weight dissatisfaction (i.e. a desired/reported weight ratio <1.00) which was augmented with increasing age (F=2.86; p<0.02). Furthermore, EAT scores well above the cut-off score (33.7; SD 17.2) were predicted by a combination of a BMI below 16, a concern about being overweight and a desired/reported weight ratio smaller than 1. In this group, an EAT-GHQ correlation of 0.56 (p<0.0001) may indicate a high level of general maladjustment. Removing the BMI<16 condition significantly lowered the EAT score (23.6; SD 11.4; t=2.66; df=115; p<0.009). Also, the EAT-GHQ correlation was lower (0.26; p<0.01). The single item responses may provide a picture of particular problems reported by the adolescents. This is shown in Table 2.

Conclusions from the study are, of course, hampered by the hazards of self-report and the flaws of the one stage design. Even when case detection is not the purpose, interviews may still increase the validity of the self-report. Also, the failure to conduct repeated measures reduces the reliability. Then, as Table 2 shows, there is a wide range in the percentage of reported eating problems (i.e. 0–49 per cent), and methodological problems may account for some of this range. However, using the methods for identifying Norwegian teenagers with suspected eating problems that may be subject to concern, one may conclude as follows:

● Using the EAT cut-point as a criterion, up to 5 per cent of the boys and 7 per cent of the girls may have unhealthy eating attitudes and behaviours.

● Possible serious eating disorder symptoms and problems seem to occur among 0.5–0.9 per cent of the boys and 0.3–1.3 per cent of the girls.

Such findings accord with the mainstream of other epidemiological studies, and may, in retrospect, seem somewhat trivial. However, when these data appeared in the 1989 report to the National Board of Health, a number of spin-off effects were observed. Judging from the numerous queries from school and health personel, the data obviously satisfied the need for information about eating disorders among Norwegian adolescents.

Table 2: Number and percentage of boys (N=819) and girls (N=874) whose answers* might indicate eating disorder problems.

	Boys		Girls	
	N	%	N	%
Highly frequent attitudes (>10 per cent of total)				
Afraid of becoming fat	186	22	455	49
Feel too heavy with present weight	151	16	429	42
Very dissatisfied with own physical appearance	114	12	272	27
Feel guilt if overeating	87	11	249	28
Go to great length to satisfy urge to binge	70	10	126	18
Worry about having no control over eating	77	9	156	17
Ashamed of own eating habits	49	6	159	17
Preoccupied with a wish to be thinner	43	5	187	19
Important to eat as little as possible	56	6	184	18
Highly frequent behaviours (>10 per cent of total)				
Turn to food for comfort	81	10	213	23
Eat more when anxious	76	9	167	17
Fasting a whole day	64	7	146	15
Periods of strict dieting	46	5	143	14
Less frequent attitudes (<10 per cent of total)				
Preoccupied with thoughts of having fat on body	33	4	130	13
Preoccupied with food	116	13	64	6
Think of burning off calories when exercising	45	5	68	7
Food controls life	49	6	55	6
Feel uncomfortable after eating sweets	18	2	37	4
Like stomach to be empty	21	2	35	4
Do not like to eat with other people	17	2	8	1
Feel guilt after eating	10	1	13	1
Have an urge to vomit after eating	14	2	11	1
Less frequent behaviours (<10 per cent of total)				
Exercise to burn off calories	48	5	39	4
Avoid eating when hungry	34	4	19	2
Unable to stop bingeing	34	4	12	1
Weigh oneself several times a day	12	1	19	2
Give too much time and thought to food	10	1	22	2
Vomit after eating	10	1	4	0

* Affirmed items from the EAT, BITE and specially designed questions.

Also, the findings stimulated and legitimated a lot of practical activities on prevention and formed a basis for lobbying to set prevention of eating disorders on the political agenda. In 1990, the Norwegian Government initiated a plan of action to increase the level of professional competence and care concerning mental health. Partly because of the documentation of the problem provided by our survey study, eating disorders were selected as one of the main targets (Gresko and Karlsen, 1994).

THE CHOICE OF PREVENTION STRATEGY

A risk strategy of prevention focus on individuals or specific groups of individuals who either already have been or are at risk of developing the illness in question. In our programme, such a strategy was chosen with respect to athletes in particular. On behalf of the Norwegian authorities, information about risk and prevention was distributed to athletes and coaches based on empirical research in support of the notion of elite athletes as a high risk group (Sundgot-Borgen, 1993; Sundgot-Borgen and Corbin, 1987). In collaboration with the Norwegian University for Sports and Physical Education, two pamphlets were distributed to all members of the Norwegian Confederation of Sports (trainers, instructors/coaches and athletes) and to teachers in physical education.

However, the main principle of our prevention programme is based on the population strategy focusing increasingly on health promotion through a general improvement of living conditions and lifestyle. Technically, of course, one may call this a risk strategy, since our programme is directed towards children and adolescents, and hence, towards an age-defined high risk group. But preventive interventions work better if spread over time, irrespective of possible biological, psychological or familial risk factors. This is particularly important since the empirical evidence for biological, psychological or familial risk factors is insufficient to justify a risk strategy. Specific preventive actions may then act as an unwanted, unhealthy and, hence, unjustified segregation of a population subgroup. We do know, however, something about the impact of cultural standards and ideals, which make risk widely diffused throughout the child and adolescent population. Then, a general preventive strategy focusing on external risk factors may include legislative or other political actions, as well as justifying psychoeducative programmes.

Already in 1975, the former Norwegian Prime Minister Dr. Gro Harlem Brundtland wrote an article, stressing schools as the important arena for health promotion and preventive efforts (Brundtland, 1975). Since all Norwegian boys and girls attend public schools, a school-based programme gives the opportunity to reach the whole child and adolescent population. Teachers are trained observers which are often more in contact with the teenagers than their parents. The school staff members are observing mood, behaviour and school performances. This provides teachers with an excellent opportunity to intervene at an early stage. Unlike many parents they have a basis for comparison to make a more qualified opinion about what is common or 'normal'. Intervening at an early stage is important to increase the likelihood of recovery. Thus, feasibility is the first argument for the school's role in the prevention work.

The school is also a powerful arena for socialization of children and adolescents into cultural standards and ideals. On the other hand, the schools should also help their pupils to take a critical look on such standards, ideals and norms relevant for eating disorders. However, the school's role is not only to promote an intellectual understanding of culture, but actually to focus on how ideals and standards 'work' within peer interactions.

As mentioned in the introduction, knowledge about, for instance, the effects of food consumption or pubertal body changes is surprisingly poor among adolescents. Lack of knowledge may lead to fear, misconceptions and cognitive illusions, which may set off dieting and other unhealthy eating behaviours. Obviously, the school should take this educational challenge seriously. We believe that for a psychoeducative programme to succeed, it is important to encourage the students to take an active part in the discussion about food, the slimming culture and the risk factors for eating disorders. Merely to present information about eating disorders is not sufficient. Moreover, to give information about eating disorders may increase the attention and acceptance of the symptoms. Eating disorders are one of the 'hot' topics in Norway and are obviously 'exciting' to many people. This can be seen in the popular press as well as in the interest in eating disorders among health and school personel. Obviously, such an increased interest should be welcomed. However, the interest should be genuine and sustained over a long time. If not, the effect could be a 'contribution' to a rise in the prevalence of symptoms, driven by 'syndrome imitation' (Habermas, 1992). Such an imitation is not factitious, but merely a response to the hidden message that 'to present with eating disorder symptoms increases the chance to get attention from someone who only then, will listen to your problems'.

Information about 'healthy' nutrition can also create problems. Various 'expert' advices about what to eat to stay healthy make girls preoccupied with foods and serve to undermine their own control and confidence about eating. This may be particularly true as such advices seem to contain a covert moralistic message. It is almost a paradox that such expert opinions and advices function almost in the same way as sociocultural pressures. When teenagers are given this kind of information along with information about eating disorders, the end result may be potentially maleficient or at least confusing. With the negative effects of knowledge in mind, such knowledge should be given in a 'normal' context, not as parts of 'lectures about eating disorders'.

However, the educational challenge goes much further. Among girls, there is a conflict between academic achievement and the wish to be popular for the boys, a conflict which many girls resolve by becoming underachievers. Young women may feel forced to choose between success at school or work, or success in relationships. This poses a dilemma, since each choice means denying many of their physical and interpersonal needs (Shisslak and Crago, 1994; Striegel-Moore, 1992). The concequences may be to produce or enlarge a basic feeling of being helpless, unable to cope with life. Such feelings may easily become a starting point for symptom development as a way to 'regain' control or autonomy.

An important condition of education in schools is that it must be embedded in a dedication to personal qualities and not only to learning a curriculum. Education should help pupils to take command of their own life, to set their own boundaries, to realise their potential, appreciate their uniqueness and worth, and to encourage their acknowledgement and expressions of their feelings. Even if such goals are met, it does not, however, protect from stress, conflicts or other negative experiences which are necessary parts of life. For this reason not only knowledge but also coping strategies should be focused on.

This educational challenge puts the school teacher in an important position as a role model, not only as an individual who provides information. Teachers must be aware of their own beliefs and behaviours with respect to dieting, self-esteem, slenderness and weight. The goal is that they can stand forth as robust and mature adults in relation to young people who are in the process of emotional and social development, and being exposed to many confusing and conflicting messages and values from the society at large.

Although the school is the important arena for primary prevention, the school system can not be viewed – and in fact does not operate – in isolation. It relates to, for instance, the health care system. A fundamental issue here is collaboration. However, while schools are everywhere, treatment units are not. While education follows detailed governmental plans, hospitals and clinics do not. The school educates people, they do not treat patients. Everyone is obliged to attend the school, while the threshold for being admitted to psychiatric treatment is still high. Hence, primary prevention does not and should not take place within the health care system. Also, treatment is not a teacher's job. On the other hand, the health care system at a primary (local community) level is governed by laws and regulations aimed to secure physical and mental health. Here, we actually have a legislative basis for general prevention.

The important question is then how health care professionals and teachers or school councellors can work together. We prefer to answer this question by referring to the practical solutions mentioned in the implementation part of our prevention model.

THE EDUCATIONAL MATERIAL

In 1992, the National Board of Health in co-operation with the Norwegian Ministry of Education and Research produced a comprehensive educational package under the editorship of the first author. Free of charge, this was distributed to all secondary schools and colleges, the school health services, advanced colleges/universities of education, and schools of nursing in Norway.

EDUCATIONAL PACKAGE

The package '*Adolescence and Eating Disorders*' contains seven chapters which we will describe in brief. Each of the chapters starts with background information intended for the teacher or school nurse, followed by various student tasks. Overheads and a few slides for use in teaching are included.

1. Introduction: This chapter gives a general introduction to eating disorders and comments on how to use the package. Also, a weight and shape attitudes test for teachers (Levine and Hill, 1991) was presented.

2. Eating disorders: This chapter provides general information on eating disorders. It describes symptoms, signs and psychological aspects of anorexia nervosa, bulimia nervosa and compulsive eating.

3. Somatic and psychological consequences of eating disorders: Many girls are anxious of becoming overweight and start vomiting at an early age. Education about the medical damages may stop this kind of self-destructive behaviour. Despite the effort to provide facts about physical consequences, not to scear people off, our experience is that such information still often do. This is particularly true with respect to the irreversible teeth damage and the cost of dental treatment.

4. Body and dieting: This chapter is made up of information and tasks to encourage respect for individual differences in body weight and body shape. Students are informed that fat is necessary for the body function, and that one's body weight is highly genetically dependent. This means that the body establishes and defends a 'set-point' weight range. Some people have a predisposition to be heavier or lighter than others. Trying to combat one's individualized set-point range of healthy body weight by dieting may lead to unwanted weight gain in the long run. This chapter also discusses the cultural factors which may invalidate the respect for individual weight differences and prompt a negative body image. We also want to create an understanding of how unjust and painful it is to be socially isolated, particularly if weight and appearance are the reasons.

5. Sociocultural factors: The goal for this chapter is to make students think for themselves in order to oppose unhealthy cultural messages about beauty, body shape and diet. By looking at how ideals for weight and shape vary through the centuries, they may come to realize the transient nature of such ideals, and that they certainly not are some kind of 'gold standards'. Another task is to discuss how teen magazines and commercials focus on body expectations and glorify thinness. Who has decided that thinness is a requirement for physical attractiveness?

6. *Puberty*: Bodily transformation during puberty may cause anxiety and eating disorder symptoms. In this chapter the goal is to demystify body fat by explaining the link to pubertal development. Moreover, the chapter points out that in the pursuit of feeling more successful and accepted, a healthy coping strategy is not to focus on body and appearance. Rather, one should try to increase self-assertion. Plots for role-playing in self-assertion are provided.

7. *What to do if you suspect an eating disorder*: This chapter provides guidelines for teachers, school nurses and counsellors for early intervention. The purpose of detection is to identify a problem and refer the student to the appropriate treatment services, not to make a clinical diagnosis. That is by no means the task of the school staff members. Part 1 of this chapter is intended for the staff member closest to a student like the class teacher, school nurse, teacher in physical education or the counsellor. Here, we present guidelines for how to reach out to a student, including students who are resistant or otherwise defensive. The main task is to communicate care and concern, and if necessary, refer the student to the school health system or other professionals which can provide adequate help. We recommend the teachers to describe specific observations which have caused their concern, like, for instance, 'I've noticed that you have lost weight lately, that you haven't eaten your school meal for two weeks, and that your school performance has been a bit up and down lately'. It is important that the problem should be evaluated by a professional, and that the parents must be informed. The school staff member should never moralize, try to become the persons therapist or act as some kind of 'saviour'. Teachers are also guarded against intiating confessions from students with a suspected eating disorder. Confessions can glamorize eating disorders, and school staff cannot know the effects a confession may have on the sufferer. Part 2 of the chapter provides guidelines for the school staff member who, for some reasons, has to take care of the student in

the time interval between treatment referral and the first session. Here it is important to agree upon the frequency, length and content of the contact.

VIDEO

A video '*This is my life*' is especially made for the programme and provides information of eating disorders, the medical complications and the cultural preoccupation with slenderness. Sufferers of both genders are interviewed, and we follow a young girl in her development of an eating disorder. This video is produced for sale.

PAMPHLET FOR THE HEALTH SERVICES

The quality of the health services depends on the level of knowledge of health care professionals. The basic knowledge of eating disorders should be provided in the professional education. In Norway this has been rather the exception, not the rule. Professionals in general feel helpless when faced with an eating disorder patient, or they may be ignorant of early signs and symptoms. Based on the results of a survey on this problem carried out in all colleges within the Norwegian professional health education system, recommendations regarding educational plans were made. The Norwegian Board of Health has also produced an instructive pamphlet entitled '*Serious eating disorders: A guide for health service in treatment of anorexia nervosa and bulimia nervosa*'.

In addition, the school health services also received a textbook '*Fight for the Body*' which includes a lot of specific examples. Together with the book a circular adviced the school health personnel on how they should relate to children and youths with eating disorders of varied severity. Suggestions for adequate referral procedures and treatment settings are also made.

THE USE OF THE MATERIAL

To produce and distribute materials is of course an important task. However, one need to be sure that materials actually are being used. Too often various materials are 'stuffed away', either due to misunderstandings or to a general 'overload' of 'outside' information to the schools. Building on the experiences from the 1992 project period, a follow-up project was organized in the period 1993–1995 under the responsibility of the Norwegian Ministry of Education and Research and the National Board of Health. Our goals were to ensure the practical use of materials, to meet the need for further professional training, and to improve coordination between professionals and institutions. The follow-up project consisted of four different components.

COMPONENT I: 'DRIVING RULES'

A survey which was conducted revealed a strong demand to clearify the role of different professions and to establish a co-ordinated referral procedure to secure prompt help at an adequate level of care. Such procedures must involve teachers, the school health system, and the general primary and secondary health care services. It may seem simple, but it was a problem to get helpers to understand their role and what they are supposed to do in the various situations that may occur. One reason for this could be that in general, the school and the health care system are quite separated. For this reason we developed what we called 'Driving-rules' for teachers and school nurses. Comments on a draft version were given by the union of teachers and nurses as well as by The National Board of Health and by the national parent representatives. A final version was then distributed free of charge by the regional health and school authorities. We can summarize the tasks of the different services like this:

Teachers
1. *Identification*
2. *Communication of care and concern*
3. *Contact parents*
4. *Referral to school health service*

School health service
1. *Identification*
2. *Communication of care and concern*
3. *Treatment*
4. *Referral to secondary health care system*

Secondary health care system
1. Treatment
2. Guiding teachers, counsellors, school nurses/doctors

COMPONENT 2: RAISING THE COMPETENCE

An education programme for school and health care personnel was carried out to increase their knowledge and competence of eating disorders. Courses were offered to school and health care personnel in all the 19 counties in Norway, and except from one county they all accepted to take part. In fact some counties wanted several courses. At times we were not able to meet the demand. Totally we lead 136 courses in the project period, attended by about 10,000 school and health care personnel.

COMPONENT 3: SUPPORT GROUPS

A main part of the follow-up project was to establish support groups for students who are preoccupied with food, eating, dieting, weight and body shape. Such problems disturb their school performance, interpersonal relations and affect general mental and physical health. Students with such 'subclinical' problems may get little help. They are seldom accepted for treatment in the health care system. Also, counsellors and school nurses have had little to offer. To resolve this problem, support groups in the secondary schools have been set up, based on the self-help groups of a national self-help organization for women in Norway and on the support groups of The Anorexia and Bulimia Association in Norway. The main target is to provide the students with a 'safe place' to discuss problems and, if necessary, as a forum to motivate them for professional treatment.

Secondary schools and (limited to Buskerud county) the school health service were invited for a two-days course about group leadership. To qualify as a participant in the course, a person had to have basic skills about eating disorders. To qualify as a group leader, counsellors, health care personnel or teachers had to get specific training in psychology and communication enabling them to focus on group processes that would facilitate emotional expression. Also, they should familiarize themselves with referral procedures in the health care system and 'the way around' in the health care system in their county. In total, 16 persons qualified as group leaders.

THE GROUP MODEL

The groups are voluntary and limited to 10 weekly meetings each of about 90–120 minutes. The groups consist of 5–8 members with eating disorder problems and two group leaders. At each session specific teaching materials are used. Group meetings also give members the opportunity to share their experiences and feelings. For each of the 10 sessions, a particular issue guided the discussions:

1. Why are we here?
2. Eating disorders
3. Food
4. Culture
5. Body image
6. Communication
7. Self-assertion
8. Stress management
9. Self-esteem
10. 'On our own'

The choice of topics was based on the assumption that dieting and fear of fat are developed from our cultural context, characterized by prejudice against non-slender people and that women's success in school, work and relationships is much more dependent on physical appearance than what is the case for men.

In total, 14 adolescents attended the groups. Most of them were caught up in a self-destructive cycle of dieting and overeating. For some, self-induced vomiting was a problem. Only few of the group members were restrictive dieters. We were surprised that more than 50 per cent were totally confused about healthy nutrition and, hence, needed information about how many calories they should eat. Another observation was the pressure on their academic performance. This pressure was one of the factors that inevitably lead them to (increased) binge-eating.

What kind of experiences appeared from this activity? In the final session, most of the group members reported that they easier accepted themselves, with less feelings of being 'abnormal' or ashamed. All group members found the meetings warm and supportive, and were grateful for the confidential setting. Most of the girls reported less symptoms. None of the participants reported increased problems. Several felt happy about the education they were given on eating disorders and especially nutrition. Some group members realized that their eating problems were not just connected to a strong desire for slenderness, but even more to 'how you feel about yourself'.

How beneficial are these support groups? Obviously, there are many flaws and demand characteristics in self-report of satisfaction taking place within the groups. Also, we had no information about the stability of the positive changes reported. Despite these limitations the qualitative reports formed the basis for manualization of the group model. The manual was distributed free of charge by the regional school and health authorities.

A STUDY ON THE RELATIONSHIP BETWEEN THE PREVALENCE OF
SERIOUS EATING DISORDER SYMPTOMS, PSYCHOLOGICAL FACTORS,
AND PREVENTION STRATEGIES

In 1994, we performed a two-stage study of a representative sample of adolescents aged 15 years, to gain a more empirical basis for deciding which areas to focus on in further preventive strategies. We designed questions about height and weight to calculate BMI values. We also asked questions about knowledge of eating disorders and the source of information. In addition, questions were also asked about academic and social performance at school. We used scales from the Eating Disorder Inventory (EDI; Garner, Olmstead and Polivy, 1983) and the 'perfectionism' and 'general dissatisfaction' scales from the Setting Conditions for Anorexia and Bulimia Scale (SCANS; Slade and Dewey, 1986; Slade, Dewey, Kiemle and Newton, 1990). Possible clinical significant eating problems were defined as scores above 10 on the EDI scale 'drive for thinness'. A semistructured, standardized clinical interview modified after Johnson (1985) was performed for all participants satisfying this criterion plus a sample of participants with scores below the criterion. The sample of low scorers were matched to the high scorers with respect to age and sex.

Originally, 1,000 pupils were approached. The final sample consisted of 678 pupils. The drop-out rate was caused by lack of consent from pupils and parents, to some extent also due to misunderstandings in the distribution of questionnaire forms from some schools. Only in 6 per cent drop-out could most certainly be attributed to the presence of eating problems. In the final sample 462 girls and 216 boys took part.

Indications of some kind of eating disorder were found in 8.8 per cent of the girls and 0.9 per cent of the boys. Most of them had bulimic symptoms. It was alarming that none of the pupils with some kind of eating disorders had been identified by school or health care personnel prior to the study. We do not know whether this could be attributed to the secrecy of bulimia, or to lack of competence among school and health care personnel.

In the total material, compared to the boys the girls scored statistically significantly higher on the EDI scales 'bulimia', 'drive for thinness' and 'body dissatisfaction'. Such a difference was also found on the 'general dissatisfaction' scale of the SCANS. On the 'perfectionism' scale of the SCANS, extremely elevated scores were found for boys and girls. Such a drive for perfectionism was high irrespective of whether pupils had a suspected eating disorder or not. Hence, this finding was contrary to qualitative self-report obtained in the group model. Furthermore, we found that 99 per cent of the girls and 89 per cent of the boys could name signs and symptoms of eating disorders and that 97 per cent of the girls and 88 per cent of the boys had knowledge about risk factors. On the other hand, girls had statistically significantly more knowledge about consequences of eating disorders (69 per cent) than the boys (41 per cent). For 53 per cent of the girls and 43 per cent of the boys the school was the source of their information. Limited by the lack of baseline data, these results can be interpreted as an indirect evidence of the effect of the activities in the educational part of our programme, particularly since the school was the main scource of information. On the other hand, the effect of psycho-education can be questioned. First, a relatively high percentage of pupils with knowledge of eating disorders was found irrespective of whether pupils had some kind of eating disorder or not. Secondly, the percentage of pupils with serious eating disorder symptoms were fairly similar to the figures from our 1989 survey, even when we now used a more reliable research design. Recent controlled studies (Carter, Stewart, Dunn and Fairburn, 1997, Killeen, Taylor, Hammer, et al., 1993, Smolak, Levine and Schermer, 1998) have corroborated this suggestion of symptom information as useless, or perhaps even as harmful inspiration to symptom development (Habermas, 1992).

A striking result was that almost 40 per cent of the whole sample reported a very poor social performance at school. This may indicate that general maladaption should be a major focus in preventive work. An even more striking result was that pupils with an eating disorder actually reported a better social and academic performance at school.

RECENT DEVELOPMENTS OF THE PREVENTION MODEL: FROM DISEASE PREVENTION TO HEALTH PROMOTION

A final question remains: What have we gained in experience and understanding about how to conduct prevention and how has the experience formed our future goals and activities? In particular, we have become increasingly interested in how to set up goals for prevention which may take both general and specific aspects into consideration. In this respect, we have taken our point of departure from research related to the defining of characteristics of patients with eating disorders and to criteria for improvement.

The psychological differences between dieters and patients with eating disorders reported by Noordenbos (1994) can be converted into the following goals for prevention:

1. To increase self-esteem and self-confidence
2. To increase the sense of control
3. To make young people more independent
4. To reduce ambitions and perfectionism
5. To make adolescents more assertive and expressive
6. To enhance a more positve body experience on others

These points fit well with the following suggested criteria for treatment effects (Rosenvinge, 1996):

1. Development of a broader emotional register and a better contact with own feelings
2. Alternative and more functional coping strategies than symptoms of eating disorders
3. Recognize and assert own needs
4. Increased self respect
5. Connect self-esteem to other factors than weight and appearance
6. Orienting towards less narcissistic goals of life
7. Healthier eating habits
8. Improved body-image and body experience
9. More functional relations within the family

10. An awareness or insight with respect to the connection between eating disorders, and specific events, sometimes of a traumatic nature

We believe that these themes may be important in preventive work on eating disorders, especially because they correspond to many years of experience from educational practice in the secondary school system. All students will benefit from focusing on these themes. Such a focus may eliminate objections like the adverse effects of social learning of symptoms, and that talking about eating disorders may increase the attention and acceptance of symptoms in a way that increases the incidence rate.

The information package *'Adolescence and Eating Disorders'* became very popular and the high demand called for a new release. We then decided to make a thorough revision, based on our most recent ideas about prevention as well as on the official view on health politics and prevention (Report to the Storting, (Norwegian Parliament) 1992–1993). The new material is called *'About Culture, Body and Communication – a preventive material on eating disorders'* (in short: 'The OK-material'). The outline of the new package is as follows:

Introduction to youth culture and aspects of primary prevention
    General part
1.1 Adolescence
1.2 Self-esteem
1.3 Communication
1.4 Self-assertion
1.5 Stress management
1.6 What the body needs: About food and dieting
1.7 What the body likes: About training and sports
    Specific part
2.1 About eating disorders: Symptoms, somatic and psychological consequences
2.2 Sociocultural factors in eating disorders
    Introduction to secondary prevention
2.3 What to do if a person shows sign of eating disorders
2.4 About the two interest groups for persons with eating disorders, and about the treatment services available

While still containing some information about eating disorders, this material obviously is far more general in perspective adopting a health promotion model to replace the disease prevention model. Hopefully, the package will become even more popular than the 'old material', and more easily incorporated into the school curriculum. This revised version has now been released. A prospective evaluation of the effects of this material is an important future task. Positive effects of preventing anxiety (Dadds, Spence, Holland, et al., 1997) and depression (Gillham, Reivich, Jaycox, et al., 1995) focusing on health promotion and stress management, give hope for similar results on eating disorders. Apart from this, a number of indirect effects of the prevention programme have appeared, proving the importance of a long-term focus on prevention strategies:

• Prevention of eating disorders along our way of thinking has been set on the political agenda. For instance, in the forthcoming Report to the Storting (Norwegian Parliament) on psychiatry and on child and youth politics, prevention is specifically mentioned.

• The first regional center for treatment and prevention of eating disorders has been founded in Northern Norway, financed by the Royal Ministry of Social and Health Affairs and run by a collaboration between county health authorities, the Asgard University Hospital and the University of Tromsø.

• At present, eating disorders and health promotion have begun to appear in the educational curricula for the health professions.

• The National Board of Health initiated a nation-wide study of how their recommendations with respect to the organisation of treatment services have been carried out. The results show that implementation of treatment recommendations depends on the annual number of referrals of patients with eating disorders.

CONCLUSIONS

Concerning the content of prevention, it seems clear that we do not prevent eating disorders by just talking about it. Pure information is highly insufficient in terms of primary prevention. Rather, prevention strategies means to give back to the children their self-confidence and belief in their own intrinsic value to counterbalance the adverse sociocultural factors. Thus, we have come to believe that health promotion should be at focus, not the 'prevention' of a particular illness. In this way, we may be guarded against negative effects of interest and actions related to a particular, and hence, a 'popular' illness like eating disorders. We must then influence general social conditions and living conditions. Secondly, prevention strategies must influence the individual's choices and behaviours and encourage people to take charge of their own health.

Concerning the organization of prevention, we need to take an active role towards the political system and argue for the long-term cost-effectiveness of prevention. The authorities should not be allowed to avoid the problems or pass the bill to, for instance, voluntary work altogether. In the struggle for economical resources, it is essential to point out the 'silent' and 'invisible' effect of prevention as opposed to clear-cut and short-term effects with respect to treatment. Then, we may move away from the short-lived political populism of various 'task forces', and towards a genuine, long-term prevention strategy.

Secondly, we must ensure that economic resources stimulate preventive efforts and local initiatives. This implies, for example, monitoring how the funds are channelled to municipal and county services, particularly with respect to the services provided by general practitioners. Regular, ongoing evaluation of what the health services are *expected* to do and what they *actually* do is important. The health authorities must put more emphasis on teaching both 'the sick and the healthy' on how to act to prevent illness, injury and relapse after treatment. The watchdog role of the health authorities as regards public health hazards must also be further strengthened. At the local level, it is important to break down barriers between sectors and professions to make prevention work. Hence, we do good prevention by political actions, and by influencing political decisions regarding financial priorities and public health. However, when a plan of action is agreed upon, one should not remain in opposition at any cost, but rather contribute to its implementation at a local, regional or national level.

At last, we must curb the trend whereby the health care system is held responsible for solving problems which are best taken care of through normal interpersonal relations. The bottom line is to continuously argue that prevention is important. The importance of preventive work only shows when it isn't done but then the long-term consequences of such a failure could become disasterous.

REFERENCES

Brundtland, G.H. (1975) 'Skolen – et sentralt angrepspunkt i forebyggende helsearbeid' [The school as entrance for preventive health care]. In Larsen, Ø (ed) *Forebyggende medisin* [Preventive medicine] (pp. 67–73), Oslo: Universitetsforlaget.

Carter, J.C., Stewart, D.A., Dunn, V.J. and Fairburn, C.G. (1997) Primary prevention of eating disorders: might it do more harm than good? *International Journal of Eating Disorders*, 22: 167–72.

Dadds, M.R., Spence, S.H., Holland, D.E., Barrett, P.M. and Laurens, K.R. (1997) Prevention and early intervention for anxiety disorders: a controlled trial. *Journal of Consulting and Clinical Psychology*, 65: 627–35.

Frombonne, E. (1995) 'Anorexia nervosa: No evidence of an increase'. *British Journal of Psychiatry*, 25: 525–34.

——(1996) 'Is bulimia nervosa increasing in frequency?' *International Journal of Eating Disorders*, 19: 287–96.

Garner, D.M. and Garfinkel, P.E. (1979) 'The Eating Attitudes Test: An index of the symptoms of anorexia nervosa'. *Psychological Medicine*, 9: 273–9.

Garner, D.M., Olmstead, M.P. and Polivy, J. (1983) 'Development and validation of a multidimensional eating disorder inventory for anorexia nervosa and bulimia'. *International Journal of Eating Disorders*, 2: 15–34.

Gillham, J.E., Reivich, K.J., Jaycox, L.H. and Seligman, M.E.P. (1995) Prevention of depressive symptoms in schoolchildren: two-year follow-up. Psychological Science, 6: 343–51.

Goldberg, D. and Hillier, V.F. (1979) 'A scaled version of the General Health Questionnaire'. *Psychological Medicine*, 9: 139–45.

Gresko, R.B. and Karlsen, A. (1994) 'The Norwegian program for the primary, secondary and tertiary prevention of eating disorders'. *Eating Disorders: The Journal of Treatment and Prevention*, 2: 57–63.

Habermas, T. (1992) 'Possible effects of the popular and medical recognition of bulimia'. *British Journal of Medical Psychology*, 65: 59–66.

Henderson, H. and Freeman, C.P.L. (1987) 'A self-rating scale for bulimia: The BITE'. *British Journal of Psychiatry*, 150: 18–24.

Johnson, C. (1985) 'Initial consultation for patients with bulimia and anorexia nervosa'. In Garner, D.M. and Garfinkel, P.E. (eds) *Handbook of psychotherapy for anorexia nervosa and bulimia* (pp. 19–51), New York: Guilford Press.

Killeen, J.D., Taylor, C.B., Hammer, L.D., Litt. I., Wilson, D.M., Rich, T., Hayward, C., Simmonds, B., Kraemer, H. and Varady, A. (1993) An attempt to modify unhealthful eating attitudes and weight regulation practices of young adolescent girls. *International Journal of Eating Disorders*, 13: 369–84.

Levine, M. and Hill, L. (1991) *A 5 day lesson plan on eating disorders*, Columbus (Ohio): National Anorexic Aid Society.

Noordenbos, G. (1994) 'Problems and possibilities of the prevention of eating disorders'. *European Eating Disorders Review*, 2: 126–42.

Report to the Storting No. 37 (1992–93) *Health promotion and prevention: Challenges*, Oslo: Royal Ministry of Health and Social Affairs.

Report on the Public Health in Norway (1996) *Statement of the Minister of Health to the Storting by 30th April 1996*. Oslo: Royal Ministry of Health and Social Affairs.

Rosenvinge, J.H. (1994) *Eating disorders in clinical and non-clinical samples*, Doctoral dissertation, Institute of Psychology, University of Oslo.

——(1996) 'Treatment of anorexia nervosa'. *Norwegian Journal of Psychology*, 33: 309–15.

Shisslak, C.M. and Crago, M. (1994) 'Toward a new model for the prevention of eating disorders'. In Fallon, P., Katzman, M.A. and Wooley, S.C. (eds) *Feminist perspectives on eating disorders* (pp. 419–38), New York: Guilford Press.

Slade, P.D. and Dewey, M.E. (1986) 'Development and preliminary validation of SCANS: A screening instrument for identifying individuals at risk of developing anorexia nervosa and bulimia nervosa'. *International Journal of Eating Disorders*, 5: 517–38.

Slade, P.D., Dewey, M.E., Kiemle, G. and Newton, T. (1990) 'Update on SCANS: A screening instrument for identifying individuals at risk of developing eating disorders'. *International Journal of Eating Disorders*, 9: 583–4.

Smolak, L., Levine, M.P. and Schermer, F. (1998) A controlled evaluation of an elementary school primary prevention program for eating problems. *Journal of Psychosomatic Research*, 44, 339–53.

Steiger, H., Leung, F.Y., Ross, D.J. and Gulko, J. (1992) 'Signs of anorexia and bulimia nervosa in high school girls reporting combinations of eating and mood symptoms: Relevance of self-report to interview-based findings'. *International Journal of Eating Disorders*, 12: 143–9.

Striegel-Moore, R.H. (1992) 'Prevention of bulimia nervosa'. In Crowther, J.H., Tennenbaum, D.L., Hobfoll, S.E. and Stevens, M.A.P. (eds) *The etiology of bulimia nervosa* (pp. 203–24). Washington, D.C.: Hemisphere Publishing Corporation.

Sundgot-Borgen, J. (1993) 'Prevalence of eating disorders in elite female athletes'. *International Journal of Sport Nutrition*, 3: 29–40.

Sundgot-Borgen, J. and Corbin, C.B. (1987) 'Eating disorders among female athletes'. *Physician and Sports Medicine*, 15: 33–5.

CHAPTER FIVE

Experience with a school-based eating disorders prevention programme

Anne Stewart

INTRODUCTION

Eating disorders are a significant health problem amongst females in developed countries. In most cases the onset is in adolescence or early adult life. A recent Swedish study found the prevalence rate of anorexia nervosa to be 0.7 per cent for girls up to the age of 16 (Rastam, Gilberg and Garton, 1989). Studies on bulimia nervosa indicate prevalence rates of 1–2 per cent amongst young women (Fairburn and Beglin, 1990). Lucas and coworkers (1991) found anorexia nervosa to be the third most common chronic illness in adolescence. Morbidity and mortality in eating disorders have been shown to be high (Keilen, Treasure, Schmidt and Treasure, 1994; Zilber, Schufman and Lerner, 1989) and these disorders can persist for years disrupting many aspects of the woman's life and those around her.

Given these facts, there has been growing interest in developing school-based programmes to prevent the development of eating disorders. However, to date there are few published controlled studies of the effectiveness of such programmes. The first part of this chapter focuses on some of the problems and challenges of designing prevention programmes. Previous research studies of prevention programmes are reviewed briefly, noting their limitations. The second part of the chapter involves a discussion of the theoretical and practical aspects of designing and carrying out a new primary prevention programme which attempts to take into account the drawbacks of previous programmes. A detailed description of the school-based primary prevention programme developed by the author and her colleagues in Oxford, UK, is included. The research methodology of an evaluation of this programme is described. However, the results of the evaluation are not presented as the research is still in progress. Finally, there is a discussion of possible future directions in school-based primary prevention.

PROBLEMS AND CHALLENGES OF DESIGNING A PREVENTION PROGRAMME

Primary prevention of eating disorders (i.e. preventing the onset of eating disorders), requires knowledge of the factors which contribute to the development of eating disorders as well as a knowledge of factors which might protect against an eating disorder developing. A prevention programme may then attempt to modify these factors. Unfortunately, our knowledge of the risk factors in eating disorders is still limited and the knowledge of protective or resilience factors is virtually non-existent.

There is a considerable body of research on the aetiology of eating disorders, however, much of the research has major limitations, such as a focus on clinical samples, lack of appropriate control groups and insufficient attention paid to the timing of potential aetiological factors (Fairburn et al., 1997). Moreover, very few studies have tried to tease out the specific risk factors in eating disorders, as compared to risk factors in general psychiatric problems. Fairburn and colleagues (1997) have overcome many of the limitations of previous studies in their recent large case-control study. In this study the main risk factors found to be significant in the development of bulimia nervosa were: parental and personal history of obesity, parental and personal history of affective disorder, critical comments by family about shape, weight or eating, family history of eating disorder, negative self-evaluation, parental alcoholism, and certain adverse childhood experiences. Rastam and Gilberg (1992) in a case-control study focusing on background factors in anorexia nervosa found that early feeding problems, obsessive compulsive traits and death of a close relative early in childhood were all more common in the anorexia nervosa group. A limitation of this study, however, was the small number of cases studied. Apart from these two studies there is very little focus in the research literature on community samples of those with eating disorders, using case-control design. There are also few prospective studies of risk factors in eating disorders. A recent prospective study (Button, Sonuga-Barke, Davies and Thompson, 1996) found that girls with low self-esteem at age 11–12 were at greater risk of developing eating disorders four years later. Other general risk factors suggested by a number of studies include being female and being subject to Western sociocultural pressures where thinness is held out as an ideal (Striegel-Moore, Silberstein and Rodin, 1986). In general, primary prevention of eating disorders is constrained by our limited knowledge of risk factors. Moreover, many of the risk factors described may be difficult to address through a school-based prevention programme or indeed through any prevention programme.

The challenges of designing a prevention programme are, firstly, to identify from our limited knowledge those risk factors that are potentially modifiable in a programme and, secondly, to design a programme that is developmentally appropriate, has potential to induce change and is feasible within a school context.

One risk factor that is potentially modifiable is dieting. A number of research studies have suggested that dieting is an important risk factor in eating disorders (Polivy and Herman, 1985; Patton et al., 1990). Indeed it can be seen as a behavioural precursor of eating disorders in some people (Cooper, 1995). Patton et al. (1990) found that most cases of eating disorder are preceded by dieting and that the risk of developing eating disorder following a history of dieting is increased eight fold. Of course, many people diet and do not develop eating disorders, but it is possible that decreasing dieting in a vulnerable group (i.e. adolescent girls) may eliminate some cases of the disorder. Research has not yet clarified how the risk factors in eating disorders operate, however, it is likely that they operate at a number of levels, contributing to the development of dieting in the first place as well as increasing the likelihood of dieting leading to eating disorders. The aims of a prevention programme would thus be to reduce the prevalence of dieting, and to prevent unhelpful eating attitudes and behaviour from even developing. In designing a programme the risk of sensitising girls to issues relating to weight control and body image, making them more vulnerable to dieting, needs to be taken into account (Carter et al., 1997).

Finally, a school-based programme needs to be evaluated effectively. One of the problems with primary prevention of eating disorders is that eating disorders are not common enough to detect changes in their prevalence without very large numbers. Dieting, however, is relatively common in adolescence (Hill 1993), and any changes are therefore more easily measured.

REVIEW OF PREVIOUS PROGRAMMES

There are only a handful of published studies evaluating the success of primary prevention programmes in schools (Killen et al., 1993; Moreno and Thelen, 1993; Moriarty, Shore and Maxim, 1990; Paxton, 1993; Rosen, 1989; Shisslak, Crago and Neal, 1990) (see Table 1). In general, previous programmes have focused, firstly, on imparting information about eating disorders and the adverse effects of dieting and other weight regulation behaviours, and secondly, on developing skills to resist social pressures to diet. All of these studies showed an increase in knowledge following the programme, however, none of the studies to date have been able to show a change in eating behaviour following the intervention. There are a number of limitations with these studies, both with respect to research methodology and the design of the programmes.

The only large long term controlled study was by Killen et al. (1993). They developed an 18 session programme providing information on the harmful effects of unhealthy weight regulation, education concerning healthy eating behaviour and skills training for resisting social pressures to diet. However, although there was an improvement in knowledge, there was no effect on eating attitudes or behaviour.

Moreno and Thelen (1993) used a minimal intervention (6.5 minute video followed by a 30 minute discussion) with 80 12–14 year old girls. Knowledge, eating attitudes and behavioural intentions were measured two days before, two days after and one month after the presentation. An improvement in eating attitudes was reported at two day follow-up, however the intervention did not have significantly different effects over time in the target versus control group.

Moriarty et al. (1990) developed a programme that was designed to change attitudes to sociocultural pressures, but did not include active techniques to change eating behaviour. This study only looked at short term effects and did not show a positive change in eating attitudes.

Paxton (1993) did a 12-month follow up but did not find any changes in eating attitudes or behaviour. Her programme consisted of five structured classes, presenting information for discussion on weight regulation, biological factors, cultural factors and emotional eating. However, there were minimal active techniques. The study was carried out on 107 14–15 year old girls and no effect was found on body dissatisfaction, drive for thinness, eating or weight control behaviour.

Rosen (1989) in his study aimed to decrease weight reduction behaviour and improve body image. He included information about eating disorders and dieting as well as procedures to counteract negative body image. However, he did not use active techniques to change eating behaviour. The evaluation involved 100 boys and girls randomly assigned to an eight session programme or no intervention. The result was an increase in knowledge but no reduction in the incidence of weight reduction behaviours.

The study by Shisslak et al. (1990) used small numbers (50 pupils) and did not in fact assess eating attitudes and behaviour. The intervention was an eight session programme, primarily imparting information about eating disorders along with a consultation component (see also Chapter by Shisslak et al. in this book).

Despite the largely negative results of previous studies, schools remain an important arena where it is possible to target those most at risk from developing an eating disorder (i.e. adolescent females). The task is to design a programme which draws on the strengths of previous programmes, but which includes additional components to produce changes in attitudes and behaviour which are maintained in the long term. In the present project, recently undertaken in Oxford, we attempted to develop a programme that was research-based, that drew on previous programmes, but which included active strategies for modifying attitudes and behaviour within a developmental framework. The programme was developed jointly by the author and Jacqueline Carter. The following section will describe how this programme was devised and carried out.

TABLE 1 – Previous Research Studies Evaluating School-Based Prevention Programmes

AUTHORS	GOALS	CONTENT	TECHNIQUES	No. OF SESSIONS	SUBJECTS	EVALUATION
Killen et al., 1990	To modify unhealthful eating attitudes & weight regulation practices of young adolescent girls.	1. Information on the harmful effects of unhealthy weight regulation. 2. Education concerning healthy eating behaviours & exercise habits. 3. Development of coping skills for resisting socio-cultural influences.	Presentation of information through slide shows & stories. Discussion. Role plays. Assignments.	18	931 11-13 year old girls randomly assigned to intervention & control groups.	Increase in knowledge. No change in eating attitudes/behaviour.
Moreno & Thelen, 1993	To increase knowledge and improve eating attitudes & intentions to diet.	Description of eating disorders & effects. Socio-cultural attitudes. Suggestions for healthy eating. Suggestions for resisting peer pressure to diet.	6.5 minute video of a conversation between 2 girls followed by 30 minute discussion.	1	80 junior High school students in intervention group. 139 in control group.	Increase in knowledge. No difference between intervention and control groups over time in attitudes or behavioural intention.
Moriarty, Shore & Maxim, 1990	To increase knowledge & change attitudes towards socio-cultural pressures relating to eating disorders.	Educational curriculum on dieting and eating disorders, and socio-cultural influences.	Discussion groups. Role plays. Assignments.	15 (girls) 11 (boys)	315 elementary & high school students. (91% intervention 9% controls)	Increase in knowledge of dieting & eating disorders. No change in eating attitudes & behaviour.

TABLE 1 – Previous Research Studies Evaluating School-Based Prevention Programmes (*Cont.*)

AUTHORS	GOALS	CONTENT	TECHNIQUES	NO. OF SESSIONS	SUBJECTS	EVALUATION
Paxton, 1993	To reduce moderate & extreme weight loss behaviours, disordered eating & low body image.	Cultural ideas about beauty. Determinant of body size. Healthy & unhealthy weight control methods. Emotional eating.	Written information presented by class leader. Small group & individual research & discussion activities.	5	125 girls in intervention group. 34 girls in control group. Mean age 14.1.	Increase in body dissatisfaction across all subjects at 1 year follow up. No change in eating attitudes or behaviour.
Rosen, 1989	To decrease weight reduction attempts.	Physical development in adolescence. Body image. Weight modification. Guided decision making.	Lectures. Class discussion. Homework assignments.	8	100 boys & girls randomly assigned to intervention and control groups.	Increase in knowledge. No reduction in incidence of abnormal eating behaviour.
Shisslak, Crago and Neal, 1990	To educate students about eating disorders.	Descriptive information about eating disorders.	Presentation of information about eating disorders. Consultation & referral service. Education for staff.	8	50 high school students in intervention group. 131 students in control group.	Increase in knowledge. Eating attitudes and behaviour not measured.

THEORETICAL FRAMEWORK OF THE PROGRAMME

The overall aim of the programme was to prevent the development of eating disorders such as anorexia nervosa and bulimia nervosa by reducing the prevalence of dietary restraint and the level of concern about shape and weight. The methods by which we attempted to do this were: through increasing knowledge about dieting, eating disorders and related issues: by using procedures designed to produce attitudinal and behavioural change: and through attempting to address factors leading to the onset of dieting.

The factors addressed were: the developmental challenges for girls, sociocultural pressures, negative thinking, response to stresses, and adverse comments about shape and weight, all of which can contribute to the development of eating problems in some girls. These are described in more detail later in the chapter.

General aims were: to create a culture where pupils support each other not to diet, and to encourage pupils to seek help early on if an eating problem should develop. There is evidence in anorexia nervosa that if the interval between the onset of symptoms and the beginning of treatment is short, a favourable prognosis is more likely than if there is a long delay before treatment (Steinhausen, Rauss-Mason and Seidel, 1991). In our programme the pupils were given information on how to get help for eating disorders and there was discussion of factors which may delay help seeking (Fairburn, 1995), in the hope of increasing the motivation for early intervention if an eating problem should develop.

There has been much discussion in the literature concerning the most appropriate age for delivery of a prevention programme. Some investigators have highlighted the importance of preventative strategies with pre-pubertal school children (Smolak and Levine, 1994b). However, we felt that as eating disorders are rare in younger children, many of the issues commonly addressed in prevention programmes would have less relevance for them. Many studies have indicated that eating disorders become more common with the start of puberty (Killen et al., 1992; Koff and Rierdan, 1993; Hill, 1993). We decided to target 13–14 year old girls which is the age range at which abnormal eating attitudes and behaviour typically start to appear. Although this age range is strongly susceptible to peer influences, it is also an age at which the cognitive and behavioural skills are present to make changes, and attitudes can potentially be influenced before becoming more entrenched in later adolescence. Epidemiological data suggests that eating disorders are approximately ten times more frequent in females (Rastam et al., 1989; Lucas et al., 1991). It was, therefore, decided to design a programme for use in girls' schools.

Some researchers have suggested that it would be more beneficial to target high risk groups (Killen et al., 1993). We decided not to do this for a number of reasons: Firstly, since few risk factors for eating disorders are known with any confidence, it is difficult to clearly define a high risk group. Secondly, a significant proportion of people who develop eating disorders do not come from known high risk groups, therefore these people would not have the potential benefit of taking part in the programme. Thirdly, from a practical point of view, it is much easier to include the whole class in a session that is incorporated in the regular curriculum. Inviting high risk pupils to take part in a separate session would involve issues of consent and it is possible that those pupils who are at high risk would be hesitant to take part. Another advantage of targeting a general risk group (i.e. adolescent girls) rather than selecting a high risk group, is that there is the possibility of changing the culture in the particular year group by promoting awareness of eating problems and building peer support in resisting the pressures to diet.

The programme was designed within a developmental framework, taking account of the normal process of development in young adolescent girls (see Figure 1). As already mentioned, eating disorders are approximately ten times more likely to occur in girls than boys (Rastam et al., 1989; Lucas et al., 1991). Normal adolescent development involves a number of tasks and challenges which can be difficult to negotiate, particularly for girls. These include adjusting to the biological changes of puberty, establishing relationships, developing skills, becoming independent, and developing a sense of identity. Alongside these challenges girls have to contend with the sociocultural messages suggesting that happiness and success are obtained by having a body weight and shape similar to the slender models portrayed in the media. These multiple pressures can lead to the development of low self-esteem and a feeling of loss of control. Additional external stresses, such

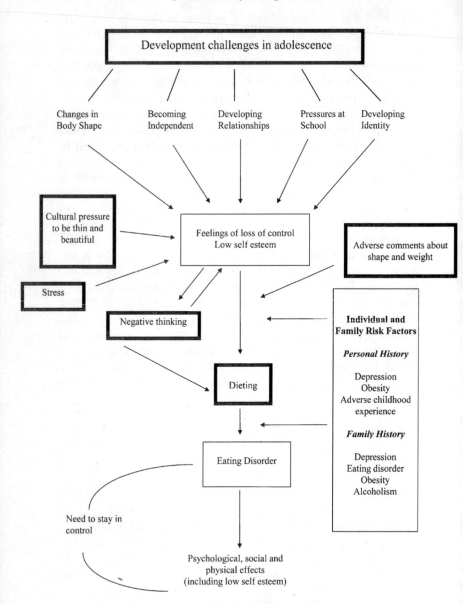

FIGURE 1. Conceptual framework for development of eating disorders indicating the factors (in bold squares) that were addressed in the programme

as family break-up, may contribute to these feelings. In some girls, perhaps those who already have the personal and family risk factors described earlier, negative thinking and in particular overconcern about shape and weight can develop which may lead to dieting. Adverse comments about shape and weight at this vulnerable time may also contribute to the onset of dieting.

As described earlier, adolescents who diet have an increased risk of developing an eating disorder (Patton et al., 1990). Once eating disorders are established they appear to be maintained by the psychological, physical and social effects of eating disorders which contribute to further loss of self-esteem and the need to stay in control. In addition, the diet-binge-vomit cycle is self-perpetuating and contributes to continuing low self-esteem and overconcern about shape and weight (Fairburn, Cooper and Cooper, 1986).

The potential risk factors for eating disorders such as a family history of eating disorders and obesity, or a previous history of depression and obesity, contribute to this model, but cannot be addressed through a school-based programme. This programme is designed to address the developmental challenges for girls, socio-cultural pressures, negative thinking, and response to stresses and adverse comments about shape and weight, all of which can lead to low self-esteem, disturbed body image and eating problems in some girls. These factors will now be described in more detail linking them to the way the programme was devised (see table 2).

ADOLESCENT DEVELOPMENTAL TASKS

Adjusting to the biological changes of puberty. The changes in body shape and increase in body fat in puberty can be particularly challenging for girls as their bodies develop in a way which is opposite to the sociocultural norms of beauty as portrayed in the media. The situation for boys is quite different since, for them, puberty brings them closer to the cultural ideal of masculinity (i.e. a well developed muscular body) (Striegel-Moore, 1993). Following puberty, girls' body image often deteriorates and an overconcern about physical appearance, including feelings of fatness, becomes common (Shore and Porter, 1990). Attie and Brooks-Gunn (1989) showed that girls who, in early adolescence, felt most negatively about their bodies were more likely to develop eating

TABLE 2 – Aims of Programme

MAIN AIM	
To prevent the development of eating disorders such as anorexia nervosa and bulimia nervosa by reducing the prevalence of dietary restraint and the level of concern about weight and shape.	
SPECIFIC AIMS	TECHNIQUES
1. To address adolescent developmental challenges	
a. To improve knowledge on the biological changes in puberty	Providing information through use of overheads, a story and handouts. Small and large group discussion about the difficulties of the biological changes and how to cope.
b. To encourage development of strategies to cope with interpersonal pressures.	Use of a story to illustrate difficulties in relationships and to stimulate discussion on ways of coping. Teaching skills to counteract peer pressure, including role play.
c. To encourage pupils to set realistic goals.	Small and large group discussion to help pupils feels good about themselves in other ways besides through high achievement.
d. To encourage awareness of the influence of family attitudes	Use of a story, discussion and role play focusing on the influence of families.
e. To help pupils feel good about themselves.	Providing information on the links between body image and self esteem. Teaching skills to challenge negative thoughts and attitudes. Encouraging pupils to listen to and value each other. Home activities designed to promote awareness of positive attributes.

TABLE 2 – Aims of Programme (*Cont.*)

SPECIFIC AIMS	TECHNIQUES
2. To address socio-cultural influences	
a. To develop a critical awareness of the cultural factors which promote dieting, weight concern and insecurity about appearance.	Use of slides depicting different views of beauty across cultures and in different times. Discussion of contemporary beauty ideals. Use of advertisements. Small and large group discussion about the influences of the media.
b.To encourage pupils to challenge media messages about thinness and dieting.	Small group exercises and home activities designed to help pupils challenge the media messages.
3. To encourage pupils to develop strategies about shape and weight.	Small and large group discussion and role play focusing on how to deal with negative comments.
4. To encourage pupils to develop strategies for dealing with stress.	Small and large group discussion promoting ideas on how to deal with stress.
5. To encourage pupils to challenge negative thinking.	Cognitive restructuring techniques.
6. To improve eating habits & lifestyle.	Providing information on the possible consequences of dieting and eating disorders, and information on healthy eating and life styles. Use of a story to illustrate these aspects. Self monitoring to encourage change in eating habits. Self monitoring to promote healthy exercise. Home activities.
GENERAL AIMS	
1. To create a culture where pupils do not encourage each other to go on diets.	Helping pupils be aware of each other. Building peer support. Providing information for a whole year group.
2. To encourage pupils to seek help early on if they develop eating problems.	Providing information about help available. Handout on how to get help. Discussion about possible difficulties in accepting help.

problems two years later. A number of studies have found that eating problems increase substantially at puberty (e.g. Levine et al., 1994; Killen et al., 1992; Koff and Rierdan, 1993). Some studies suggest that early puberty is a risk factor for later eating disorders (Fairburn et al., 1997). Levine et al. (1994) found that girls who were beginning to date at the same time that they started menstruation were at greater risk from eating problems. Our intervention was targeted at girls who were in the process of going through puberty. The programme provided information on the biological changes in puberty and gave the pupils an opportunity to discuss and reflect upon coping strategies during this transition.

Developing relationships (including sexual relationships). Girls report more social anxiety than boys (Allgood-Merton, Lewinsohn and Hops, 1990). For girls, a sense of identity is closely linked to interpersonal success and they are more likely to attribute a failure in relationships to an inadequacy in themselves (Grotevant and Cooper, 1985). Perceptions of physical attractiveness play a powerful role in achieving a good sense of self and success in interpersonal relationships. Bush and Simmons (1987) found that girls experience dating as more stressful than boys. The programme gave pupils the opportunity to discuss these pressures and develop strategies to cope with the pressures. Relationships with peers become increasingly important in adolescence. Conformity within a peer group is important, particularly for girls (Peterson and Hamburg 1986). In our prevention programme the aim was to encourage peer support to counteract the pressures to diet, and to help the pupils develop ways of approaching others who may have developed eating disorder symptoms. We attempted to create a culture where pupils did not encourage each other to go on diets. Pupils also learned skills to counteract peer pressure to start dieting. Research on prevention of substance abuse suggests that learning skills to counteract social pressure can be effective (Hansen, 1992). This strategy has been used in previous eating disorder prevention programmes (e.g. Killen et al., 1993) which were not successful in changing eating behaviour. We used this strategy in combination with other active techniques.

Developing skills. Girls in early/mid adolescence become increasingly concerned with achievement. Many girls feel under pressure to be high achievers as well as beautiful. Unrealistic expectations have been suggested as playing a part in the development of eating disorders (Striegel-Moore et al., 1986). Clinical experience suggests that perfectionism may be involved in the development of eating disorders. The programme attempted to address this by helping girls develop other ways of feeling good about themselves besides setting themselves often unrealistic goals.

Relationships with families – developing independence.   Families are very important in early/mid adolescence, but this is also a time when adolescent girls are beginning to explore the process of becoming independent from the family. Compared to boys adolescent girls have been found to report more interpersonal stresses related to the their relationship with their parents (Windle, 1992). There is no conclusive research showing a link between disordered family functioning and development of eating disorders (Vandereycken, Kog and Vanderlinden, 1989). However, research does show a link between a family history of eating disorders and the development of eating disorder (Strober et al., 1990). Although this cannot be addressed specifically in the programme there was a discussion on family attitudes to eating and how this may affect the adolescent girl.

Developing a sense of identity.   Low self-esteem has been suggested as a possible risk factor for eating disorder (Button et al., 1996; Fairburn et al., 1997). The self-image of girls appears to be more interpersonally orientated than that of boys (Striegel-Moore et al., 1986). Girls are more likely to define themselves in terms of physical appearance, and when this becomes extreme, eating disorders may develop. Button et al. (1996) suggest that there is a role for enhancement of self-esteem in the prevention of eating disorders. Improving self-esteem is an ambitious aim for a short-term school-based programme, however a component of our programme was to explore the links between body image and self-esteem and encourage positive change in these factors.

SOCIOCULTURAL PRESSURES

It is widely thought that exposure to media images of slender models contributes to the development of poor body image, along with abnormal eating attitudes and behaviour. Although much research in this area is inconclusive there is some support for this idea. Shaw and Waller (1995) suggested that media images can exacerbate body dissatisfaction in those adolescents who already have poor body image. There is some evidence that young adolescent girls who focus on media images show a tendency to have more abnormal attitudes about weight and shape (Levine, Smolak and Hayden, 1994). Given the suggestion in the literature that media images may have an impact on, at least, a sub group of girls, it was felt that sociocultural factors and the role of the media should be addressed in the programme. The girls were taught to be aware of, and to challenge, the media messages which emphasise slenderness as a goal.

ADVERSE COMMENTS ABOUT SHAPE AND WEIGHT

Clinical experience suggests that teasing about body shape and weight can often precipitate dietary restraint. There is some confirmation for this finding in the research literature. Thompson and Heinberg (1993) found that a history of having been teased about one's weight was a significant predictor of body dissatisfaction and eating problems. Fairburn et al. (1997) also found that critical comments about shape and weight were a risk factor in the development of bulimia nervosa. In the programme teasing was addressed directly by encouraging the girls to develop strategies to deal effectively with negative comments about shape and weight.

STRESS

There are some studies suggesting a link between stressful life events and the onset of eating disorders. Strober (1984) found that there was an increased incidence of severe life stresses in the 18 months prior to the development of eating disorder. Levine, Smolak and Hayden (1994) found that if changes of school were accompanied by other life stresses there was a higher incidence of eating problems. Our prevention programme included discussion of how to develop strategies for dealing with mild stress, although it was beyond the scope of the programme to deal with reactions to severe stress.

NEGATIVE THINKING

Negative cognitions about shape and weight are well recognised in eating disorders and there is a suggestion in the literature that negative cognitions may contribute to the development of eating disorders. Attie and Brooks-Gunn (1989) found that girls who had negative cognitions about their bodies were more likely to develop eating disorders two years later. Although the prevention programme was designed for a non-clinical group of girls, experience with normal adolescents suggest that negative cognitions about shape and weight occur commonly from time to time in adolescent girls. In some girls a pattern of negative cognitions may become established which can contribute to the onset of dieting. At this age, with the increased capacity for abstract thinking, it is possible to teach the girls skills to challenge negative cognitions (McAdam, 1986). In this programme the pupils were taught how to challenge negative thinking using cognitive restructuring techniques (to be described in the next section).

EATING BEHAVIOUR

As well as addressing the potential factors contributing to the development of dieting we also focused directly on eating habits. In our intervention we attempted to change dietary restraint through a number of means. Firstly, we provided information on the possible consequences (physical, psychological and social) of dieting and eating disorders, and information on healthy eating and life style. The programme focused more on immediate consequences than long term consequences, bearing in mind the research in the field of substance use prevention, suggesting that a focus on immediate consequences is more likely to have an effect (Botvin et al., 1990). Secondly, the programme aimed to foster actual change in eating habits and attitudes through a variety of active techniques, including self-monitoring.

STYLE OF THE PROGRAMME

The main strength of this programme, and where it differs from some of the programmes in existence is the focus on encouraging the development of skills and changes in behaviour by using active techniques. Skills are developed through a variety of strategies including cognitive-behavioural techniques, role play, home activities and self-monitoring. The style of the programme was interactive rather than didactic, making extensive use of group discussion and role play. The pupils were actively encouraged to make changes in their eating habits and exercise patterns.

Cognitive-behavioural strategies form an important component of the programme. The main assumptions in cognitive behaviour therapy are as follows. Firstly, the way an individual thinks about his/her experiences influences the way he/she feels and behaves, which in turn influences cognitions in a cyclical way. Secondly, psychological disturbances frequently involve cognitive distortions which can contribute to the development and maintenance of other symptoms (Beck, 1976; Beck, Rush, Shaw and Emery, 1979). Modification of cognitions can therefore be a useful place to intervene in the cycle. People with eating disorders show characteristic cognitive distortions and this observation has led to successful application of this model in the treatment of patients with bulimia nervosa (Fairburn, Cooper and Cooper 1986). In our programme we attempted to teach the girls the skills to challenge negative thinking, using this cognitive model. Active exercises were done to enable the girls to see the connection between thoughts, feelings and behaviour, and to identify and challenge negative automatic thoughts, particularly thoughts about shape and weight, substituting them with more adaptive thoughts. Other active techniques included self-monitoring of eating habits (Fairburn 1981).

A variety of educational techniques were used, including the use of overheads, flip charts and handouts. At the end of each session a summary sheet was handed out covering the main points from the session. As far as possible ideas were elicited from the girls and sharing of information with each other was encouraged. A story about a teenage girl the same age as the pupils was used throughout the course to illustrate the points addressed in the course. This was to enable pupils to identify closely with the issues without feeling personally threatened. Throughout the course a key strategy was to help the pupils feel good about themselves. This was done through active self-affirmation as well as indirectly by valuing contributions and ideas and encouraging pupils to listen to each other.

FITTING INTO THE SCHOOL TIMETABLE

The schools approached for inclusion in the project were very positive about introducing an eating disorder prevention programme into the curriculum, despite the inroads this made on other subjects. This interest reflected the general anxiety that these schools had about eating disorders in the school and the desire to address the problem. In most of the schools that participated, the programme was fitted into the curriculum in the time normally devoted to personal and social education.

The programme ran for six sessions. This is a realistic section out of the school curriculum, can be completed in half a term (in the UK) and appears to be a good time span to hold the pupils interest. The length of each session was determined by the existing lesson plan of the schools. Schools were able to offer a maximum of forty five minutes per session. Ideally, the sessions could have been a little longer to allow more time for group discussion. In order to foster a consistent and safe environment where the girls felt they could discuss personal issues it was planned that all the sessions had consistency of room, time of day and class teacher.

ROLE OF THE TEACHER

The programme was developed for use by school teachers. A clinical knowledge of eating disorders is not necessary to deliver the programme, although it is important that the teacher is familiar with the course material and has good facilitation skills. A comprehensive manual has been written (Stewart and Carter, 1995) which includes background information for teachers, as well as a detailed lesson plan. The issues discussed in the sessions are of a very sensitive and emotional nature, such as body weight and shape, body image and self-esteem. Thus, it is important that teachers examine their own beliefs and attitudes about eating and weight as well as becoming knowledgable in this area. Non-verbal as well as verbal behaviour may influence the way students respond to the programme. The main aim of the teaching was to facilitate ideas from the pupils rather than to present information didactically.

For the research evaluation of the programme four different tutors (all female) from a range of backgrounds were used. The majority of the teaching was done by a mature psychology graduate with no clinical experience but with skills in working with young adolescents. Three other members of the research team also took part in the teaching. They included a clinical psychologist, a research psychologist and a child and adolescent psychiatrist. It was planned that the usual class teacher also remained in the class during sessions. The regular class teacher's role was to contribute to the smooth running of the session and in particular to facilitate small group discussion.

Most of the teaching was carried out successfully by a person without clinical knowledge of eating disorders. In view of this, it is feasible for the programme to be presented by normal school teachers, assuming that they familiarise themselves with the material contained in the manual, have good facilitation skills and have normal eating attitudes and behaviour themselves.

INVOLVEMENT OF SCHOOL TEACHERS AND PARENTS

Alongside the prevention programme an information session on eating disorders was developed for all the teachers in a participating school. There are a number of reasons for this. Firstly, the aim was to educate teachers so that they will be more likely to identify early on those pupils who are developing eating problems. A second aim was to increase awareness in teachers of how to approach pupils with eating disorders and what help is available. Another aim was to help create a culture in the school where teachers are aware of the pressures on girls to start dieting, and are able to contribute to positively fostering the girls self-esteem and body image.

Information about the prevention programme was also sent home to parents along with a leaflet on eating disorders. The aim of this was to raise awareness in the parents about eating disorders and also to generate discussion between pupils and their parents about the topics covered in the programme.

The programme will now be described in detail focusing on the goals and content of each session.

DETAILED DESCRIPTION OF THE PROGRAMME

SESSION I. SOCIOCULTURAL FACTORS

Goals:

1. To promote interest in the programme
2. To develop a critical awareness of cultural factors which promote dieting, weight concern and insecurity about appearance.
3. To raise awareness of how these factors affect the pupils personally.
4. To encourage the girls to challenge media messages about thinness and dieting.

Content:

It is important in the first session to engage the pupils and promote interest in the programme. Issues of confidentiality are discussed. The girls are reassured that what they say will be kept private unless there is an indication of serious harm.

As an ice-breaking exercise, the pupils are then asked to form into small groups to discuss the question: 'Does it matter what weight and shape we are?' Feedback from each group leads to discussion about different attitudes to weight and shape and the effect these attitudes can have on people. Girls are encouraged to begin to question social attitudes.

In the next part of the session there is a focus on beauty ideals for women. The girls are shown, through a series of slides, how, in different time periods, and in other cultures, a wide variety of body types have been admired as beautiful. There is discussion about contemporary beauty ideals and the effect this has on women. In small groups the pupils are given a selection of advertisements, with the task of identifying the message about physical appearance in the advert and how this affects the way they feel about themselves. For their home activity the girls are asked to collect adverts for either diet weight loss products or beauty products, and answer questions on a handout concerning the message in the adverts – the aim being to encourage the girls to begin to challenge the narrow and unrealistic beauty ideals that are portrayed in the media.

At the end of the session the class is introduced to a fictional girl called Laura whom they will hear more about in future sessions.

SESSION 2. BODY IMAGE, BODY WEIGHT REGULATION AND THE EFFECTS OF DIETING

Goals:
  1. To provide information on the factors which determine body weight and the concept of natural weight range.
  2. To discuss the changes in body shape and body fat composition in puberty.
  3. To discuss and challenge popular myths about dieting and weight control.
  4. To promote awareness of harmful weight control practices and their effects.
  5. To encourage respect for individual differences in weight and shape.
  6. To define and discuss body image.

Content:
At the start of the session the home activity is reviewed with pupils describing the messages contained in the adverts and how these make them feel. Pupils are encouraged to challenge these messages. This is followed by a general discussion of dieting. Examples of dieting behaviour are given, such as missing meals, avoiding certain types of foods, or going for long periods without eating. The difference between dieting, eating a special diet, for example a diabetic diet, and eating a healthy diet is clarified.

The first part of the story about Laura is read. Laura is a school girl the same age as themselves who is struggling with aspects of growing up and dealing with herself and her family. Laura is dismayed by the changes her body goes through in puberty and begins to feel bad about her appearance. This leads to a discussion about body image and how this relates to actual physical appearance. Changes of body shape in puberty for males and females are then described, referring back to Laura. The pupils become aware that for girls the body shape in puberty is in direct conflict with the thin images put across in the media, leading commonly to a feeling of poor body image. The various functions of body fat are discussed.

In small groups the pupils are given a list of popular beliefs about weight control, dieting and body shape with the task of deciding whether they agree or disagree. Examples of these popular beliefs include: 'being thin will lead to happiness and success', 'people have complete control over their weight' and 'dieting is an effective way of losing weight'. Feedback from the small groups leads to discussion about weight regulation and the effects of dieting. The important role of heredity is emphasised. Pupils are shown that the healthy weight range is broader than many people believe, and they are encouraged to respect individual differences in weight and shape.

The home activity as preparation for the next session, consists of writing down the personal costs and benefits of dieting as well as re-reading Laura's story and identifying some of the problems she is facing.

SESSION 3. EATING DISORDERS

Goals:

1. To educate the pupils about the nature of anorexia nervosa and bulimia nervosa.
2. To promote awareness of the problems associated with eating disorders.
3. To promote awareness of the causes of eating disorders.

Content:

The session starts with a review of the home activity. Ideas from pupils on the advantages and disadvantages of dieting are discussed as a group. The first small group session involves the group making a list of the problems that Laura is facing. Feedback from this leads to general discussion of problems and changes that adolescent girls face as they go through puberty: adjusting to the biological changes, developing skills, developing relationships (including sexual relationships), becoming independent and developing a sense of their own identity.

The next section of Laura's story is read, in which Laura begins to develop symptoms of anorexia nervosa. In small groups pupils discuss what is happening to Laura and the group leader guides a discussion of the main features of anorexia nervosa and the physical, psychological, social and behavioural consequences. A further section is read from Laura's story in which she develops symptoms of binge eating and vomiting. In small groups the pupils discuss the effect of this on Laura and her life. The tutor summarises the main features and consequences of bulimia nervosa.

In the final part of the session there is an open discussion of the way dieting can develop as a response to some of the pressures, particularly for girls, in adolescence. The point is made that in some girls this can lead to eating disorders. The links between low self-esteem and overconcern about shape and weight which can lead to extreme dieting, binging and purging are discussed. The maintenance cycle described by Fairburn (1981) in his cognitive-behavioural model of bulimia nervosa is described.

The home activity for the next session consists of writing down a list of triggers which precipitated Laura's dieting and then rewriting the second part of Laura's story, indicating what she could have done differently and to have avoided developing an eating disorder. An alternative to rewriting the story is to make a list of what Laura could have done differently.

SESSION 4. EARLY INTERVENTION IN EATING DISORDER

Goals:

1. To provide information on the early warning signs of eating disorders.

2. To provide information on what help is available and how to access it.

3. To foster ways of supporting and helping friends who may have an eating problem.

4. To help pupils develop the ability to challenge negative thoughts about oneself.

5. To help pupils discover ways of improving body image and self-esteem.

Content:

The session starts with a review of the early warning signs of eating disorders. The home activity is reviewed leading to general discussion about what triggered Laura's extreme dieting. The pupils inevitably bring up issues such as low self-esteem, poor body image, worries about puberty, school pressures, pressures from the media, anxieties about relationships and negative thoughts. The pupils have further discussion about the links between low self-esteem, overconcern about weight and shape and development of extreme dieting.

The main part of this session involves an introduction to the cognitive model in which thoughts, feelings and behaviour are connected. Pupils are able to identify thoughts that Laura had about herself and discuss how this made her feel and behave. The circular nature of the model is emphasised and also the fact that thoughts are often automatic. In small groups, pupils are given the task of helping Laura challenge her negative automatic thoughts and come up with more helpful thoughts. As a large group other examples of negative thoughts from the pupils own experience are elicited and alternative thoughts written up on the flip chart. Towards the end of the session, the home activity is reviewed. An overhead is projected, summarising the solutions that the pupils came up with themselves. The session ends with a discussion of how to get help for eating problems, what the difficulties might be in getting help, and what the benefits are. Pupils invariably want to know how to help a friend and this is discussed.

The home activity for the following week is to make records of food eaten on two days during the week as well as making a list of their own positive attributes. The tutor also makes a record of the food she has eaten. Along with the home activity and summary sheet the pupils are given an information sheet on how to obtain help for an eating disorder.

SESSION 5. HEALTHY EATING AND LIFE STYLE: A NON-DIETING APPROACH

Goals:
1. To promote a non-dieting approach to eating.
2. To provide guidelines for healthy eating habits according to the National Food Guide of the UK (Health Education Authority, 1994).
3. To encourage healthy exercise habits.

Content:
The session starts with a review of the list of positive attributes. The pupils often find that their view of themselves varies from day to day depending on circumstances; this is discussed. This is followed by a discussion of the food records made by the pupils (and tutor). Usually there are plenty of volunteers to read out their food records but if not, the tutor starts with her own record. There is discussion about the types of food and proportions, any attempt to resist food, skip meals, etc. The pupils discuss the effect of skipping meals.

A non-dieting healthy approach to eating is defined and discussed. This involves eating according to feelings of hunger and fullness rather than following dietary rules, eating normal moderate amounts of all foods in the balance recommended by the National Food Guide [The suggested proportions for the daily food intake are: one third – fruit and vegetables; one third – bread, cereals and potatoes; the remaining third – meat, fish and alternatives, milk and dairy foods, and fatty and sugary foods], having regular meals, not going for long periods without eating and eating enough food to satisfy energy needs. The costs and benefits of a non-dieting healthy approach to eating are discussed. It is emphasised that different people have different nutritional needs depending on age, gender, activity level, body type, genetics and metabolic rate.

The role of exercise is discussed including the value of physical activity in stress reduction. It is suggested that with regular exercise and healthy eating habits a young person can stay at a healthy weight without dieting. It is emphasised that the healthy weight range is very broad. There is some discussion about what people who are overweight can do to minimise the health risks. This involves adopting a healthy life style (eating according to the National Food Guide and taking regular exercise). It is suggested that a person who is extremely overweight may need to consult their doctor for medical and nutritional guidance. However, it is emphasised that dieting amongst normal weight people is problematic.

At the end of the session Part 3 of Laura's story is read. In this section of the story Laura receives help for her eating disorder, addresses her problems and begins to adopt a healthy eating pattern and life style. The pupils discuss the ways in which Laura's life now changes. Ideas from the group are written up on a flip chart and usually include: increased self-esteem, better concentration at school, better relationships, happier feelings, more energy, improved sleeping, improvement in physical state.

For the next home activity pupils are asked to repeat the food records over the next week, particularly thinking how they might begin to make changes in line with the discussion in the session. They are also asked to take part in physical activity on three occasions during the week and note the effect it has on them.

SESSION 6. HEALTHY EATING: RESISTING PRESSURES TO DIET

Goals:
1. To review changes in eating and exercise habits in the past week.
2. To raise awareness of the social pressures to diet and discuss ways of resisting these pressures.
3. To develop strategies for dealing with stress.
4. To summarise and revise the main issues covered by the course.
5. To discuss how to maintain changes made during the course.

Content:
The session starts with a brief review of the previous session. The food records are then reviewed particularly noting the way some pupils have begun to make changes. Pupils are asked what advantages they see in a non-dieting healthy eating approach. They also give feedback on the effect of regular exercise. This is

followed by a discussion about the social pressures to diet. Family and friends attitudes towards weight and dieting are talked about and ideas are shared on how to deal with teasing. The pupils are encouraged to look at ways of resisting pressures to diet. This is done by means of a role play in which pupils learn to challenge pressure from others to diet.

Referring back to Laura there is discussion about the difficulty Laura had in coping with the stresses in her life. The pupils are encouraged to consider healthy ways of coping with stress. They are given the message that feelings can be confronted, experienced and dealt with. The links between body image and self-esteem are recapped and the pupils are asked to come up with ways of boosting body image and self-esteem. Pupils are reminded of the links between thoughts, feelings and behaviour and the skills of challenging negative thoughts. Finally, in small groups they think about what they have learnt in the course, what they will do differently as a result of the course and what difficulties they might encounter in trying to maintain changes. Pupils are encouraged to support each other in challenging the popular beliefs about dieting and weight in order to keep healthy. At the end pupils are given positive feedback for the contribution they have made to the course.

RESEARCH EVALUATION OF THE PROGRAMME

Prior to mounting and evaluating the prevention programme described in this chapter, we evaluated the feasibility of carrying out a programme of this kind in a small uncontrolled pilot project (Carter et al., 1997). The programme was delivered to two classes with an assessment of eating attitudes and behaviour before, after and at six-month follow-up. Immediately after the programme there was an improvement in eating attitudes and behaviour, however, this improvement was short-lived as by six-month follow-up, overall scores on measurements of eating attitudes and behaviour had returned to baseline. Moreover the level of dietary restraint was statistically significantly higher than baseline, although the actual size of the difference was not large. There was, however, no control group, thus it was not possible to determine whether the increase was due to the effects of the programme or whether it was due to developmental or societal factors. The programme was modified following this pilot, for example it was shortened from eight to six sessions and more active cognitive-behavioural techniques were included. In order to evaluate the effectiveness of the programme described in this chapter a research study has been carried out. It was a large controlled study with a six-month follow-up.

The programme was administered in three different types of schools (a private and a state girls' school both selecting on ability, and a state girls' comprehensive school). Three similar schools acted as controls. All girls aged 13–14 in the three intervention schools received the intervention as part of the normal school curriculum (459 girls). In each intervention school the programme was delivered over a period of six weeks and consisted of six forty-five minute sessions.

Outcome measures included the Eating Disorder Examination Questionnaire (Fairburn and Beglin, 1994), the children's version of the Eating Attitudes Test (Garner et al., 1982; Maloney, McGuire and Daniels, 1988), the Piers-Harris Self Concept Scale (Piers, 1969) and a knowledge questionnaire devised by the authors of the programme. The knowledge questionnaire was based on the educational component of the questionnaire and included questions on healthy eating as well as questions on eating disorders. It was designed to measure how much the subjects learned about the various topics as covered in the programme (a copy of this knowledge questionnaire is available on request). The questionnaires were administered, in both index and control schools, one week before the intervention, one week afterwards, and at six-month follow-up. The results of this study are not yet available. The aim of the next section is to report on our practical experience in carrying out the programme.

EXPERIENCE IN CARRYING OUT THE PROGRAMME

RESPONSE OF THE PUPILS

In general the pupils responded well to the programme. They particularly enjoyed the small group exercises, the role play and the cognitive restructuring. Laura's story worked well in that it held their interest and stimulated discussion. The session which dealt with the consequences of eating disorders was perceived as upsetting by some of the pupils and needed to be handled sensitively by the tutor. On occasions pupils brought up personal issues about themselves and their friends, and commonly would approach the tutor at the end of the session to ask for advice. Girls were advised where they could go for help. A number of girls reported eating problems and one girl who disclosed that she had an eating disorder was able to be referred for appropriate help. Another girl disclosed physical abuse within the family which was able to be taken up by the school. The programme appeared to facilitate disclosure of problems which could be seen as a strength of this programme, provided that there is a way to respond to the problems that are brought up.

DIFFICULTIES ENCOUNTERED

When conducting field research, it is inevitable that there will be some inconsistency between the implementation of the programme as planned, and the actual practice of carrying it out. The material presented in the sessions was reasonably constant, as it was presented by members of the research team, rather than by regular class teachers. However, the setting was not always consistent. In one school, due to the way the school curriculum was organised, the sessions were held in different classrooms on different days each week, sometimes with a different class teacher present. All this made the process of engagement more difficult. Where the regular class teacher was both consistent and enthusiastic about the programme the effect on the girls was very positive.

Unfortunately some girls were absent from one or more of the sessions. This created an inevitable lack of continuity for these individuals as the sessions were designed to follow on from each other. The use of summary handouts after each session went some way to filling the gap for students who had missed classes. In one school the last two or three sessions of the programme coincided with the end of year examinations. This provided competition for the girls when completing their home activities. The limited amount of time available often curtailed useful group discussions. It would have been preferable to have had another 15 or 20 minutes at the end of each session.

As stated earlier, family or individual problems were often raised either in the class discussions or privately at the end of sessions. It was very apparent that outside the programme there were strong influences on the girls' well-being which could not be adequately addressed within the scope of this programme.

With regards to the practical use of the manual, our experience indicated that more flexibility could be usefully built into the programme. The sessions were well-structured to fit in with a consistent research protocol, however in practice there needs to be greater flexibility and adaptation to the needs of the group that are actually being taught. There is inevitably a conflict between producing a well-controlled programme which can be evaluated and having the flexibility to adapt to the needs of the group. Ideally the class teacher who is experienced with a particular group of pupils could be involved in planning individual sessions with that group.

The questionnaires filled in by the girls as part of the research evaluation inevitably identified serious problems with eating in some of the girls. We had already made it clear to the girls that we would maintain confidentiality in the responses they made in the questionnaires, and therefore did not inform teachers or parents about these problems. We carefully considered the ethical issues involved here (as indeed the local Ethics committee did) and felt that it was ethical to honour confidentiality, given that the programme itself dealt with how girls could seek help for eating problems. In addition, ample opportunity was given to the girls to bring up concerns about eating problems both in the class and privately at the end. It is unlikely that we would have obtained accurate response from the girls if the answers were potentially not kept confidential.

CONCLUSION AND DISCUSSION

This programme has now been carried out in three schools with a total of 459 girls. The results of the evaluative study are not yet available, however, the experience of doing the programme has raised a number of issues. Firstly, an intervention of this sort cannot adequately address all potential risk factors. There are many powerful external influences on adolescent girls (family, peer group, school and wider society) which are largely unmodifiable through the programme. Ways of challenging sociocultural influences were explored in the programme, however, the pressures in Western society to be unhealthily slim remain unabated and can be a source of considerable stress for some adolescent females. Alongside attempts to develop prevention programmes there may need to be intervention at a socio-political level to address these societal pressures.

Our experience working with the schools has highlighted the importance of the influence and attitudes of teachers. Perhaps further preventative efforts need to include a more detailed educational training for teachers. In Norway a nationwide intervention programme is being introduced which includes full education for teachers (Gresko and Karlsen, 1994), although results of the evaluation of this programme have not yet been published.

Research studies suggest that a family history of eating disorder may be an important risk factor in eating disorder (Strober et al., 1990; Fairburn et al., 1997). Moreover, clinical experience suggests that families may unknowingly collude with the development of eating problems (Crisp, 1979) and may play a part in the maintenance of eating problems. Our experience of working with the girls and hearing their comments about attitudes within their families suggests that it may be helpful for further interventions to develop a way of involving the families, for example by setting up educational sessions for parents.

It was clear that some of the girls in our programme were already showing abnormal attitudes to eating. Consideration should be given to developing programmes that are applicable to younger age groups. Studies looking at the prevalence of dieting have found significantly high levels of dieting in prepubertal children (Hill, 1993). Eating disorders, although rare, do occur before puberty. Epidemiological studies have been hampered by the difficulty in applying adult diagnostic criteria to children. Therefore it is not known exactly how common they are. It may be helpful for preventative education to start at an earlier age with booster sessions given throughout the school years, focusing on different aspects according to the child's developmental level. In this way ideas and skills learned could be consolidated and reinforced over the period of growing up. However, there needs to be further research evaluating the effect of such a prolonged and intensive intervention. Logistically this would be difficult research to carry out.

The cognitive-behavioural element in the programme appeared

to work well in that the pupils grasped the ideas fairly easily and enjoyed the tasks. However, realistically, a greater input may be needed for the girls to develop long lasting skills in challenging negative cognitions. Perhaps in future programmes the teaching in this area could be increased with an evaluation of the effectiveness of this part of the programme.

The response of the pupils in bringing up a variety of problems with eating, as well as in other areas, suggests that it may be useful to have a counselling component linked to the programme. Shisslak et al. (1990) incorporated a counselling component into her pilot eating disorders project which was taken up by six out of fifty pupils. Ideally this could be built-in to future programmes.

Our programme was designed for use with girls only, but there may be scope for developing programmes which include boys. For most children in the UK the school environment is mixed sex and there may be advantages in encouraging communication between the sexes on the issues developed in the programme.

In conclusion, there has, to date, been very little systematic evaluation of primary prevention programmes in schools. This programme was designed to draw on the strengths of previous programmes and overcome some of the limitations. The results of the evaluation of the programme are in progress and will be reported at a later stage.

ACKNOWLEDGEMENTS

This project was funded by a Research and Development grant from the Oxfordshire Regional Health Authority. I am very grateful to the pupils and staff of all the schools involved for their interest and contributions. I am indebted to Jacqueline Carter, who co-authored the programme and jointly conducted the research project with me, and to Jonquil Drinkwater and Jane Hainsworth for their contributions to the development and carrying out of the project. Valerie Dunn, Zafra Cooper, and staff at the Highfield Family and Adolescent Unit, particularly Lyndell Costain, Mike Kent, Tony James, Judy Mann and Fiona Springthorpe have all given helpful advice in the development of the programme. Christopher Fairburn has given invaluable advice and support at all stages of the project. Finally, Jacqueline Carter, Zafra Cooper and Jonquil Drinkwater have provided very useful comments on this chapter.

REFERENCES

Allgood-Merten, B., Lewinsohn, P.M. and Hops, H. (1990) 'Sex differences and adolescent depression'. *Journal of Abnormal Psychology,* 99: 55–63.

Attie, L. and Brooks-Gunn, J. (1989) 'Development of eating problems in adolescent girls: A longitudinal study'. *Developmental Psychology,* 25: 70–9.

Beck, A.T. (1976) *Cognitive Therapy and Emotional Disorders.* New York: International Universities Press.

Beck, A.T., Rush, A.J., Shaw, B.F. and Emery, G. (1979) *Cognitive Therapy of Depression,* New York: Guilford Press.

Botvin, G.J., Baker, E., Dusenbury, L., Tortu, S. and Botvin, E. (1990) 'Preventing adolescent drug abuse through a multimodal cognitive-behavioural approach: Results of a 3-year study'. *Journal of Consulting and Clinical Psychology,,* 58: 437–46.

Bush, D.M. and Simmons, R.G. (1987) 'Gender and coping with entry into early adolescence'. In Barnett, R.C., Biener, L. and Baruch, G.K. (eds) *Gender and Stress* (pp. 185–217), New York Free Press.

Button, E.J., Sonuga-Barke, E.J.S., Davies, J. and Thompson, M. (1996) 'A prospective study of self-esteem in the prediction of eating problems in adolescent school girls: Questionnaire findings'. *British Journal of Clinical Psychology,* 35: 193–203.

Carter, J.C., Stewart, D.A., Dunn, V.J. and Fairburn, C.G. (1997) 'Primary prevention of eating disorders: Might it do more harm than good?' *International Journal of Eating Disorders,* in press.

Crisp, A.H. (1979) 'Early recognition and prevention of anorexia nervosa'. *Developmental Medicine and Child Neurology,,* 21: 393–5.

Cooper, Z. (1995) 'The development and maintenance of eating disorders'. In Brownell, K.D. and Fairburn, C.G. (eds) *Eating Disorders and Obesity* (pp. 199–206), New York: Guilford Press.

Fairburn, C.G. (1981) 'A cognitive behavioural approach to the management of bulimia'. *Psychological Medicine,* 11: 697–706.

——(1995) 'Prevention of eating disorders'. In Brownell, K.D. and Fairburn, C.G. (eds) *Eating Disorders and Obesity* (pp. 289–93), New York: Guilford Press.

Fairburn, C.G. and Beglin, S.J. (1990) 'Studies of the epidemiology of bulimia nervosa'. *American Journal of Psychiatry,* 147: 401–8.

——(1994) 'The assessment of eating disorders: Interview or self report questionnaire'. *International Journal of Eating Disorders,* 16: 363–70.

Fairburn, C.G., Cooper, Z. and Cooper, P.J. (1986) 'The clinical features and maintenance of bulimia nervosa'. In Brownell, K.D. and Foreyt, J. (eds) *Handbook of Eating Disorders: Physiology, Psychology and Treatment of Obesity, Anorexia and Bulimia* (pp. 389–404), New York: Basic Books.

Fairburn, C. G., Welch, S. L., Doll, H., Davies, B. O'Connor, M. E. (1997) 'Risk factors for bulimia nervosa: A community-based case-control study'. *Archives of General Psychiatry*, in press.

Garner, D.M., Olmstead, M.P., Bohr, Y. and Garfinkel, P.E. (1982) 'The eating attitudes test: Psychometric features and clinical correlates'. *Psychological Medicine*, 12: 871–8.

Gresko, R.B. and Karlsen A. (1994) 'The Norwegian programme for primary, secondary and tertiary prevention of eating disorders'. *Eating Disorders*, 9: 501–12.

Grotevant, H.D. and Cooper, C.R. (1985) 'Patterns of interaction in family relationships and the development of identity exploration in adolescence'. *Child Development*, 56: 415–28.

Hansen, W.B. (1992) 'School based substance abuse prevention: A review of the state of the art in the curriculum, 1980–1990'. *Health and Education research*, 7: 403–30.

Health Education Authority (1994) *The National Food Guide: Information for educators and communicators*, United Kingdom.

Hill, A. (1993) 'Pre-adolescent dieting: Implications for eating disorders'. *International Review of Psychiatry*, 5: 87–100.

Keilen, M., Treasure, T., Schmidt, U. and Treasure, J. (1994) 'Quality of life measurements in eating disorders, angina and transplant candidates: Are they comparable?' *Journal of the Royal Society of Medicine*, 87: 441–4.

Killen, J.D., Hayward, C., Litt, I., Hammer, L., Wilson, D., Miner, B., Taylor, C., Varady, A. and Shisslak, C. (1992) 'Is puberty a risk factor for eating disorder?' *American Journal of Diseases of Children*, 146: 323–5.

Killen, J.D., Barr Taylor, C., Hammer, L.D., Litt, I., Wilson, D.M., Rich, T., Hayward, C., Simmonds, B., Kraemer, H. and Varady, A. (1993) 'An attempt to modify unhealthful eating attitudes and weight regulation practices of young adolescent girls'. *International Journal of Eating Disorders*, 13: 369–84.

Koff, E. and Rierdan, J. (1993) 'Advanced pubertal developmental and eating disturbances in early adolescent girls'. *Journal of Adolescent Health*, 14: 433–9.

Levine, M.P., Smolak, L. and Hayden, H. (1994) 'The relation of sociocultural factors to eating attitudes and behaviours among middle school girls'. *Journal of Early Adolescence*, 14: 472–91.

Levine, M.P., Smolak, L., Moody, A., Shuman, M. and Hessen, L. (1994) 'Normative developmental challenges and dieting and eating disturbances in middle school girl'. *International Journal of eating Disorders,* 15: 11–20.

Lucas, A.R., Beard, C.M., Fallon, W.M. and Kurland, L.T. (1991) '50 year trends in the incidence of anorexia nervosa in Rochester: a population based study'. *American Journal of Psychiatry,* 148: 917–22.

Maloney, M., McGuire, J. and Daniels, S. (1988) 'Reliability testing of a children's version of the Eating attitudes test'. *Journal of the American Academy of Child and Adolescent Psychiatry,* 5: 541–3.

McAdam, E.K. (1986) 'Cognitive behaviour therapy and its application with adolescents'. *Journal of Adolescence,* 9: 1–15.

Moreno, A.B. and Thelen, M.H. (1993) 'A primary prevention programme for eating disorders in a junior high school population'. *Journal of Youth and Adolescence,* 22: 109–24.

Moriarty, D., Shore, R. and Maxim, N. (1990) 'Evaluation of an eating disorder curriculum'. *Evaluation and Programme Planning,* 13: 407–13.

Patton, G.C., Johnson-Sabine, E., Wood, K., Mann, A.H. and Wakeling, A. (1990) 'Abnormal eating attitudes in London school girls – a prospective epidemiological study: Outcome at twelve month follow-up. *Psychological Medicine,* 20: 383–94.

Paxton, S.J. (1993) 'A prevention programme for disturbed eating and body dissatisfaction in adolescent girls: A one year follow-up'. *Health Education Research,* 8: 43–51.

Peterson, A.C. and Hamburg, B.A. (1986) 'Adolescence: A developmental approach to problems and psychopathology'. *Behavior Therapy,* 17: 480–99.

Piers, E.V. (1969) *The Piers-Harris Children's Self Concept Scale,* Los Angeles, California: Western Psychological Services.

Polivy, J. and Herman, C.P. (1985) 'Dieting and binging: A causal analysis'. *American Psychologist,* 40: 193–201.

Rastam, M., Gilberg, C. and Garton, M. (1989) 'Anorexia nervosa in a Swedish urban region: a population-based study'. *British Journal of Psychiatry,* 155: 642–6.

Rastam, M. and Gilberg, C. (1992) 'Background factors in anorexia nervosa: A controlled study of 51 teenage cases including a population sample'. *European Journal of Child and Adolescent Psychiatry,* 1: 54–65.

Rosen, J.C. (1989) 'Prevention of eating disorders'. *National Anorexic Aid Society Newsletter,* 12: 1–3.

Shaw, J. and Waller, G. (1995) 'The media's impact on body image: implications for prevention and treatment'. *Eating Disorders: The Journal of Treatment and Prevention*, 3: 115–23.

Shisslak, C., Crago, M. and Neal, M.E. (1990) 'Prevention of eating disorders among adolescents'. *American Journal of Health Promotion*, 5: 100–6.

Shore, R.A. and Porter, J.E. (1990) 'Normative and reliability data for 11–18 year olds on the Eating Disorder Inventory'. *International Journal of Eating Disorders*, 9: 201–7.

Smolak, L. and Levine, M.P. (1994b) 'Towards an empirical basis for primary prevention of eating problems with elementary school children'. *Eating Disorders: The Journal of Treatment and Prevention*, 2: 293–307.

Steinhausen, H.C., Rauss-Mason, C. and Seidel, R. (1991) 'Follow-up studies of anorexia nervosa: A review of four decades of outcome research'. *Psychological Medicine*, 21: 447–51.

Stewart, D.A. and Carter, J.C. (1995) *Eating Disorder Prevention: A Six Session Education Programme for Use in Schools*, Oxford: Warneford Hospital.

Striegel-Moore, R.H., Silberstein, L.R. and Rodin, J. (1986) 'Towards an understanding of risk factors for bulimia'. *American Psychologist*, 41: 246–63.

Striegel-Moore, R.H. (1993) 'Etiology of binge eating: A developmental perspectives'. In Fairburn, C.G. and Wilson, G.T. (eds) *Binge Eating: Nature, Assessment and Treatment* (pp. 144–72), New York: Guilford Press.

Strober, M. (1984) 'Stressful life events associated with bulimia in anorexia nervosa. Empirical findings and theoretical speculations'. *International Journal of Eating Disorders*, 3: 3–17.

Strober, M., Lampert, C., Morell, W., Burroughs, J. and Jacobs, C. (1990) 'A controlled family study of anorexia nervosa: evidence of familial aggregation and lack of shared transmission with affective disorders'. *International Journal of Eating Disorders*, 9: 239–53.

Thompson J.K. and Heinberg, L. (1993) 'Preliminary test of two hypotheses of body image disturbance'. *International Journal of Eating Disorders*, 14: 59–63.

Vandereycken, W., Kog, E. and Vanderlinden, J. (1989) *The Family Approach to Eating Disorders: Assessment and treatment of Anorexia Nervosa and Bulimia*, New York-London: PMA Publishing.

Windle, M. (1992) 'A longitudinal study of stress buffering for adolescent problem behaviours'. *Developmental Psychology*. 28: 522–30.

Zilber, N., Schufman, N. and Lerner, Y. (1989) 'Mortality among psychiatric patients: the groups at risk'. *Acta Psychiatrica Scandinavica*, 79: 248–56.

CHAPTER SIX

Lessons from lessons: An evaluation of an elementary school prevention program

Linda Smolak, Michael P. Levine and Florence Schermer

INTRODUCTION

Recently there have been calls for the development of programs for the primary prevention of eating problems aimed at elementary school students (Shisslak, Crago, Estes, and Gray, 1996; Smolak and Levine, 1994b; Thompson, Heinberg, and Clarke, 1996). There are several reasons for this interest, including the limited success of primary prevention programs for middle and high school students (ages 11–18) and accumulating evidence that poor body esteem and weight reduction behaviors are not uncommon among elementary school children (ages 6–11). Unfortunately, research on eating problems among elementary schoolers and, importantly, their relationship to the development of disordered eating in adolescence and adulthood is sparse. Indeed, we do not yet possess the measures to adequately assess the childhood precursors of eating disorders; nor do we have models which clearly specify the childhood-adolescence eating disorders links (Smolak, 1996; Smolak and Levine, 1994a).

This chapter considers some of the factors important in the development of elementary school prevention programs, and describes an experimental evaluation of such a program [this research was supported by a Nutrition Education Training Grant from the Ohio Department of Education]. The chapter is divided into four major sections. The first section is an attempt to define terms and provide theoretical background concerning factors which might be addressed in a primary prevention program. This includes a consideration of the meaning of risk factors and protective factors. In the second section, we review relevant empirical data on behavior, attitudes, and knowledge concerning body image, weight and shape, and weight control among elementary school children. The third section describes the specific content of the experimental curriculum, while the fourth presents the results of the evaluation of the program.

RISK AND PROTECTIVE FACTORS AMONG ELEMENTARY SCHOOL CHILDREN

Primary prevention programs aim to reduce the likelihood of the onset of a problem, in this case eating disturbances. This is accomplished by decreasing influences which initiate and support the problem behavior, while increasing the impact of factors which *deter* the development of the behavior. So, for example, many cigarette smoking prevention programs try to simultaneously reduce peer influence while increasing the knowledge that peer use is non-normative (see, e.g. Schinke, Botwin, and Orlandi, 1991). Thus, ideally, prevention programs would address both *risk* and *protective* factors involved in the development of eating disorders and problems. Furthermore, it is important to distinguish risk factors from symptoms of the problem. This raises the thorny issue of whether there is a continuum linking 'normative' behaviors (Rodin, Silberstein and Striegel-Moore, 1985), such as dieting or body dissatisfaction, to clinically severe eating disorders (Levine and Smolak, 1992; Heatherton and Polivy, 1992).

Risk factors are any influence or variable which predates the problem of interest and increases the likelihood that the problem behavior will develop (Kraemer et al., 1997). We can distinguish a causal risk factor from fixed and variable markers (Kraemer et al., 1997). A causal risk factor is one that can vary, whereas a fixed marker can not vary, although it is still a risk factor. So, for example, sex can not be varied but it is a risk factor for anorexia nervosa and bulimia nervosa. Thus, sex is a fixed marker. Most importantly, manipulation of causal risk factors creates a change in the incidence of the problem behavior (Kraemer et al., 1997). Therefore, if an educational program successfully raises body satisfaction and that in turn is associated with a decline in eating problems, then body satisfaction may be considered a causal risk factor (assuming that poor body dissatisfaction preceded the eating problems). We should emphasize that causal risk factors need not be necessary or sufficient causes. Indeed, causal risk factors for a given disorder may vary across ethnic groups, developmental levels, and times of measurement (Kraemer et al., 1997; O'Connor and Rutter, 1996). In a dramatic example of this, marriage appears to be a risk factor for suicide among adolescent girls, but a protective factor for women (Kraemer et al., 1997).

In addition, there is little reason to suspect that there is a single crucial cause of eating disorders. Rather, there is a complex interaction of causes, typically postulated to include personality factors such as anxiety (e.g. Crisp, 1988), family dysfunction such as enmeshment (Strober and Humphrey, 1987), sociocultural factors such as media (see Chapter by Levine and Smolak in this volume) and teasing (Heinberg, 1996), and physical factors such as a genetic propensity toward being overweight (Crisp, 1988). The definition of causal factors is further complicated by the fact that there are likely multiple pathways to the development of eating disorders (Smolak and Levine, 1994a). Certainly, there are differences in the development of bulimia nervosa, anorexia nervosa and binge-eating disorder. But even within each disorder, there are multiple pathways. For example, binge-eating disorder may be rooted in dieting or in emotional overeating (Striegel-Moore, 1993). Similarly, Stice, Nemeroff, and Shaw (1996) have presented evidence of two distinct pathways to the development of bulimia nervosa. Thus, the risk factors may differ somewhat across cases (though there are not an infinite number of risk factors nor an infinite number of possible combinations of risk factors).

There are several multidimensional theories of the etiology of eating disorders which identify numerous risk factors. Unfortunately, few of these models have been empirically tested, especially in the type of prospective research that we usually rely on to distinguish causal precursors from correlates. The prospective data which are available (Smolak, 1996) typically focus on adolescent rather than elementary school girls. Currently, then, we are hard pressed to distinguish true causal risk factors from correlates of eating problems, especially among younger girls. In other words, it is probable that some of the variables currently thought of as risk factors are actually correlates of either other risk factors or of eating problems.

Teasing about weight and shape, for example, is related to appearance dissatisfaction, body image disturbances, and eating problems (Cattarin and Thompson, 1994; Heinberg, 1996). Does teasing increase the likelihood of eating problems? Or is it the case that people who are heavier are more likely to be teased (Cattarin and Thompson, 1994) and therefore it is really the above-average body mass index which creates the risk? Or, given that people with eating problems overvalue weight and shape, is it possible that they tend to overinterpret even innocent comments as being about their weight? At this point, we are unable to determine which role teasing plays and, hence, can not say whether it is a risk factor or a correlate.

DISTINGUISHING SYMPTOMS FROM RISK FACTORS

Early dieting has been linked to the later development of eating disorders (Tobin et al., 1991). However, dieting is part of the symptomology of anorexia nervosa and is frequently a correlate of bulimia nervosa and binge-eating disorder (American Psychiatric Association, 1994; Beumont, 1995). Similarly, body dissatisfaction, particularly when integrated into self-definition, appears to be a risk factor for eating disorders (e.g. Attie and Brooks-Gunn, 1989). But, it is also a symptom of both anorexia and bulimia nervosa. When do these 'causal risk factors' become early forms of symptoms or symptoms themselves? This question requires substantial research and is beyond the scope of this chapter. We can, nonetheless, note that behaviors and attitudes that may eventually be symptoms may be risk factors when they appear in children. In either case, preventing the onset of these behaviors and attitudes, including dieting and body dissatisfaction, is a reasonable goal of prevention.

PROTECTIVE FACTORS

We might make similar comments about protective factors, which have received far less attention than risk factors have. A protective factor is one which, in the face of one or more risk factors, decreases the likelihood that the disorder will develop. Protective factors may include responses to risk factors, including adaptation and coping (O'Connor and Rutter, 1996). One important question is whether a factor truly affords special protection or whether it is simply the absence of a risk factor. For example, if we say that a woman who does not invest in the appearance ideal set forth by society is 'protected,' is that different from saying she does not have the risk factor of investment in or overconcern with weight and shape? Compare this, for example, to the possible protective factor of having parents and peers who actively endorse diversity of body shapes, as appears to be true in parts of the African-American community (Striegel-Moore and Smolak, 1996). This seems different from simply not receiving the direct parental pressure about weight and shape that may be a risk factor for the development of eating problems (Pike and Rodin, 1991). It is important to identify true protective factors. Otherwise, we are in the awkward position of needing to erase variable risk factors which, as we discuss below, can be an insurmountable task for a school-based primary prevention program.

Clearly there are serious questions as to what constitutes risk and protective factors for eating disorders and problems. One could reasonably argue, then, that we are in no position to design primary prevention programs (Vandereycken and Meermann, 1984). We certainly agree that more basic research concerning both risk and protective factors is crucial. However, we would also argue that we do have a substantial amount of information about factors which are related to eating problems. Furthermore, the paucity of well-established causal models has not hindered the development of fairly effective therapies such as cognitive behavior therapy for bulimia nervosa (Pike, Loeb, and Vitousek, 1996). Even if some of the putative etiological factors are ultimately found to be correlates rather than causes, interfering with the development of the complex web of inter-related factors may be enough to reduce the likelihood of eating problems. Furthermore, we have increasingly clear and specific theories to guide us, some of which have received at least some empirical testing (e.g. Levine and Smolak, 1992; Silverstein and Perlick, 1995; Smolak and Levine, 1996a; Stice, et al., 1996; Thompson, et al., 1996). By carefully designing experimental evaluations of prevention programs, including curricula, researchers can actually contribute to the risk and protective factor literature. In fact, the critical questions of which factors can be modified and the optimal approaches to achieve such changes are probably best answered within experimental prevention research.

A MODEL OF RISK AND PROTECTION

Figure 1 presents our model of the development of eating problems (Levine and Smolak, 1992; Smolak and Levine, 1994a, 1996a). The model emphasizes pathways to eating problems during the early adolescent transition, a high risk period for the development of these problems, including body dissatisfaction, restrictive dieting, and anorexia nervosa. We propose that predispositions (e.g. need for social approval), which may constitute causal risk factors, interact with precipitators (e.g. pubertal changes) to lead to interpretations of or reactions to developmental tasks and demands. These reactions constitute various potential outcomes which vary in degree of adaptiveness. In other words, the model outlines developments in elementary school (and before) which shape reactions to the adolescent transition. Some of these predispositions would be targets of elementary school prevention programs. In addition, information about some of the precipitators might be provided in order to prepare the children for the demands of the early adolescent transition. Thus, the model provides a good basis for programs attempting to prevent the initiation of eating problems in early adolescence. Given that the effects of risk and protective factors may vary with stage of development (Kraemer et al., 1997; O'Connor and Rutter, 1996), other models may be more useful in designing prevention programs aimed at other age groups.

Figure 2 represents an adaptation of the Figure 1 model. It emphasizes the aspects of the original model which might guide a prevention program, trying to be fairly specific in terms of behaviors and attitudes which might be addressed. We have also added several protective factors which might be discussed. Note that this is still a fairly general model which would need to be modified depending on the specific grade for which the curriculum is being developed. Thus, for example, discussions of puberty should definitely be included in fifth grade (ages 10–11) curricula but probably not in first grade (ages 5–6).

Certainly all of the components of the model outlined in Figure

2 are potentially important. We urge, however, that special emphasis be given to the *thinness schema*. The thinness schema is a cognitive network that interrelates beliefs about the importance of attractiveness, the importance of thinness to attractiveness and personal success, and ways to achieve thinness and attractiveness. The term 'importance' implies both the perceived importance of the thinness schema to success in career and social achievement and its importance to self-definition. Specific components might include what would happen with a gain (or loss) of a few pounds, the likelihood of being successful if one was overweight, and how controllable weight and shape are. The thinness schema is comparable to the cognitive schemas described by Crisp (1988) and Vitousek and Hollon (1990), as well as the weight concerns proposed by Killen and colleagues (1994). It may represent the core of the eating disorders, especially anorexia and bulimia nervosa, and may be the motivation for subthreshold disorders, restrictive dieting, and compulsive exercise.

One important question that prevention research can address is whether breaking down components of the thinness schema (as opposed to trying to attack the entire schema) can sufficiently undermine its power and hence prevent eating problems. This is a relevant question because of pragmatic concerns (number of lessons possible, type of information which can be conveyed, etc.). Moreover, the limited research on what elementary school children know about dieting, weight, etc., suggests that their thinness schema may still be forming (Shisslak et al., 1997; Smolak and Levine, 1994b, 1996b).

A developmental approach may partially explain why certain variables pertaining to the thinness schema are more highly intercorrelated among adolescents and adults than in children. For example, Striegel-Moore and colleagues (1995) found no correlation between drive for thinness and calorie restriction among 9–10-year-old black or white girls. Gustafson-Larson and Terry (1992) reported a correlation of −.11 between 'wanting to be thinner' and 'avoiding foods that make you fat', while Hill, Draper and Stack (1994) reported correlations of −.26 and −.25 respectively, between body shape satisfaction and restraint and between body esteem and dietary restraint in eating among 9 year old children. However, Stice et al. (1996), using a sample of college women, reported a correlation of .53 between body dissatisfaction

FIGURE 1 – A Model of Risk for the Development of Eating Problems at the Early Adolescent Transition (From: Smolak & Levine, 1996a, p. 214)

Predispositions	Precipitators or Triggers	Developmental Tasks	Mediators	Outcomes
Individual	*Individual*	Adjusting to adult physical (reproductive, body size, strength) features	Simultaneity of task demands	*Most Adaptive*
Personality	Awareness of ending childhood: puberty, school changes, parent relationship changes		Timing of puberty	In the absence of individual predispositions, tasks may be positively interpreted ? body satisfaction, positive self esteem, mature interpersonal relationships, achievement motive
Thinness schema		Begin heterosocial relations		
Perfectionism	*Stressful or Unanticipated Life Events*			
Need for social approval	Sexual abuse or harassment	Begin realistic career exploration ('tracking' toward high school)		*Moderate*
Body dissatisfaction	*Social Systems*	Assess relationship with family vs. peers		With presence of thinness schema and non-simultaneous tasks, simple dieting, w/o notable pathology. With thinness schema, simultaneous events → disturbed eating with dieting, and reduced self-esteem, due to body dissatisfaction
Dieting	↑ Peer interaction	Gender-role intensification		
Self-esteem	↓ Parental support & influence			
↑				
Interacts with	↓ Teacher support			
↓	↑ Pressure from coaches, teachers			*Least adaptive*
Systems	↑ Exposure to media messages			Presence of thinness schema and three simultaneous, esp. early, tasks → subthreshold eating disorders.
Family enmeshment				
Family hostility				Presence of several personality predispositions and three simultaneous tasks → eating disorder
Peer pressure				
Teasing				
Family attitudes & behaviors concerning weight & shape				

FIGURE 2 – Components of risk factor model which might be included in elementary school primary prevention programs.

	Predispositions: Individual Personality	Predispositions: Systems	Precipitators/ Triggers	Developmental Tasks
Reducing Risk Factors	Provide information about effects and effectiveness of dieting	Discourage peer and family teasing and criticism	Discourage sexual harassment	Provide information about pubertal weight changes
	Provide information about genetic effects on weight and shape	Discourage negative parental modeling of weight concerns	Media Literacy	Discourage gender stereotyping
Enhancing Protective Factors	Provide role models of all sizes and shapes who are praised for accomplishments *and* appearance		Provide support and information to parents concerning adolescents and resources	Explore pathways to success not related to beauty/ appearance
	Encourage definitions of 'beautiful' that focus on self-respect, assertiveness and generosity of spirit			Help provide support from adults
	Teach problem-oriented coping			Help organize peer support
	Teach assertiveness			
	Focusing on health, functionality, and self-respect in developing positive body image			

and restraint. Furthermore, in the Hill et al. (1994) study, the combination of body mass index, body shape satisfaction, body esteem, and age accounted for only 17 per cent of the variance in restrained eating scores among 9-year-old girls. Among a sample of 10th graders (ages 15–16), body esteem, ideal shape, and current shape (the last two variables together are conceptually related to body mass index and body dissatisfaction) accounted for 31 per cent of the variance in dieting attitudes and behaviors (Gralen, Levine, Smolak, and Murnen, 1990). Of course, measurement differences may account for some of the variation in results. Nonetheless, these results raise the possibility that the link between children's attitudes about body and dieting behavior is relatively weak. Prevention efforts may inhibit the development of such links and, hence, of the full-blown thinness schema.

DIETING AND BODY CONCERNS AMONG ELEMENTARY SCHOOL CHILDREN

Several researchers have examined body image, dieting, and weight/shape concerns among elementary school children (see Table 1). Typically, the samples in these studies are late elementary school children (fourth and fifth graders, ages 9–11). There are fewer data available on first through third graders. A number of tentative conclusions can be drawn based on the extant data.

First, it is clear that elementary school children do diet. About 40 per cent of late elementary school Caucasian girls report ever having dieted, although estimates are as high as 53 per cent (Gustafson-Larson and Terry, 1992; Maloney, McGuire, Daniels, and Specker, 1989; Smolak and Levine, 1994b). Younger elementary school girls may diet less frequently. For example, Thelen, Powell, Lawrence and Kuhnert (1992) reported that 27.5 per cent of the second graders in their sample had ever dieted. On the other hand, Smolak and Levine (1994b) found no signficant grade differences in reports of dieting or weight loss attempts. Children also report using exercise to control their weight and shape (Smolak and Levine, 1994b), as well as more severe weight loss techniques such as vomiting (Maloney et al., 1989; Shisslak et al., 1996).

Second, children's knowledge of dieting exceeds their use of it. Fully 90 per cent of the fourth and fifth graders and about two-

Table 1: Findings from Studies of Dieting and Weight/Shape Concerns among Elementary School Children

Study	Sample	Findings
Childress et al (1993)	1599 girls in grades 5–8	33% of black girls and 45% of white girls had tried to diet
deCastro & Goldstein (1995)	30 prepubertal girls (M=9.7 yrs); 28 postpubertal girls (M=15.2 yrs)	2 of the prepubertal (6.7%) and three of the postpubertal (10.7%) reported they were currently dieting on their own to lose weight
Gustafson-Larson & Terry (1992)	Caucasian boys (238) and girls (219) ages 9–11 yrs	40% reported 'going on a diet' at least sometimes; 33% of girls and 17% of boys reported they were 'very often' worried about being fat.
Hill et al. (1992)	British, Caucasian girls: 84 ages 8–10; 86 ages 14–15.5	15 (18%) of the girls (mean age = 9.1) had DEBQ restraint scores equal to the top quartile of scores for the older sample
Hill et al. (1994)	213 girls and 166 boys; British, 80% Caucasian; mean age = 10 yrs	no gender main effect for body esteem; 20% of the girls who were slightly overweight to underweight had a fairly high restraint score on the DEBQ
Maloney et al. (1989)	244 children in grades 3–5 (53% girls; 92% Cauc.)	40 of 4th and 5th grade girls (vs. 27 and 29% of boys) had tried to lose weight; 11% of 4th grade and 7% of 5th grade girls (vs. 3% and 0% of boys) had ChEAT scores > 20
Mellin et al. (1992)	all girls; 66% Caucasian; 9–11 yrs	approx. 30% at age 9, 55% at age 10, and 65% at age 11 worry that they are too fat; approx 45% at age 9, 80% at age 10, and 80% at age 11 responded 'yes' to at least 1 of 5 questions pertaining to 'restrained eating'
Koff & Rierdan (1991)	481 5th–8th graders 243 girls, 238 boys	almost 15% of the fifth grade girls reported 'extreme' weight and eating concerns; older girls reported more concerns and girls reported more concerns than boys
Schreiber et al. (1996)	2379 girls ages 9–10 yrs	40% of the girls were trying to lose weight
Shisslak et al. (1998)	523 girls aged 9–15 years	among the elementary school girls, nearly 40% reported eating less to lose weight, about 56% had exercised to lose weight, almost 51% reported using diet pills and 5.8% had used laxatives to lose weight
Smolak & Levine (1994b)	187 Caucasian boys & girls in grades 1–5	interviews indicated that 40% of girls and 25% of boys had tried to lose weight at least once; 25% of the girls and 14% of the boys reported altering or restricting eating as a weight loss method

Striegel-Moore et al. (1995)	311 Black & 302 Caucasian girls 9 or 10 yrs	40% had an EDI drive for thinness (DT) score of 0; dietary patterns did not correlate with DT score; black girls had a higher DT score than White girls, although body esteem predicted drive for thinness only for White girls
Thelen et al. (1992)	74 2nd gr., 54 4th gr., 63th gr.; lower SES; 74% Caucasian	27.5% of 2nd grade girls, 33.3% of 4th grade girls, and 34.5% of 6th grade girls indicated they had dieted; compared to 2nd grade girls, 4th and 6th grade girls were more concerned about overweight and had a stronger desire to be thin(ner)
Wood et al. (1996)	109 boys & 95 girls, ages 8–10	55% of the girls and 35% of the boys were dissatisfied with their size; most of the dissatisfied girls wanted to be thinner while about equal numbers of dissatisfied boys wanted to be heavier vs thinner

thirds of the first through third graders in Smolak and Levine's (1994b) study believed that people could do something to lose weight if they really wanted to do so. Children mentioned dieting, eating differently (e.g. fewer desserts and more vegetables), and exercising as possible weight reduction techniques, with the older children more likely than the younger ones to mention dieting and exercise.

Third, there is a sizeable group of girls who worry about being too fat, show high restraint scores, or have elevated scores on the Children's Eating Attitudes Test (ChEAT; Maloney et al., 1989). For example, one-third of the 9-to-11-year-old girls in Gustafson-Larson and Terry's (1992) sample reported that they worried about being fat 'very often', while 55 per cent of the 10-year-olds and 65 per cent of the 11-year-olds in Mellin, Irwin, and Scully's (1992) study worried that they were too fat.

The concerns about weight, as well as the weight control attempts, may be motivated in part by dislike of, and even disgust for, body fat. By age six, children tend to associate negative personality characteristics with obesity (Lerner and Jovanovic, 1990; Staffieri, 1967). Such attitudes are not clearly related to self-esteem or sociometric status in childhood indicating, once again, the relatively weak links among aspects of the thinness schema (Cohen, Klesges, Summerville and Meyers, 1989; Mendelson and White, 1985). However, older children with higher body mass index do appear to be teased more frequently about their weight and shape (Cattarin and Thompson, 1994). Hence, there clearly is awareness and some enforcement of the norm concerning the preference for thinness. This norm may form the foundation of the thinness schema. Prevention programs may realistically aim to provide information which counters these erroneous stereotypes concerning personality characteristics of fat people.

Finally, even among elementary school children, girls are much more likely than boys to report such weight/shape concerns and attempts at weight reduction. Typically, nearly twice as many girls as boys report concerns about their weight or attempts to lose weight (Gustafson-Larson and Terry, 1992; Smolak and Levine, 1994b). Evidence does not, however, clearly indicate that girls have lower overall body esteem and body satisfaction than boys do. For example, Wood, Becker and Thompson (1996) reported higher body dissatisfaction among 8–10-year-old girls than boys. But, in a sample of British children, Hill et al. (1994) found no gender differences in overall body esteem. Smolak and Levine (1994b) reported a similar finding. Unfortunately, only a handful of studies have looked at both boys and girls.

Several caveats are important here. The data concerning dieting among elementary school girls have been primarily collected from Caucasians. It is possible that African-American girls are more similar to African-American adolescents and women (Striegel-Moore and Smolak, 1996) than to white girls and so may diet less. In fact, Striegel-Moore et al. (1995) found that 9–10-year-old black girls did not diet more than white girls, although the black girls had significantly higher body mass indices. Given that some researchers have called for targetted rather than general popula-tion prevention programs (Killen, 1996), it is important that data on this issue be collected. Furthermore, data concerning groups of girls who demonstrate more positive body image and less dieting behavior may be helpful in identifying *protective factors* that might be encouraged or facilitated by prevention programs.

A second problem with these data is that they are virtually all self-report. In addition to the usual problems with self-report data (O'Connor and Rutter, 1996), it is not always clear that a young child's meaning of 'eating less' or 'exercising' to lose weight is synonymous with an adult's. Having interviewed elementary school children (Smolak and Levine, 1994a; Smolak and Levine, 1996b), we have little doubt that children know something about dieting. They name commercial diet programs and specific exercise machines. They can enumerate what foods they believe they are supposed to avoid (e.g. sweets) and which ones to eat (e.g. vegetables). We do not know how extensive their knowledge is (e.g. do they know how to count calories?). Nor do we know whether their attempts to lose weight are stopped or at least truncated by their parents, teachers, and other adults. It is possible that elementary school girls parrot what they hear older girls and women say. Hill and Robinson (1991) found that young girls (9-years-old) who score high on a measure of restrained eating actually eat fewer calories than do other girls (although all girls had adequate diets), but Striegel-Moore et al. (1995) found no relationship between EDI-scale 'Drive for Thinness' and diet as recorded in food diaries. Considerably more research, including food diaries and parental reports of actual eating, is needed to clarify what children do when they alter or reduce food intake to lose weight.

Risk factor models suggest that early dieting, poor body esteem, fear of fat, and investment in thinness and attractiveness are important components of self-definition which might set the stage for the development of eating problems and disorders in adolescence. A growing body of data indicates that a sizeable minority of elementary school girls exhibit such behaviors and attitudes. Furthermore, one small study (Smolak and Levine, 1996c) has linked elementary school dieting to elevated ChEAT scores in middle school. Finally, there is limited evidence that all of the components of eating problems – including dieting, body dissatisfaction, and investment in thinness – may not be as clearly linked in elementary school children as they are in adolescents or adults (Shisslak et al., 1996; Smolak and Levine, 1994a). In other words, a child's 'thinness schema' may be less consolidated and hence more susceptible to intervention. All of this makes elementary school prevention efforts seem particularly important.

PROGRAM CONTENT

Prevention programs must start with a statement of goals. More specifically, careful consideration needs to be given to what aspects of eating problems are amenable to change (Neumark-Sztainer, 1996; Smolak and Levine, 1994b). Clearly, a school-based set of lessons is not likely to ward off personality disorder or family enmeshment, although both of these might be important contributors to at least some cases of eating problems. Similarly, primary prevention programs are not likely to change existing behavior (Neumark-Sztainer, 1996). Those children who are already dieting, then, may need support and guidance beyond the classroom lessons in order to reduce the risk that they will develop eating problems. Primary prevention programs *can* be helpful in such cases albeit in indirect ways. For example, dieting children might be identified either because their friends express new concerns about their dieting or because they self-identify. Thus, they are more likely to receive the help they need.

What exactly should we expect to change in an intervention program? First and foremost, we might change *knowledge*. Myths concerning fat people (e.g. that they have high rates of psychopathology), body fat (especially its dangerousness and malleability via will power), and dieting abound (Faith and Allison, 1996; Smolak and Levine, 1994b; Yucker and Allison, 1994). As Neumark-Sztainer (1996) has noted, knowledge is not a sufficient condition for preventing poor body esteem, restrictive dieting, and so on, but it is a necessary one. The importance of proper information concerning body shape, fat, dieting, and exercise is underscored by the relative success of cognitive approaches in treating eating disorders (Pike et al., 1996). Thus, we might expect that the increase in dieting at adolescence might be smaller among children who have accurate information about dieting.

Second, efforts might also be directed at *altering children's body esteem and body image*. Although such attitude change is difficult to achieve within a classroom curriculum (Rosen, 1989), body image and esteem issues are arguably at the core of eating problems (Faith and Allison, 1996; Thompson, 1996). The limited attempts to alter body image as part of the treatment of eating disorders and obesity which have met with some success (Thompson, et al., 1996). These might serve as models for body image lessons in primary prevention programs. As was true of dieting, primary prevention programs may be more helpful in *preventing poor esteem* (which is not a given even among overweight children in elementary school; see, e.g. Mendelson and White, 1985) than in altering it. But school based primary prevention programs may lead to the 'secondary' identification of children with body esteem problems, who might then receive the support and assistance necessary to ward off full-blown eating disorders later on.

Thus, the first goal of our curriculum was designed first to increase *knowledge* about nutrition, exercise, body fat and body weight, dieting, and media as a sociocultural factor in the promotion of unhealthy eating. Another core goal was changing *attitudes* toward fat, fat people, and the value of slenderness. There were also some exercises to try to reduce teasing and to improve body esteem. The methods by which we hoped to accomplish these goals included provision of information, learning exercises (e.g. role-playing and problem-solving), student creation of art work, and creative homework assignments involving parents and students.

EATING SMART, EATING FOR ME

The 'Eating Smart, Eating for Me' fourth-grade curriculum (Levine, Schermer, Smolak and Etling, 1995; for a description of the fifth-grade curriculum and data, see Smolak, Levine and Schermer, 1998) was designed for use with all students, i.e. it was intended to be be used with both boys and girls of all weights, social classes, etc. While some have argued that prevention efforts ought to be directed at high risk groups (e.g. Killen, 1996), others have noted that the sociocultural changes needed to reduce eating problems are really everyone's responsibility (e.g. Levine, 1994; Neumark-Sztainer, 1996). So, for example, the teasing which appears to be associated with a range of body image and eating problems (Faith and Allison, 1996; Heinberg, 1996) can only be reduced by informing all children.

GOALS

The 'Eating Smart, Eating for Me' curriculum embodied six goals (see Table 2) which were translated into ten lessons. First, we wanted to encourage *healthy eating*. More specifically, lessons concerning the United States Department of Agriculture (USDA) Food Guide Pyramid were developed. In addition to specific information concerning the Pyramid's guidelines for type and number of daily servings of the major food categories, these

Table 2: Goals of the 'Eating Smart, Eating for Me' fourth-grade curriculum

1. To explain the importance of proper nutrition, including that fat is a nutrient, and to explain how to use the USDA Food Guide Pyramid to achieve healthy nutrition.
2. To encourage healthy, moderate exercise on a regular basis.
3. To teach students and parents about the diversity of body shape.
4. To encourage the development of a positive body image.
5. To encourage healthy eating rather than calorie-restrictive dieting.
6. To encourage critical evaluation of media messages about body shape and nutrition.

lessons aimed to send salient messages about the importance of variety and moderation in eating choices. The lessons contained no references to calorie or fat gram counting. They noted that all foods were permitted under the pyramid guidelines, i.e. there were no 'forbidden foods.' In fact, the lessons included information about the value of fats and carbohydrates – some of the food nutrients children often think they should avoid – in our diets.

Second, two lessons emphasized *healthy exercising*. These lessons, offered as part of the children's physical education classes, focussed on the value of regular moderate exercise, discussing both aerobic and strength-building activities. Again, moderation and variety were the key. There was no discussion of how many calories were burned during exercise or how exercise might be used to lose weight. We tried, in fact, to downplay that aspect, given earlier data (Smolak and Levine, 1994b) indicating that elementary school girls especially considered exercise a primary weight loss technique.

A third goal was to *decrease prejudice concerning body fat and fat people*. Research has long and consistently indicated (Staffieri, 1967; Wardle, Volz, and Golding, 1995) that children associate negative characteristics and behaviors with body fat. This may contribute to the teasing of heavier children which may in turn be associated with emotional and eating problems (Faith and Allison, 1996; Heinberg, 1996). Among adults, higher body mass index is associated with greater perceived pressure to lose weight which in turn is associated with body dissatisfaction, dietary restraint, and bulimic symptomology (Stice, 1994; Stice et al., 1996). Thus, the comments of others appear to be potentially powerful contributors to a range of eating problems and are therefore important targets for prevention programs. The lessons concerning body fat also included some information about the genetics of body weight and shape. These lessons, then, were aimed at inhibiting the development of components of the thinness schema, especially fear of fat.

Fourth, as part of the effort to decrease prejudice concerning fat, we were interested in *encouraging children to accept their own bodies*. Exercises for self-acceptance as well as messages of tolerance of diversity were included in these lessons.

Fifth, we sought to *educate the children about dieting*. As reviewed above, many elementary school children believe that dieting is an effective way to lose weight and, apparently, keep it off. The extant data led us to believe that children had little information about either the immediate negative effects of dieting or its relative ineffectiveness in long-term weight reduction.

Finally, we firmly believe that most eating problems are primarily socioculturally rooted. Indeed, such an assumption is a virtual necessity for interest in developing a prevention program. Those researchers who believe that eating problems are primarily the outcome of individual or familial pathology would not typically endorse school-based primary prevention efforts (see, e.g. Neumark-Sztainer, 1996, for a discussion of these differing perspectives). Thus, our sixth goal was to *educate the children about cultural, and particularly the media, messages concerning the body*. More specially, the media lesson focused on television and magazine portrayals of body diversity.

Several of these goals, particularly the first two, are consistent with Ohio curricular guidelines. Hence, we did attempt to integrate the lessons with state recommendations concerning health education.

CURRICULAR DEVELOPMENT

Drawing from several existing curricular models (e.g. Carney, 1986; Levine and Hill, 1991; Shisslak and Crago, 1994), we developed ten lessons. A certified physical education teacher (Charlotte Ettling) designed the exercise lessons. The initial drafts of the lessons were examined by a community advisory panel, consisting of parents, teachers, nutritionists, physicians, and a counseling psychologist. Revisions were made based on their input and the program was pilot tested in three fourth-grade classrooms. Pre- and post-curriculum data were collected for the test classrooms and were compared to pre-post data for children (in the same schools) who did not receive the curriculum. The children in these control classrooms did, however, receive the typical nutrition education for fourth graders in Ohio. Based on the comparisons of the experimental and control classrooms in the pilot phase, the lessons were again revised. These revisions also considered comments from the teachers who had used the curriculum, as well as a more thorough review by a specialist in nutrition education.

STRUCTURE OF THE LESSONS

The ten fourth-grade lessons are listed in Table 3. The lessons were quite detailed. Each began with a statement of the rationale for that lesson. This was followed by a general goal and three to five specific objectives for the lesson. These objectives were presented in the form of things the children would be able to do after completing the lesson, such as listing three functions served by body fat or being able to identify five things children can do to keep their bodies fit.

Instructions were then provided as to how the teacher needed to prepare for the lesson. For some lessons, this meant assembling food, for others assembling magazine advertisements or provided materials, and for some simply preparing a pre-lesson homework assignment. Detailed instructions were then given as to how to conduct the lesson. These instructions usually included several options as to how points might be made. This permitted the teacher to tailor the lesson to her/his personal style as well as to the level and interests of the class. Each lesson concluded with a summary statement of the key points pertaining to the lesson's specific objectives. This was followed by a homework assignment which, in most cases, involved parent-child interaction.

Teachers did, indeed, make some changes in the lessons (and even omitted some lessons). While this feature probably made the program more attractive to educators, it almost certainly introduced error variance from an experimental perspective. Although sending people in to teach the lessons insures a more controlled

Table 3: Parent Newsletter Topics and Curriculum Lessons in 'Eating Smart, Eating for Me'

Newsletter	Topic	Children's Lesson #
1	Introducing 'Eating Smart, Eating for Me'	None
2	The Food Pyramid	1: Learning How to Climb the Food Pyramid; 2: Making the Pyramid Work for You; and 9: Handling the Snack Attack
3	Nutrients	2: None
4	Myths re: Body Fat	3: Myths About Fat
5	Body Image	4: Body Shape: Tolerance of Differences and 5: Positive Body Image
6	Exercise	6 and 10: Eating and Exercising for You and Your Health
7	Dieting	7: Dieting
8	Media	8: Media Literacy
9	Eating Problems	None

experimental design, we would argue that our approach constitutes a more ecologically valid evaluation. While outsiders might be able to present one lesson or lecture to a class, a program of this length (ten lessons) is most likely to be presented by the classroom teacher. Because this curriculum experiment was supported by a grant, each teacher was provided cooking equipment and money for purchasing food. Stickers, posters, and other teaching aids were given to the teachers.

The present chapter focuses on the effectiveness of the lessons concerning nutrition, exercise, body diversity and acceptance, dieting, and body esteem. These lessons deal most directly with attitudes and behaviors that are precursors to or components of eating problems.

THE ROLE OF PARENTS

We have argued elsewhere (Smolak and Levine, 1994b) that elementary school prevention programs must include the parents. Many of the decisions concerning what food is available to elementary school children are made by parents. Furthermore, parents' comments about children's weight and shape, as well as parental modelling of both eating patterns and body esteem, may influence children's eating attitudes and behaviors (Heinberg, 1996; Pike and Rodin, 1991). Parents of children in the curriculum classrooms received nine newsletters. These newsletters paralleled the curriculum lessons (see Table 3). The set also included an introduction to the 'Eating Smart, Eating for Me' curriculum, as well as a newsletter discussing eating problems (anorexia nervosa, bulimia nervosa, and obesity). Data were collected from some parents of the curriculum and non-curriculum classroom children both prior to and after the curriculum was instituted. Due to space limitations, these data will not be discussed here.

ASSESSMENT OF THE 'EATING SMART, EATING FOR ME' CURRICULUM

The curriculum program was presented to eight fourth-grade (ages 9–10) classrooms from six of the seven elementary schools within one rural school district. Three fourth-grade classes from the same set of schools constituted the control group. Teachers were not required to use the curriculum, so the assignment of experimental and control classrooms was not random.

There were 299 children surveyed at the pretest. Of these, 156 were boys and 143 were girls. About 65 per cent of the children were in classrooms receiving the curriculum, while the remainder served as controls. Virtually all of the children were white. Of these 299 children, 266 (89 per cent) were available for post-testing. The complete pre- and post-tested sample contains 129 girls and 137 boys. Following the ethical guidelines of the American Psychological Association (1992), children were told that they were not required to answer all questions (although they were encouraged to do so). Many of the children did opt to skip certain questions and so many of the analyses are based on fewer than 266 children.

PROCEDURE

Most of the children were tested in their classrooms with their classmates. The exceptions to this were children who were absent during their class' testing time. Some were tested in larger rooms (e.g. a cafeteria) with two or three classrooms together. In all cases, the classroom teacher and one or two members of the research team were available to answer questions. Unless the classroom teacher objected, the survey was read to the children.

The survey was approximately seven pages long and took about 30 minutes to complete. The same survey was used at pre- and post-testing. The only changes were in the holidays used to anchor the few questions using a time frame. For example, we were interested in whether the children had tried to lose weight 'recently' (about the past four or five months). In the fall, they were asked whether they had tried since the 4th of July, whereas in the winter the anchoring holiday was Thanksgiving.

The survey covered all ten lessons and was primarily geared towards testing curriculum content. Thus, for example, children were asked specific questions about numbers of servings of foods recommended in the USDA Food Guide Pyramid. In addition, food choices were evaluated by asking the children to check off which foods they had eaten the previous day, a method adapted from Domel and colleagues (1994). A similar technique was used to assess exercise patterns, although here the question covered yesterday and the day before. Body esteem was measured using seven items from the Body Esteem Scale for Children (BES; Mendelson and White, 1993), although this was reduced to six in the analysis in order to increase the available number ($\alpha = .82$). Children were also asked their attitudes about fat people. Both weight loss attempts and concern about weight were assessed. Children were asked whether they were teased about their weight and whether they teased other children. The full survey is available from the first author.

RESULTS

Results will be presented in terms of the curriculum's major goal areas: nutrition education (including increasing fruit and vegetable consumption), exercise patterns, beliefs about body fat and fat people, the behavior of teasing fat children, body esteem, and, finally, beliefs about and use of weight reduction techniques. For each area, baseline information is first presented because such information is important in interpreting the meaning of the pre-post assessment. It is important to keep in mind that approximately two-thirds of the children were in curriculum classrooms. Thus, the expected representation of children giving any particular answer to a specific question is approximately two-thirds curricular and one-third control.

Nutrition education

Variety and moderation were emphasized in the nutrition lessons. At the pre-test, 37 per cent of the children knew that you could eat 'at least some of any kind of food.' Of the children (n = 89) who changed from an incorrect to a correct answer to this question, nearly 80 per cent were in the curricular classroom [χ^2 (1) = 12.53, p < .001; with Yates Continuity Correction, which was used in all reported chi-square tests]. At the pre-test, almost all of the children (80 per cent) correctly chose that we eat a variety of foods to 'get lots of nutrients.' Not surprisingly, then, the curriculum had no statistically significant effect on this question.

Three questions asked about servings of foods based on the Food Guide Pyramid. At the pre-test, 62 per cent of the children knew the number of vegetable servings suggested, while 49.5 per cent knew how many servings of meat were suggested. About one-third of the children understood that always eating the same fruit did not meet the criteria of the fruit intake guidelines in the Pyramid. Post-test data showed no significant effect of the curriculum on knowledge concerning vegetable servings. There was a marginal improvement in knowledge concerning the appropriate number of servings of meat [χ^2 (1) = 3.54, p = .06]. Of the children (n = 73) who changed to a correct answer on this question, 75 per cent were from curriculum classrooms. There was also a significant effect for the 'same fruit' question [χ^2 (1) = 3.71, p = .05]. At the post-test, 76 per cent of the children (n = 72) who changed to a correct answer on this question were from the curriculum classes.

Finally, children used a 59-item checklist to report how many servings of fruits and vegetables they had eaten during the preceding day. At the pre-test, the mean number of vegetables eaten was 2.23 (sd = 3.16) and the mean number of fruits eaten was 2.57 (sd = 3.26). A mixed design MANOVA (sex X curriculum time of testing) revealed no sex nor curriculum exposure effects on these variables.

Exercise
At the pre-test, the children reported a mean of 5.8 activities (of at least 20 minutes duration) during the preceding two days. We should emphasize that these data, like all of the other information here, are self-report and have no corroborating evidence. A mixed design MANOVA again revealed neither sex nor curricular effects.

Beliefs about fat and fat people
Over half of the children originally reported that people were fat because they ate 'all of the time.' At the post-test, 90 children had changed to the correct answer. Of these, 76 per cent were in the curriculum classroom while 60 per cent of those who had not changed to a correct answer were in these classes [χ^2 (1) = 5.88, p < .02]. Similarly, about 50 per cent of the pretested children thought that people did not inherit their body shapes. At the post-test, 73 changed their answer to be correct. Again, compared to the children who did not change, more of these were in the curricular classrooms [χ^2 (1) = 5.14, p < .03].

Children also checked off which, if any, of six negative (e.g. mean, lazy) and six positive (e.g. friendly, smart) characteristics they thought distinguished fat and thin people. At the pretest, they checked an average of 1.32 negative and .94 positive characteristics. Mixed design ANOVAs showed that while the number of negative characteristics decreased and the number of reported positive characteristics increased significantly, these changes were not attributable to the curriculum. Children in both curricular and non-curricular classrooms showed these changes.

Teasing
Over three quarters of the pretest children claimed they never teased other children about being too fat. The mean score (on a 4-point scale with 1= never and 4 = all the time) on the teasing others question was 1.24 at the pretest and 1.38 at the posttest [F

Table 4: Total Body Esteem Scores (Means and Standard Deviations)

	Pre-Test		Post-Test	
	Boys	Girls	Boys	Girls
Curriculum	10.77	10.32	11.04	10.28
	(1.70)	(2.02)	(1.44)	(2.10)
No Curriculum	11.13	10.12	11.18	10.71
	(1.24)	(2.07)	(1.52)	(1.91)

$(1, 253) = 11.02$, $p = .001$]. This increase was evident for both boys and girls in both types of classrooms.

Body esteem
A four point scale (1 = no concern) was used to assess concern about weighing too much or being too fat. Concern did not change from pre to post test. However, at both times of testing, girls reported more concern about being fat than did boys [$F (1, 247) = 4.67$, $p < .05$]. It is noteworthy that for the girls the mean was 1.90, indicating that on average they were 'a little bit concerned' about their weight.

A short version of the BES (Mendelson and White, 1993) was also used to examine body esteem. Again, a mixed design ANOVA showed that across the board the boys reported higher body esteem [$F (1, 210) = 8.35$, $p < .01$]. There was also a significant pre-post change [$F (1, 210) = 4.01$, $p > .05$], and a significant sex X curriculum X pre-post interaction [$F (1, 210) = 4.28$, $p < .05$]. The boys in the curriculum classes and the girls in the non-curricular classrooms showed an increase in BES scores. The means, standard deviations, and numbers for these effects are shown in Table 4.

Weight loss and dieting
In the fall, children were asked to rate the frequency of their weight loss attempts since the 4th of July on a scale ranging from 1 = never to 5 = always. Of the 296 children who answered this question, 152 (51 per cent) said 'never' (compared to 235 children saying they 'never' tried to gain weight in a separate question). The average rating was 2.36, which declined to 1.96 at the post-

Table 5: Frequency of Changing from Incorrect to Correct Answer on Question Concerning the Effects of Dieting

	Curriculum	No Curriculum	Total
From incorrect to correct	67	18	85
Other	104	66	170

test [F (1, 252) = 18.61, p < .001]. The mixed design ANOVA indicated neither sex nor curriculum effects and no significant interactions. Those 144 children who reported they had attempted to lose weight were asked, in an open-ended question, how they had tried to do this. At the time of the pre-test only 6 said they dieted, 13 said they changed their eating habits, and 104 stated they exercised to try to lose weight. In terms of knowledge about dieting, 137 children at the pretest indicated that healthy eating was better than dieting in order to lose weight. On the other hand, only 63 knew that dieting would make you cranky and tired (see Table 5). The curriculum appeared to affect the latter but not the former. At the posttest, 79 per cent of the children (n = 85) who changed to a correct answer concerning the effects of dieting had been through the curriculum [χ^2 (1) = 7.21, p < .01].

SUMMARY

The 'Eating Smart, Eating for Me' curriculum had its clearest effects on the children's knowledge. Of the ten variables measuring knowledge, the children who had the curriculum showed positive changes on six of them. These knowledge improvements were spread across the domains, including nutrition, dieting, and body fat information, including beliefs about fat people.

On the other hand, the curriculum had no discernable effect on dieting, teasing, eating, or exercising behavior. Indeed, teasing actually increased in both the curricular and control classrooms at the post-test. It is possible that some of the children gained weight during from fall to winter and hence were teased more frequently. Or the increase in teasing may be a function of increased familiarity (and hence comfort with teasing) as the school year progressed. Attitudes about fat people were not affected nor were concerns about becoming fat.

Body esteem did appear to increase for boys in the curriculum classrooms. However, this meaning of this effect is unclear since girls in the non-curriculum, but not curriculum, classrooms similarly increased in body esteem. This latter effect is especially disturbing because it raises the possibility that even discussing the issues of body fat, weight, and shape with girls of this age may heighten their negative feelings about their own bodies. This issue deserves further research attention. It should be noted, however, that this was the only variable for which such an anomalous effect occurred. Therefore, it is possible that it is a random finding or is attributable to some unmeasured variable.

We have no effective way of gauging how much the children in the curriculum classrooms discussed what they were learning with the control children. It is possible, then, that the control children 'learned' some of the lessons, hence negating a curricular effect. However, our results are generally fairly consistent with those of other controlled curriculum evaluations (Shisslak et al., 1996). Hence, we tend to believe that the curriculum did not directly affect these behaviors and attitudes. As we noted above (and discussed below), it is reasonable to expect little direct effect on existing behavior. Instead, the goal is to modify (i.e. prevent) future negative attitudes and behaviors.

CONCLUSIONS

Evidence continues to accumulate indicating that there is a strong sociocultural component in the development of eating problems (e.g. Heinberg, 1996; Murnen and Smolak, 1997; Stice et al., 1996). If this is indeed the case, one might expect that primary prevention programs could be effective in undermining the development of eating disorders. Certainly such programs could not reverse major social trends (e.g. sexism as a contributor), but they might serve to decrease some of the specific behaviors reflecting social trends (e.g. teasing as an indicator of weightism) as well as some specific behaviors (e.g. dieting) which might lead directly to eating disorders (Stice et al., 1996).

Developmental psychopathology models are becoming more influential in explaining the etiology of eating disorders (Smolak, Levine, and Striegel-Moore, 1996). Moreover, although genetics may play a role in eating disorders (Rende, 1996), eating disorders seem to reflect a variety of acquired patterns of thinking and behaving (Pike et al., 1996). Therefore, it seems not only reasonable but important to intervene with children and early adolescents who either have not developed or are in the early phases of these problems.

Several primary prevention programs have been developed for use with middle and high school students (see Shisslak et al., 1996, for a review). These programs differ in length, format, and emphasis. Yet, the results of systematic evaluations, when they are available, are remarkably similar. The programs measurably affect knowledge but have little or no impact on attitudes and behaviors. Whether these programs actually *prevent* eating problems is unclear since follow-ups of more than a year are rare (and the follow-up period is typically shorter than one year). In other words, we do not know whether children, especially girls, who go through these curricula ultimately develop eating problems at the same rate as those who do not. Nonetheless, these programs have frequently been interpreted as relative 'failures.'

The 'failure' of the adolescent programs, coupled with disturbing data concerning eating attitudes and behaviors among elementary school children, led to calls for the development of prevention programs for younger children. Data linking elementary school behaviors and attitudes to adolescent eating problems are severely limited. Nevertheless, there are theoretical models suggesting what the relationships might be. Using these models as well as the available data, we developed 'Eating Smart, Eating for Me', a primary prevention program for use with fourth and fifth graders. An experimental evaluation, however, yielded results similar to those for the adolescent programs. Knowledge, but not attitudes and behaviors, was partly changed by the curriculum.

One interpretation of the extant studies is that primary prevention does not work very well, if at all. Either we do not have enough information about risk and protective factors to design effective programs or the factors which shape eating disorders are not amenable to intervention. We believe that it is certainly premature to argue the latter and possibly the former. We do not yet know whether 'Eating Smart, Eating for Me' prevented eating disorders. To ascertain that, we are planning to re-evaluate the children, especially the girls, in middle or high school. This need for longitudinal data is underscored by the low rate of dieting among the children in this sample. Even if we include children who said they 'ate less' to lose weight, only 19 of the original 299 children reported any form of dieting. The crucial question then is not whether our curriculum changed those children's behavior. From a statistical perspective, that was virtually impossible. The question is whether girls start to diet in adolescence.

We must be cautious, however, not to be overly optimistic about prevention possibilites. The data, indeed, suggest that our current curricular programs are not very effective. New programs need to consider factors not included in many of the current programs such as gender role issues, life skills to resist peer pressure, and, perhaps, coordinating curricular interventions with system-wide changes in the schools' culture and with community and mass media efforts. Thus, eating disorders prevention programs need to be multidimensional (Neumark-Sztainer, 1996), as is true of the more successful drug prevention programs (Donaldson et al., 1996). Again, longitudinal evaluation of such programs will be crucial.

Equally importantly, research is needed which more clearly establishes what the risk factors and protective factors are for eating problems. Such data are crucial if we hope to design prevention programs. Research is also needed concerning what children know and do in regard to eating and weight management. In the present study, we were surprised by the low rate of dieting. While methodological differences (especially the phrasing of questions concerning dieting) may account for the relatively low rate of dieting in the present sample, it is also possible that samples of children will vary considerably in rates of body dissatisfaction, dieting, and so on. Understanding such differences will also be critical in the development of effective primary prevention programs.

REFERENCES

American Psychiatric Association (1994) *Diagnostic and statistical manual of mental disorders (4th edition)*, Washington, D.C.: Author.
American Psychological Association (1992) *Ethical principles in the conduct of research with human participants*. Washington, D.C.: Author.
Attie, I. and Brooks-Gunn, J. (1989) 'Development of eating problems in

adolescent girls: A longitudinal study'. *Developmental Psychology,* 25: 70–9.

Beumont, P. (1995) 'The clinical presentation of anorexia and bulimia nervosa'. In Brownell, K. and Fairburn, C. (eds) *Eating disorders and obesity: A comprehensive handbook* (pp. 151–8), New York: Guildford

Carney, B. (1986) 'A preventive curriculum for anorexia nervosa and bulimia'. *Canadian Association for Health, Physical Education and Recreation Journal,* 52: 10–14.

Cattarin, J. and Thompson, J.K. (1994) 'A three-year longitudinal study of body image, eating disturbance, and general psychological functioning in adolescent females'. *Eating Disorders: The Journal of Treatment and Prevention,* 2: 114–25.

Childress, A., Brewerton, T., Hodges, E. and Jarrell, M, (1993) 'The Kids Eating Disorders Survey (KEDS): A study of middle school students'. *Journal of the American Academy of Child and Adolescent Psychiatry,* 32: 843–50.

Cohen, R., Klesges, R., Summerville, M. and Meyers, A. (1989) 'A developmental analysis of the influence of body weight on the sociometry of children'. *Addictive Behaviors,* 14: 463–76.

Crisp, A. (1988) 'Some possible approaches to prevention of eating and body weight/shape disorders, with particular reference to anorexia nervosa'. *International Journal of Eating Disorders,* 7: 1–17.

de Castro, J. and Goldstein, S. (1995) 'Eating attitudes and behaviors of pre- and postpubertal females: Clues to the etiology of eating disorders'. *Physiology and Behavior,* 58:, 15–23

Domel, S., Baranowski, T., Davis, H., Leonard, S., Riley, P. and Baranowski, J. (1994) 'Fruit and vegetable food frequencies by fourth and fifth grade students: Validity and reliability'. *Journal of the American College of Nutrition,* 13: 33–9.

Donaldson, S., Sussman, S., MacKinnon, D., Severso, H., Glynn, T., Murrary, D. and Stone, E. (1996) 'Drug abuse prevention programming: Do we know what content works?' *American Behavioral Scientist,* 39: 868–83.

Faith, M. and Allison, D. (1996) 'Assessment of psychological status among obese persons'. In Thompson, J.K. (ed) *Body image, eating disorders, and obesity: An integrative guide for assessment and treatment* (pp. 365–88), Washington, D.C.: American Psychological Association.

Gralen, S., Levine, M.P., Smolak, L. and Murnen, S. (1990) 'Dieting and disordered eating during early and middle adolescence: Do the influences remain the same?' *International Journal of Eating Disorders,* 9: 501–12.

Gustafson-Larson, A. and Terry, R. (1992) 'Weight-related behaviors and concerns of fourth-grade children'. *Journal of the American Dietetic Association,* 92: 818–22.

Heatherton, T. and Polivy, J. (1992) 'Chronic dieting and eating disorders: A spiral model'. In Crowther, J., Tennenbaum, D., Hobfoll, S. and Stephens, M. (eds) *The etiology of bulimia nervosa: The individual and familial context* (pp. 133–56). Washington, D.C.: Hemisphere.

Heinberg, L. (1996) 'Theories of body image disturbance: Perceptual, developmental, and sociocultural factors'. In Thompson, J.K. (ed) *Body image, eating disorders, and obesity: An integrative guide for assessment and treatment* (pp. 27–48), Washington, D.C.: American Psychological Association.

Hill, A., Draper, E. and Stack, J. (1994) 'A weight on children's minds: Body shape dissatisfactions at 9-years-old'. *International Journal of Obesity,* 18: 383–9.

Hill, A. and Robinson, A. (1991) 'Dieting concerns have a functional effect on the behaviour of nine-year-old girls'. *British Journal of Clinical Psychology,* 30: 265–7.

Killen, J. (1996) Development and evaluation of a school-based eating disorder symptoms prevention program. In Smolak, L., Levine, M. and Striegel-Moore, R (eds) *The developmental psychopathology of eating disorders: Implications for research, prevention, and treatment* (pp. 313–40), Mahwah, NJ: Erlbaum.

Killen, J., Taylor, C., Hayward, C., Wilson, D., Hammer, L., Robinson, T., Litt, I., Simmonds, B., Haydel, F., Varady, A. and Kraemer, H. (1994) 'The pursuit of thinness and the onset of eating disorder symptoms in a community sample of adolescent girls: A three year prospective analysis'. *International Journal of Eating Disorders,* 16: 227–38.

Koff, E. and Rierdon, J. (1991) 'Perceptions of weight and attitudes toward eating in early adolescent girls'. *Journal of Adolescent Health,* 14: 433–9.

Kraemer, H., Kazdin, A., Offord, D., Kessler, R., Jensen, P. and Kupfer, D. (1997) 'Coming to terms with the terms of risk'. *Archives of General Psychiatry*, in press.

Lerner, R. and Javanovic, J. (1990) 'The role of body image in psychosocial development across the life span: A developmental contextual perspective'. In Cash, T. and Pruzinsky, T. (eds) *Body images: Development, deviance, and change* (pp. 110–27), New York: Guilford.

Levine, M.P. (1987) *Student eating disorders: Anorexia nervosa and bulimia*, Washington, D.C.: National Education Association.

Levine, M.P. and Hill L. (1991) *A 5-day lesson plan book on eating disorders*, Tulsa, OK: National Eating Disorder Assocation.

Levine, M.P., Schermer, F., Smolak, L. and Etling, C. (1995) *Eating smart, eating for me: Nutrition education program for the 4th and 5th grades*, Gambier, OH: Kenyon College and the Nutrition Education Training Program of the Ohio Department of Education.

Levine, M.P. and Smolak, L. (1992) 'Toward a model of the developmental psychopathology of eating disorders: The example of early adolescence'. In Crowther, J., Tennenbaum, D., Hobfoll, S. and Stephens, M. (eds) *The etiology of bulimia nervosa: The individual and familial context* (pp. 59–80), Washington, D.C.: Hemisphere.

Levine, M.P., Smolak, L. and Hayden, H. (1994) 'The relation of sociocultural factors to eating attitudes and behaviors among middle school girls'. *Journal of Early Adolescence*, 14: 471–90.

Maloney, M., McGuire, J., Daniels, S. and Specker, B. (1989) 'Dieting behavior and eating attitudes in children'. *Pediatrics*, 84: 482–9.

Mellin, L., Irwin, C. and Scully, S. (1992) 'Disordered eating characteristics in girls: A survey of middle class children'. *Journal of the American Dietetic Association*, 92: 851–3.

Mendelson, B. and White, D. (1985) 'Development of self-body-esteem in overweight youngsters'. *Developmental Psychology*, 21: 90–6.

——(1993) *Manual for the Body-Esteem Scale-Children*. Montreal, Canada: Center for Research in Human Development, Concordia University.

Murnen, S. and Smolak, L. (1997) 'Femininity, masculinity, and disordered eating: A meta-analytic review'. *International Journal of Eating Disorders*, 22, 231–242.

Neumark-Sztainer, D. (1996) 'School-based programs for preventing eating disturbances'. *Journal of School Health*, 66: 64–71.

Nichter, M. and Vukovic, N. (1994) 'Fat talk: Body image among adolescent girls'. In Sault, N. (ed) *Many mirrors: body image and social relations* (pp. 109–31), New Bruswick, NJ: Rutgers University Press.

O'Connor, T. and Rutter, M. (1996) 'Risk mechanisms in development: Some conceptual and methodological considerations'. *Developmental Psychology*, 32: 787–95.

Pike, K., Loeb, K. and Vitousek, K. (1996) 'Cognitive-behavioral therapy for anorexia nervosa and bulimia nervosa'. In Thompson, J.K. (ed) *Body image, eating disorders, and obesity: An integrative guide for assessment and treatment* (pp. 253–302), Washington, D.C.: American Psychological Association.

Pike, K. and Rodin, J. (1991) 'Mothers, daughters, and disordered eating'. *Journal of Abnormal Psychology,* 100: 198–204.

Rende, R. (1996) 'Liability to psychopathology: A quantitative genetic perspective'. In Smolak, L., Levine, M.P. and Striegel-Moore, R. (eds) *The developmental psychopathology of eating disorders: Implications for research, prevention, and treatment* (pp. 59–76), Mahwah, NJ: Erlbaum.

Richards, M., Casper, R. and Larson, R. (1990) 'Weight and eating concerns among pre- and young adolescent boys and girls'. *Journal of Adolescent Health Care,* 11: 203–9.

Rodin, J., Silberstein, L. and Striegel-Moore, R. (1985) 'Women and weight: A normative discontent'. In Sonderegger, T. (ed) *Nebraska Symposium on Motivation: Vol. 32. Psychology and gender* (pp. 267–308), Lincoln: University of Nebraska.

Rosen, J. (1989) 'Prevention of eating disorders'. *Newsletter of the National Anorexic Aid Society,* 12, (April-June): 1–3.

——(1996) 'Body dysmorphic disorder: Assessment and treatment. In Thompson, J.K. (ed) *Body image, eating disorders, and obesity: An integrative guide for assessment and treatment* (pp. 149–70), Washington, D.C.: American Psychological Association.

Schinke, S., Botvin, G. and Orlandi, M. (1991) *Substance abuse in children and adolescents: Evaluation and interventions,* Newbury Park, CA: Sage.

Schreiber, G., Robins, M., Striegel-Moore, R., Obarzanek, E., Morrison, J. and Wright, D. (1996) 'Weight modification efforts reported by black and white preadolescent girls: National heart, lung, and blood institute growth and health study'. *Pediatrics,* 98: 63–70.

Shisslak, C. and Crago, M. (1994) 'Toward a new model for the prevention of eating disorders'. In Fallon, P., Katzman, M. and Wooley, S. (eds) *Feminist persepctives on eating disorders* (pp. 419–37), New York: Guilford.

Shisslak, C., Crago, M., Estes, L. and Gray, N. (1996) 'Content and method of developmentally appropriate prevention programs'. In Smolak, L., Levine, M. and Striegel-Moore, R. (eds) *The developmental psychopathology of eating disorders: Implications for research, prevention, and treatment* (pp. 341–64) Mahwah, NJ: Erlbaum.

Shisslak, C., Crago, M., McKnight, K., Estes, L., Gray, N. and Parnaby, O. (1998) 'Potential risk factors associated with weight control behaviors in elementary and middle school girls'. *Journal of Psychosomatic Research,* in press.

Silverstein, B. and Perlick, D. (1995) *The cost of competence: Why inequality causes depression, eating disorders, and illness in women*, New York: Oxford University Press.

Smolak, L. (1996) 'Methodological implications of a development psychopathology approach to the study of eating problems'. In Smolak, L., Levine, M. and Striegel-Moore, R. (eds) *The developmental psychopathology of eating disorders: Implications for research, prevention, and treatment* (pp. 31–56), Mahwah, NJ: Erlbaum.

Smolak, L. and Levine, M.P. (1994a) 'Critical issues in the developmental psychopathology of eating disorders'. In Alexander-Mott, L. and Lumsden, D. (eds) *Understanding eating disorders, Anorexia nervosa, bulimia nervosa, and obesity* (pp. 37–60), Washington, D.C.: Taylor and Francis.

——(1994b) 'Toward an empirical basis for primary prevention eating problems with elementary school children'. *Eating Disorders: The Journal of Treatment and Prevention*, 2: 293–307.

——(1996a) 'Adolescent transitions and the development of eating problems'. In Smolak, L., Levine, M.P. and Striegel-Moore, R. (eds) *The developmental psychopathology of eating disorders: Implications for research, prevention, and treatment* (pp. 207–34), Mahwah, NJ: Erlbaum.

——(1996b) *Body esteem and eating problems in young children: A longitudinal approach.* Paper presented at the International Society for the Study of Behavioral Development, Quebec City, Quebec, Canada.

——(1996c) *Childhood attitudes and behaviors as predictors of early adolescent eating attitudes, behaviors, and problems.* Paper presented at the Society for Research in Adolescence, Boston, Massachusetts.

Smolak, L., Levine, M.P., and Schermer, F. (1998). A controlled evaluation of an elementary school primary prevention program for eating problems, *Journal of Psychosomatic Research*, in press.

Smolak, L., Levine, M.P. and Striegel-Moore, R. (Eds.)(1996) *The developmental psychopathology of eating disorders: Implications for research, prevention, and treatment.* Mahwah, NJ: Erlbaum.

Staffieri, J.R. (1967) 'A study of social stereotype of body-image in children. *Journal of Personality and Social Psychology,* 7: 101–4.

Stice, E. (1994) 'Review of the evidence for a sociocultural model of bulimia nervosa and an exploration of the mechanisms of action'. *Clinical Psychology Review,* 14: 1–29.

Stice, E., Nemeroff, C. and Shaw, H. (1996) 'A test of the dual pathway model of bulimia nervosa: Evidence for dietary restraint and affect regulation mechanisms'. *Journal of Social and Clinical Psychology,* 15: 340–63.

Striegel-Moore, R. (1993) 'Etiology of binge eating: A developmental perspective'. In Fairburn, C. and Wilson, G. (eds) *Binge eating: Nature, assessment, and treatment* (pp. 144–72), New York: Guilford.

Striegel-Moore, R., Schreiber, G., Pike, K., Wilfley, D. and Rodin, J. (1995) 'Drive for thinness in black and white preadolescent girls'. *International Journal of Eating Disorders,* 18: 59–69.

Striegel-Moore, R. and Smolak, L. (1996) 'The role of race in the development of eating disorders'. In Smolak, L., Levine, M. and Striegel-Moore, R. (eds) *The developmental psychopathology of eating disorders: Implications for research, prevention, and treatment* (pp. 259–84), Mahwah, NJ: Erlbaum.

Strober, M. and Humphrey, L. (1987) 'Familial contributions to the etiology and course of anorexia nervosa'. *Journal of Consulting and Clinical Psychology,* 55: 654–9.

Swisher, J. (1993) 'Early adolescent belief systems and substance abuse'. In Lerner, R. (ed) *Early adolescence: Perspectives on research, policy, and intervention* (pp. 369–82). Hillsdale, NJ: Lawrence Erlbaum Associates.

Thelen, M., Powell, A., Lawrence, C. and Kuhnert, M. (1992) 'Eating and body image concerns among children'. *Journal of Clinical Child Psychology,* 21: 41–6.

Thompson, J.K. (1996) 'Introduction: Body image, eating disorders, and obesity-An emerging synthesis'. In Thompson, J.K. (ed) *Body image, eating disorders, and obesity: An integrative guide for assessment and treatment* (pp. 1–20). Washington, D.C.: American Psychological Association.

Thompson, J.K., Heinberg, L. and Clarke, A. (1996) 'Treatment of body image disturbance in eating disorders'. In Thompson, J.K. (ed) *Body image, eating disorders, and obesity: An integrative guide for assessment and treatment* (pp. 303–20), Washington, D.C.: American Psychological Association.

Tobin, D., Johnson, C., Steinberg, S., Staats, M. and Dennis, A. (1991) 'Multifactorial assessment of bulimia nervosa'. *Journal of Abnormal Psychology,* 100: 14–21.

Vandereycken, W. and Meermann, R. (1984) 'Anorexia nervosa: Is prevention possible?' *International Journal of Psychiatry in Medicine,* 14: 191–205.

Vitousek, K. and Hollon, S. (1990) 'The investigation of schema content and processing of eating disorders'. *Cognitive Therapy and Research,* 14: 191–214.

Wardle, J., Volz, C. and Golding, C. (1995) 'Social variation in attitudes to obesity in children'. *International Journal of Obesity,* 19: 562–9.

Wood, K., Becker, J. and Thompson, J.K. (1996) 'Body image dissatisfaction in preadolescent children'. *Journal of Applied Developmental Psychology,* 17: 85–100.

Yucker, H. and Allison, D. (1994) 'Obesity: Sociocultural perspectives'. In Alexander-Mott, L. and Lumsden, D. (eds) *Understanding eating disorders: Anorexia nervosa, bulimia nervosa, and obesity* (pp. 243–70), Washington, D.C.: Taylor and Francis.

CHAPTER SEVEN

A participatory approach to the prevention of eating disorders in a school

Niva Piran

INTRODUCTION

The chapter aims to describe a participatory approach to the prevention of body weight and shape preoccupation in schools. The participatory approach differs from traditional approaches to body weight and shape preoccupation, primarily in that it relies on dialogue with participants to determine the course of intervention, rather than on a predetermined professionally derived curriculum. While participatory approaches have been the method of choice for some researchers and community activists for a few decades (Reason, 1994), there is a growing trend to incorporate these principles into the mainstream of health promotion. For example, the World Health Organization has been engaged for the past few years in a world-wide 'healthy school' project which relies on dialogue with administration, teachers, parents and students to determine the course of interventions in schools (Beaudier, Fortin and Annaheim, 1995). Similarly, researchers involved in the prevention of substance abuse with youth are beginning to shift intervention strategies towards a participatory model (Green, 1995). My experience with the implementation of a participatory program in a dance school over the past decade has been successful in markedly reducing body weight and shape preoccupation and clinical eating disorders in the school (Piran, 1992). A participatory approach should therefore comprise a possible strategy for professionals planning interventions for the prevention of body weight and shape preoccupation in a school.

In this chapter I will discuss key elements of the participatory approach to inquiry and change. I will describe the professional path that has led me to choose this approach in the prevention of eating disorders in a school. I will illustrate the approach with a description of a participatory program which was implemented in a high risk setting, a competitive residential ballet school. Finally, the pros and cons of this approach to the prevention of eating disorders in a school will be briefly discussed.

PARTICIPATORY APPROACHES TO INQUIRY AND CHANGE

Participatory approaches to research and intervention may vary in underlying ideology or process of application. These approaches have evolved through a long tradition of liberationist movements and were originally centered on work in less developed areas of the world (Reason, 1994). They were then adopted by researchers and activists to address varied systems of oppression, such as those related to gender, race or poverty within Western cultures (Reason, 1994).

One important dimension of a participatory approach to community intervention involves the production and ownership of knowledge (Park, 1993). A participatory approach places primary importance on a collective process of knowledge construction by participants. The knowledge is constructed by participants through dialogue, self-inquiry and reflection and is based on their life experiences. Further, the participatory approach honors the different ways participants derive and express their knowledge, for example: discussions in community meetings, storytelling or artistic creations. In the process of knowledge construction, the researcher and activist, who may have initiated the process of inquiry, has primarily a facilitative role. The questions asked, the knowledge derived, and the actions taken are decided by participants and for participants.

The link between knowledge production and power has been addressed by writers from different outlooks including participatory, critical and feminist (Gaventa, 1993; Maguire, 1993). Engaging oppressed groups in the reflexive exploration of diverse life experiences empowers people, gives them a voice and authority, and develops community solidarity and action. Such an exploration also reveals societal systems of oppression and privilege (Roman, 1992). Knowledge derived through participatory processes can be subversive, because it is contrary to the monopoly of 'expert' knowledge held by specialists. It prioritizes experience over expertise (Gaventa, 1993).

The path from knowledge generation to knowledge utilization is direct in participatory research, since the constructed knowledge is the product of inquiry by the people whose vested interest is to transform the oppressive societal mechanisms which they identify (Reason, 1994). In addition, the participatory process involves community collaboration and solidarity which works to empower the participants towards collective action.

Another component of participatory work involves a commitment to the process of dialogue and collaboration and to the community (Reason, 1994). The dialogue is typified by equitable relationships where people's diverse wisdom is similarly valued. Maguire (1993) describes the time and nurturance required to develop meaningful relationships between facilitator and participants and among participants. She also describes the process of personal transformation which occurs internally when one does not presume to transform social structures 'out there', but rather aims to transform herself and her relationships with others.

ON BECOMING A FACILITATOR OF A PARTICIPATORY INTERVENTION

This section is written in appreciation of the varied ways in which people choose to work and the paths which lead to these choices. I include aspects of my journey into the participatory approach of intervention to describe one pathway into this method of work and describe components of the work that I have considered particularly important. Other professionals may find other pathways to the same approach, or may find that other methods of community interventions are a better fit for them.

The most influential component in choosing a participatory approach was my practice of feminist counseling. The participatory approach for health promotion seemed to be a natural extension of the feminist paradigm to counseling. Similar to feminist counseling where expertise and authority is seen to be located with the client, lived experience is seen as the key to critical understanding and the generation of contextualized solutions in participatory approaches to health promotion. This stance of exploring lived experience rather than transmitting information or conveying a particular theory of understanding has enriched participants' and my own understanding, and revealed a gap between adolescent girls' experiences and the content of didactic programs for the prevention of body weight and shape preoccupation (Piran, 1995; Piran, 1996b). Both feminist counseling and participatory approaches critically examine the many varied contextual factors which adversely affect the living conditions of participants and then target aspects of the social or political environment for direct intervention. In addition, many feminist counselors see their own involvement in social activism as extension of their practice of counseling. Similar to feminist counseling, relationships between the group facilitator and participants of a community participatory approach, involve long term commitments and personal transformations of all involved. In respecting lived experience, empowering participants, honoring relationships and diversity, minimizing power differential between counselor/ facilitator and client/participants, both approaches aim to counter oppressive societal prejudices and structures. There are therefore many parallels between a feminist counseling paradigm and a participatory paradigm to health promotion.

The consideration of issues of power is central to feminist counseling. Providing students with an experience of *empowerment* was a central goal of the participatory program at the school. The prevention program strived to provide students with experiences of power, voice, authority and safety, in order to counteract experiences of powerlessness, silencing or violation often associated for women with their bodies. One way to achieve the empowerment of students was to encourage them to identify, explore and devise strategies to change aspects of the school environment which adversely affected their experiences of their bodies. Students' action plans often involved challenging teaching and administrative staff as well as peers. Knowledge anchored in the body was therefore used to guide school wide changes. In these cycles of reflection and action, the body became a source of knowledge and power, rather than a place of vulnerability and individual struggle. The students discovered that conditions which facilitated a healthy and positive connection with their bodies related to an equitable school environment where their bodies and voices were respected and their connections nurtured. While students guided the ongoing school wide systemic interventions, some interventions with school staff were carried out prior to meeting with students in order to increase the likelihood that students' changed behaviors and reactions would be met with understanding, support and success. This work is described in the next section.

A PARTICIPATORY PROGRAM FOR THE PREVENTION OF BODY WEIGHT AND SHAPE PREOCCUPATION IN A DANCE SCHOOL

WORKING WITH STAFF

For the three years preceding the implementation of the participatory program at the school, I had the opportunity to establish strong rapport with its administration through repeated consultations with students from the school. In addition, providing counseling to students from the school, familiarized me with the school culture. Related to the general goal of transforming the school environment, I have set regular meeting times with school administration, as well as attended regular consultants' meetings where important decisions were made regarding staff and students' norms of behavior at the school. It was an opportunity to discuss staff's responsibility to students' well-being including their body and self-image and to examine disruptions to these experiences. Meetings with school administration and staff have allowed clear guidelines to be set for students to follow if problems occurred. These issues and guidelines were evaluated on an ongoing basis. In addition, specific training sessions for different staff groups, such as house parents, were set. In these training sessions, staff's responsibility to students' experiences of themselves and their bodies was highlighted. Larger cultural values and norms which could adversely affect the experiences of adolescent women and men were detailed and the role of staff members in protecting students from adverse pressures and experiences was stressed. For example, when weightist prejudices were explored with staff, it was not uncommon to find that teachers associated thinness with intelligence, motivation, or will power. Teachers then had to recognize the way they have been affected by the culture at large, and by their own training, in their perception of weight, and how these prejudices may have affected their behaviors and attitudes towards the students.

The objectification of women's bodies by the culture was discussed and staff suggested ways in which stamina and move-ment, rather than appearance, should be focused on in classes. They realized they needed to avoid comments which could be interpreted by students as related to body shape or that could be experienced as an evaluative commentary of a students' shape or attractiveness. Staff were informed about the incidence of viola-tions of children's and women's bodies and the adverse conse-quences of such intrusions. Staff had a special role in scrutinizing their own actions to avoid engaging in behaviors which could violate a student's sense of ownership of her or his body as well as staying open to communication by students that they may need support or counseling in response to having been exposed to such experiences. Since students at the school are between 10 and 18 years of age, the importance of not hindering with psychological or physical growth during this important time of change and connection with the body was highlighted. Clinical manifestations of eating disorders as well as the associated medical, psychological and social complications were described to the staff. An open line of communication between myself, other consultants and staff was established.

Ongoing contact with staff has continued throughout. As stu-dents chose to challenge staff around experiences at the school which they have identified as adversely affecting their body image, the school took steps to responsibly respond to these challenges in a way that respected students' experiences and voices. For example, when students described the damaging effects of gender and sexual harassment, the school responded by supporting the incorporation of new rules regarding harassment into the school code of ethics. Staff who were found to engage in harassing behaviors were monitored and, at times, replaced. On other occasions, students brought forwards experiences which compro-mised their sense of physical safety, for example, injuries incurred during *pas-de-deux* classes. The school responded by revising its training curriculum to assure further safety for students. When, especially female, students talked about a greater need for privacy in residence, the school provided locked spaces in residence and gave further instructions to residence staff to respect students' privacy. At times some students felt that the school favored students who were skinny by selecting these students to school shows. In those instances, the administration seriously examined its own biases and made changes accordingly. The school has removed all weight scales from its premises, besides one in the physiotherapist's office, and has implemented a body conditioning program focusing on fitness and muscle strength rather than thinness. In a similar vein, a nutrition education program focusing on physical fitness has been incorporated into the school curriculum. When female students questioned whether male students' bodies may be taken more seriously than that of females, in that condom machines were installed in all boys washrooms while female students found it hard to get supplies of sanitary napkins when they needed to, the school responded by installing relevant supplies in girls washrooms. When the students felt physical demands were too harsh, or at times damaging, the school adjusted its curriculum.

These are a few examples of a broader process whereby students' reflections and feedback to the school have been used on an ongoing basis to create school wide changes in the curriculum, training, staff education, staff replacement, and in the living conditions in its residence setting. In that process students found that their reflections and understanding of the conditions which affected their sense of well being of their body, led to the creation of a safer and more equitable setting, where their voices and authority held power.

STUDENTS' GROUPS

All students at the school participated in small (6–15 members) gender-cohesive groups 2 to 6 times annually throughout their stay at the school. Group meetings lasted between 1–2 hours and were facilitated by myself, an outside consultant to the school. Groups typically started with an inquiry about what was affecting students' experiences of their body at the school and what may affect them to want to alter their body shape and weight. Students tended to bring forth issues or situations that were acutely affecting them around the time that the groups were conducted. These could relate to peer issues, such as: a girl being ranked as '10 on the slut list' or being stalked by a boy, a girl being evaluated on her thinness or her hygiene (related to being a member of a visible minority) by another girl, or a boy being teased by other boys about 'being a sissy'. At other times the students brought forth issues related to staff, such as: a teacher who seemed to disregard the rate of physcial injuries in her class, a male teacher who consistently demeaned women, or a staff person who was leering at female students. Students also mentioned situations at home which challenged their experiences of their bodies, such as a girl describing the disturbing impact of her father's derogatory comments towards her mother's body or a girl describing her mother's advice to her to be extra thin in order to combat the prejudices she will inevitably face due to being a member of a visible minority. Other times, students addressed norms at the school which represented prejudicial treatment of males and females, such as giving boys' greater physical freedom (for example to visit other rooms in residence or to leave the premises of the school after school hours) and psychological freedom (for example to be loud, messy and rude). A thematic qualitative analysis of the many experiences and conditions which were brought forward for the past ten years by female students in these focus groups was conducted recently (Piran, 1996b). It seemed that disruptive conditions fell into three major categories: violations of the body territory and of the sense of ownership of the body, prejudicial treatment of female students and their bodies, and the constricting idealized social image of women and their bodies (Piran, 1996b).

Another important focus of discussion invovled the impact of the varied adverse conditions as discussed above on students' experiences of their bodies. Especially during the first two years of the implementation of the program, female students often described experiences of alienation and dissociation from the body, causing some of them to treat their bodies as objects that have betrayed them and therefore had to be externally managed or controlled, at times through starvation and disordered eating. However, over time the experiences of alienation from the body became quite uncommon. Instead, students seemed to take greater ownership of their bodies and to be more aware of their feelings and reactions to different experiences at the school. Reactions of shame, fear, vulnerability or helplessness were common to situations where female students' bodily boundaries were violated or they were exposed to a demeaning or prejudicial treatment as outlined above. Students who were exposed to harsh or critical treatment of their bodies by staff, peers, or family members, often internalized and expressed these experiences through self-deprecation and hatred of their bodies, or tended to neglect or harm their bodies, for example: through deprivation of nourishment or rest. Another impact of harsh or prejudicial treatment was the increased sense of depression and disconnection from peers.

Voicing and narrating adverse experiences by members of a group usually had a strong impact on the group as a whole. Experiences and conditions related to the body seemed to go unspoken or be silenced until the group meeting. Validating and amplifying these stories by other group members served to universalize the difficulties. Often, strong feelings and many related experiences and themes surfaced in the group which enriched the understanding of the nature of the events which were initially described. This process of developing the themes and reflecting about them often led to discoveries and to action plans. Discoveries were often about the high prevalence of disruptive experiences and their social or political nature. For example, a female student's hesitant disclosure about a staff member's disrespect of her privacy was responded by descriptions of similar incidents of other students with the same staff member or with other adults.

Another student's description of being blamed by her male *pas-de-deux* partner for their failed exercise (due to her weight), was found to be common to almost all students of one group. The discovery of shared disruptive experiences among peers led to reflective efforts on the part of students to understand the systemic nature of these events. The process of transforming descriptions of sporadic personal complaints to a shared political understanding of the same events has been an important process in the focus groups. For example, the staff member's disrespect of students' privacy became understood as signifying the abuse of power of an adult in a position of authority. The blaming of female students weight for failed *pas-de-deux* exercises was seen as an expression of the prejudicial treatment of women and their bodies, and of inequitable gender relations. As demonstrated through the examples above, issues of gender relations, social power, human rights, societal prejudices and roles were frequently discussed.

Interestingly, a shared observation students made was about ways in which they had been co-opted into oppressive and prejudicial systems, a process which created a rift among them.

For example, a girl who made a nasty comment about another girl's 'large boobs' realized that she was treating her friend in the same deprecating way her friend was approached by the male students at the school and feminine body parts were reacted to in the culture at large. She also found out that she feared that her own developing body would be devalued. Her teasing was therefore related to her own fears. In another group discussion, female students realized that they were evaluating each other's thinness in a way that corrupted their relationship, since evaluation involved differential power, a state which disrupts relationships. In yet another group, female students realized that they were so affected by their competition that they lost any sense of connection among themselves, a state which was wearing them down and was destructive to their welfare. Almost with no exception during a decade of work in the groups, students tended to first focus on repairing their own relationships before attempting to address the systems around them. This seemed to provide them with a supportive system of connection, a safe base from which to operate outside. Moreover, they often explicitly set new norms of relating within the groups, norms which contrasted those adhered to outside of the group. Their rules included, for example, not evaluating each other's appearance, being sincere in relationships with one another, not collude with external harsh treatment, or prioritize relationships over competition. These new group norms, which they spontaneously generated, were the norms they strived to follow in relationships with other people outside of the group.

Typically after working on repairing their own relationships, they progressed in a unified way to discuss ways in which they could address their environment. A relevant factor which they often discussed in generating an action plan was their safety: Would following the plan expose them to being emotionally or physically hurt or to risking their status at the school? Their solutions were creative, well rooted in the reality of their lives as they experienced it and far richer than a predesigned program could envision. Addressing school administration with requests for changes in training, curriculum, staffing, etc., was one method of creating change. They would address the school as a unified group in a planned way, assuring that no member would be singled out as the 'bearer' of the request. As a general rule, they found the school directors open to their concerns and requests, and their suggestions would initiate a process of change at the school. At times, based on their assessment of their need for safety or confidentiality, they asked me to intervene on their behalf. This was the case, for example, when they feared that a staff member would retaliate against their group as a whole if they were identified as requesting a change.

Addressing peers outside of the group was another way of changing the school environment. For example, related to male and female partnerships in *pas-de-deux* exercises, female students not only requested changes in training from the school which would enhance their safety and their respectful treatment by their partners, but they also informed their partners, together, outside the class that they demanded from them a stance of shared responsibility, a non-blaming style of communication, and no references to body weight or shape. The male students had an opportunity to discuss their reactions and worries in their focus groups. For example, they discussed that female partners' strength rather than weight affected *pas-de-deux* exercises and confessed their own fears about the strength of their upper bodies. They scrutinized their tendency to blame their partners for failed exercises. These exchanges about *pas-de-deux* exercises occurred simultaneously at different grade levels and powerfully created a new way of partnership in these exercises throughout the school. This is but one of many examples of changes created among peers.

To summarize students' activities, through addressing peers and adults, the students worked towards creating an environment which enhanced their experience of well-being in their bodies and in their social and personal selves. They addressed peer norms of relating, gender and racial equity, and teachers' and house parents' responsible and respectful treatment of themselves and their bodies. They also arrested instances of abuse of power expressed at times at the body domain. In the process of investigating and changing experiences anchored in their bodies, they acquired an understanding of their needs as individuals in different social systems, and they reclaimed their power.

OUTCOME EVALUATION

During the Fall of 1996, the third all-school survey of eating attitudes and behaviors will be conducted. Two previous surveys were conducted in 1987 and in 1991, during the first and fourth years of implementing the program. During the three years preceding the implementation of the program, the incidence of new cases of anorexia or bulimia nervosa was about 1.67 per year for about 100 girls aged 12–18. For the past 8 years, there has been just one case of anorexia and one of bulimia. Students who became preoccupied with shape, weight or food issues either referred themselves or were referred by staff for consultation and/ or counseling (Piran, 1996a). Surveys revealed significant reductions on body dissatisfaction and drive for thinness as well as reductions in dieting and purging behaviors. For example, the percentage of graduating students scoring above the 20-point cut-off on the Eating Attitudes Test, decreased from 47.8 per cent in 1987 to 16.7 per cent in 1991 (p<.05) and those reporting bingeing decreased form 34.8 per cent to 13.3 per cent. The school is a unique setting and no similar school could be used as a comparison group for the program. Lacking a comparison group, the changes cannot be necessarily attributed to the program. However, the changes are consistent with the goals of the prevention program.

An analysis of themes discussed in focus groups indicating qualitative changes in students' experiences of their bodies and themselves over the ten years of the operation of the program is being currently conducted by myself. Several categories indicating shifts in students experience of their body have emerged so far: from the experience of alienation from the body to that of living in the body, from an experience of the body as a site of vulenrability to the body as a site of knowledge, from a pervasive sense of fear to a demand for conditions of safety, from the body as a site of internal struggle to the body as a site of political struggle, from a compartmentalized experience of the body to a felt connection between body and voice, from a sense of external ownership to that of internal ownership. This list of themes may change as the analysis progresses. However partial, the reader may use the examples provided throughout the chapter to 'ground' the list of themes just outlined.

CONCLUSION

A participatory action approach to the prevention of body weight and shape preoccupation is proposed as one possible paradigm of intervention in schools. This method of work gives students and staff the opportunity to dialogue and work together on transforming adverse systemic conditions which affect students' experiences of themselves and their bodies. Students' voices, power, and authority are honored, their solutions respected. Oppressive, inequitable and prejudicial conditions are discussed openly and relationships deepen, making it less likely that body shape and weight preoccupation become the only venue to express and cope with adverse societal conditions. This approach, however, requires a considerable investment of time and a long-term emotional and time committment on the part of the facilitator. Strong empathic ties have to be formed between facilitator and both students and staff. Staff who hold positions of power in the system have to, at least over time, become interested and supportive of the ideas and changes generated by the program.

REFERENCES

Beaudier, F., Fortin, J. and Annaheim, J. (1995) *Promoting healthy schools*. Paper presented at the Sixth International Congress on Adolescent Health, Vancouver.

Gaventa, J. (1993) 'The powerful, the powerless, and the experts: Knowledge struggles in an information age'. In Park, P., Brydon-Miller, M., Hall, B. and Jackson, T. (eds) *Voices of Change* (pp. 21–40), Toronto: OISE Press.

Green, L. (1995) *Evaluating health education*. Paper presented at the Sixth International Congress on Adolescent Health, Vancouver.

Maguire, P. (1993) 'Challenges, contradictions, and celebrations: Attempting participatory research as a doctoral student'. In Park, P., Brydon-Miller, M., Hall, B. and Jackson, T. (eds) *Voices of Change* (pp. 157–76), Toronto: OISE Press.

Park, P. (1993) 'What is participatory research? A theoretical and methodological perspective'. In Park, P., Brydon-Miller, M., Hall, V. and Jackson, T. (eds) *Voices of Change* (pp. 1–20), Toronto: OISE Press.

Piran, N. (1992) *Can a subculture change? An evaluation of a prevention program for eating disorders in a high risk setting*. Paper presented at the Fifth International Conference on Eating Disorders, New York.

——(1995) 'Prevention: Can early lessons lead to a delineation of an alternative model? A critical look at prevention with school children'. *Eating Disorders: The Journal of Treatment and Prevention*, 3: 28–36.

——(1996a) 'On prevention and transformation'. *The Renfrew Perspective*, 2(1): 8–9.

——(1996b) *The reduction of preoccupation with body weight and shape in schools: A feminist approach, Eating Disorders: The Journal of Treatment and Prevention, 4* (4), 323–333.

Reason, P. (1994) 'Three approaches to participative inquiry'. In Denzin, N.K. and Lincoln, Y.S. (eds) *Handbook of Qualitative Research* (pp. 324–39), London: Sage Publications.

Roman, L.G. (1992) 'The political significance of other ways of narrating ethnography: A feminist materialist approach'. In Lecompte, M.D., Millroy, W.L. and Preissle, J. (eds) *The Handbook of Qualitative Research in Education* (pp. 55–594), New York: Academic Press.

CHAPTER EIGHT

The principles of screening for eating disorders

Casper Schoemaker

INTRODUCTION

The screening of eating disorders is a relatively new research area. An overview of the recent literature shows that the search for the correct methods is still going on. At this moment it is hard to get a clear picture of the efficacy of screening, as the relatively scarce amount of knowledge is spread across a wide variety of research reports. In this chapter I will therefore try to review the information on this subject in a clearly structured manner.

Like Vandereycken and Meermann (1984) and Noordenbos (1988) I will make use of the distinction between primary, secondary, and tertiary prevention. I will focus on secondary prevention, aimed at the early detection of an illness. The main goal of secondary prevention is to enhance the positive effects of treatment by means of earlier intervention. The difference between primary and secondary prevention is not always very clear. Some primary preventive interventions may have secondary preventive effects as well. The informative and educational approach, for instance, may facilitate case finding by teachers, parents and health care personnel. It may also motivate people with an eating disorder to seek help. In this chapter I will highlight two methods of secondary prevention: screening and case finding.

Screening is defined as the testing of 'apparently healthy volunteers from the general population for the purpose of separating them into groups with high and low probabilities for a given disorder' (Sackett and Holland, 1975, p. 357). In the case of screening, the initiative is not taken by the patient. The goal of screening is 'the early detection of those diseases whose treatment is either easier or more effective when undertaken at an earlier point in time' (p. 357). A familiar example of screening are the nation-wide screening programs for the early detection of breast cancer.

Case finding is defined as 'the testing of patients who have sought health care for disorders which may be unrelated to their chief complaint' (Sackett and Holland, 1975, p. 357). In this respect it is important that 'the encounter is initiated by the patient and the purpose is a comprehensive assessment of health. While the results of the manoeuvre may require long-term arrangements for clinical services, the excecution of case-finding does not carry an implied garantee that patients will benefit, only that they will receive the highest standard of care available at that time and place' (Sackett and Holland, 1975, p. 357).

In the present evaluation of the screening of eating disorders, the distinction between screening and case finding is crucial. As Cochrane and Holland (1975) have asserted: 'If a patient asks a medical practioner for help, the doctor does the best he can. If, however, the practioner initiates screening procedures he is in a very different situation. He should, in our view, have conclusive evidence that screening can alter the natural history of the disease in a significant proportion of those screened' (p. 3). In other words: the practitioner is not obliged to screen for eating disorders: if he does screen, then he should have very good reasons for doing so.

Although 'the central idea of early disease detection and treatment is essentially simple [. . .], the road to its successful achievement [. . .] is far from simple though sometimes it may appear deceptively easy' (Wilson and Jungner, 1968, p. 27). The success of a screening program depends on several factors including the incidence of the illness, the validity of the screening test, the expected effects of early intervention and the financial costs of the screening program. To complicate matters, these factors are not independent but interrelated (Williams, Hand and Tarnapolsky, 1982). In the following a framework for the consideration of these factors will be presented.

THE PRINCIPLES OF SCREENING

In 1968 a classical paper on screening for illnesses was published by the World Health Organization (WHO): 'Principles and Prac-

Table 1: Ten principles for the screening of diseases

Requirements for a suitable disease:
1. There is an agreed policy on whom to treat as patients.
2. The condition sought should be an important health problem.
3. The natural history of the disease, including latent to declared disease, should be adequately understood.
4. There should be a recognizable latent or very early symptomatic stage.

Requirements for a suitable screening procedure:
5. The organization of the screening program allows for an important part of the population to be screened.
6. There should be a suitable test or examination.
7. Screening leads to earlier treatment.

Requirements for a suitable treatment:
8. There should be an accepted treatment for patients with the recognized disease.
9. There should be an advantage to treating the disease earlier than at the stage it would present spontaneously.
10. Facilities for treatment should be available.

---

tice of Screening for Disease' written by Wilson and Jungner. In this WHO-paper several principles of screening – defined as 'points that might be regarded as guides to planning early detection of disease' – were formulated. A slightly revised and rearranged list of Wilson and Jungners principles can be found in Table 1 (for a detailed discussion of the revisions and rearrangements, see Schoemaker, 1995). It is important to keep in mind that these screening principles should not be taken as strict criteria or a simple check-list. They should be viewed within a more general framework to organize the information important to an evaluation of the effectiveness, efficiency and practicability of the screening of eating disorders.

To evaluate the *effectiveness* of a screening program the benefits are measured regardless of the costs associated with such procedure. The principles 2 and 8 are the first to be considered before the start of a screening program. The possible effectiveness of a screening program is determined by the importance of the health problem (principle 2). Whether maximum effectiveness can be reached depends on whether adequate treatment for this condition exists (principle 8). When the health problem is important and the treatment adequate, the other principles will then be considered. Principle 9 is taken next into account: There must be an advantage in treating the illness earlier than at the stage when it would present spontaneously. Given such an advantage, the question is then whether a screening procedure exists to enable the initiation of treatment at an earlier time (see principles 4, 5, 6, and 7). The other principles (1, 3, and 10) may be seen as prerequisites for an effective screening program.

In the evaluation of the *efficiency* of a screening program, the benefits will be weighed against the costs. In this cost-benefit analysis the morbidity, mortality, financial costs, and the quality of life are all taken into account (King, 1986). The screening program is efficient if the benefits at least balance the costs. The financial costs can be found in principle 6. With regard to the other costs, namely possibly inadvertent effects of screening, a single most important principle does not stand out. The potential costs will therefore be considered with the possible benefits for each of the principles. The overall evaluation of the efficiency of screening is a very complicated question (Newman, Shrout and Bland, 1990). First, the benefits and the costs are hardly comparable, as they are measured in quite different terms; it is, for example, difficult to express the quality of life in financial terms. Second, the benefits and costs are situated on different levels: on the level of the individual and the level of the society. For every screening program, a cost-benefit analysis is therefore very complicated.

In the following, each of the ten principles will be applied to the screening of eating disorders. For each principle we will first clarify the meaning of the principle and its role in the evaluation of the screening in general. Then the principle will be applied to the screening of eating disorders. At the end of each discussion, the findings will be summarized and discussed with special reference to their impact on the other principles. In order to avoid any misunderstanding, I would like to stress that I am personally convinced of the desirability of the prevention of eating disorders. The practicability, effectiveness and efficiency of screening will nevertheless be the topic of discussion. My main question is an empirical rather than an ethical one.

ARE EATING DISORDERS SUITABLE FOR SCREENING?

PRINCIPLE I: THERE IS AN AGREED POLICY ON WHOM TO TREAT AS PATIENTS.

At first sight this principle can be understood as 'there are diagnostic criteria for this illness'. This is correct in most but not all cases. Some illnesses have been given a rather broad diagnostic definition, and meeting the diagnostic criteria may not be a sufficient reason to start treatment. Other illnesses have been given a rather narrow definition, and clearly subclinical cases may nevertheless need treatment. To avoid confusion with regard to this principle, 'caseness' has been defined as 'whom to treat as patients'.

It is a generally accepted rule that anyone who meets the DSM-IV diagnostic criteria for anorexia or bulimia nervosa (American Psychiatric Association, 1994) should be treated as a patient. This does not imply that all people in the general population meeting the diagnostic criteria will be treated. In most cases, the diagnosis is simply not made (see principle 4 below) and these patients will therefore receive no treatment or only at a very late stage (Hoek, 1993). It is assumed that the majority of those meeting the criteria for eating disorders will never receive any treatment at all (Beglin and Fairburn, 1992; Fairburn and Beglin, 1990; Hoek, 1993; Patton and King, 1991). As a result of this state-of-affairs, a screening program for eating disorders may prove to be effective in at least two ways: earlier treatment of those who would have received treatment much later, and treatment of patients who would otherwise not have received treatment.

The diagnosis 'Eating Disorder Not Otherwise Specified' (EDNOS) occupies a special position in the DSM. EDNOS patients constitute an 'ill defined' (Fairburn and Beglin, 1990) heterogenous group of subclinical cases of anorexia and bulimia nervosa. For these EDNOS patients treatment is not self-evident and some of these subclinical cases are known to get better without treatment (Fairburn and Beglin, 1990; Vandereycken and Meermann, 1992). However, it remains unclear in how many of these EDNOS cases a 'spontaneous recovery' does occur (Patton and King, 1991; Shaw and Garfinkel, 1990).

In many psychiatric conditions, the diagnosis is hindered by the patients' attitudes (Williams and MacDonald, 1986). In psychiatry, anorectic and bulimic patients are known for their tendency to deny or minimize their condition (Vandereycken, 1993). In screening for eating disorders, this denial of illness should therefore be taken into account. The only way eating disorders can be reliably diagnosed is by means of a clinical, preferably structured, interview (Fairburn and Beglin, 1990; Rathner, 1992). Scores of self-report questionnaires are no reliable basis for the diagnosis (Fairburn and Beglin, 1990; Garfinkel, 1992; Vandereycken and Vanderlinden, 1983; Williams, Hand and Tarnapolsky, 1982).

In conclusion we can say that in case of anorexia and bulimia nervosa there exist clear criteria as to whom should be treated as patients. The physician is clearly dependent on the cooperation of the patient for making a diagnosis, although some eating-disordered patients may be unwilling to cooperate.

PRINCIPLE 2: THE CONDITION SOUGHT SHOULD BE AN IMPORTANT HEALTH PROBLEM.

This is the most complicated principle. A particular condition may constitute an important health problem for several reasons. For the sake of clarity, the effects of an illness on the individual and the society as a whole should be separated. For the individual, the morbidity and impact on the quality of life determine the importance of the health problem. For society as a whole, the importance of the health problem will be determined by the importance for the individual, the prevalence of the illness, and the costs of treatment. The importance of the health problem can be regarded as the upper limit to the potential benefits and effectiveness of screening.

Eating disorders may have serious consequences. The mortality in anorexia nervosa patients is very high compared to other psychiatric conditions (Herzog, Keller and Lavori, 1988; Herzog, Rathner and Vandereycken, 1992). Little is known about the mortality rate in bulimia nervosa, as long-term follow-up studies are scarce (Russell, 1992). Anorectic and bulimic patients clearly suffer from their eating disorder; their quality of life is seriously affected (Garfinkel and Garner, 1982). As eating disorders may show a chronic course over several years, with a high relapse rate, the conditions produce long-lasting serious suffering, including both somatic and psychosocial impairment (Garfinkel and Garner, 1982; Shisslak, Crago, Neal and Swain, 1987; Herzog, Rathner and Vandereycken, 1992). In summary, on the level of the individual patient, eating disorders appear to constitute an important health problem.

Whether eating disorders constitute a significant problem for the community as well mainly depends upon the frequency of occurrence. It still is difficult to get a clear picture of the incidence – defined as the number of new cases in the population in a specified period of time – of eating disorders in the general population. 'Because the incidence of eating disorders are low, studies on their incidence in the general population are lacking. It is impossible to screen a large population, for instance 100,000 people, for a year or longer. Therefore, the incidence rates have been based on cases presenting to health care' (Hoek, 1993, p. 62). According to several studies of registrated cases, the incidence of anorexia nervosa in the community is about 8 per 100,000 per year (Hoek, 1993). But these studies underestimate the true incidence in the community because not all cases are referred to health care services. The incidence of bulimia nervosa is higher and has been estimated at 11.4 per 100,000 per year (Hoek et al., 1995). This figure should be interpreted with caution, however: 'Because of the lack of data, the greater taboo around bulimia nervosa and its smaller perceptibility compared to anorexia nervosa, the true incidence rate of bulimia nervosa seems still as much a secret as the syndrome itself is for many patients' (Hoek, 1993, p. 64).

There have been a lot of studies on the prevalence of eating disorders (for review: see Fairburn and Beglin, 1990; Hoek, 1993; Rathner, 1992). The prevalence rate – defined as the actual number of cases in a defined community at a particular point in time – is probably a more reliable estimate of the frequency of eating disorders in the community than the incidence rate. Given the low frequency of eating disorders in the general community, most of these prevalence studies have been conducted in high-risk populations: young females between 15 and 25 years. Hoek (1993) reviewed nine two-stage surveys of the prevalence of anorexia and bulimia nervosa among young females and came to the following estimates: an average prevalence of anorexia nervosa of about 0.3 per cent and an average prevalence of bulimia of 1 per cent among young females. These prevalence rates may nevertheless be an underestimation of the true rate, as a result of denial and non-cooperation of the patients (Fairburn and Beglin, 1990; Hoek, 1993).

In sum, eating disorders appear to constitute an important health problems on the level of the individual. This is reflected by the serious suffering, decreased quality of life, chronicity and mortality. For the community as a whole, however, the incidence and prevalence of these disorders are rather low and, hence, the number of deaths per year is comparatively small. Compared to other illnesses on the level of the community, eating disorders do not constitute a particularly important health problem. This conclusion should not be interpreted as an impetus to abandon all prevention activities in the area of eating disorders. It does have consequenses for the benefits that the screening of eating disorders can be expected to produce. No matter how succesful screening may be on an individual level, the effects will always be modest on the level of the community. In order for the screening of eating disorders to be efficient, the costs should be kept as low as possible. Otherwise the costs will simply outweigh the benefits. Moreover, the screening of eating disorders should be restricted to the risk groups, in order to be efficient and practicable (Patton and King, 1991).

PRINCIPLE 3: THE NATURAL HISTORY OF THE DISEASE, INCLUDING LATENT TO DECLARED DISEASE, SHOULD BE ADEQUATELY UNDERSTOOD.

In order to change the course of an illness, it is important that its natural course be understood. Knowledge about the beginning, cause and preclinical phase of an illness may highlight potential risk factors and risk groups and therefore facilitate the screening. Much has been written about the possible causes of eating disorders. But none of the many theories is able to predict whether someone will develop an eating disorder or not (Fairburn and Beglin, 1990; Garner, 1993; Russell, 1992). This is probably related to the multifactorial etiology (Garfinkel and Garner, 1982; Katz, 1985).

Most knowledge about etiology and early course of eating disorders has been based on retrospective studies of relatively serious cases treated in specialized centers. In this respect three possible sources of distortion have been mentioned: the causal interpretation of strictly correlational relations, hindsight interpretation, and negative selection (Cohen and Cohen, 1984; Shaw and Garfinkel, 1990; Vandereycken and Meermann, 1992). Although empirical evidence with regard to the non-representativeness of the clinical populations is scarce, it is generally assumed that such negative sampling-biases exist, and that no valid conclusions about the etiology can be made on the basis of studies in clinical populations (Fairburn, Welch, Norman, O'Connor and Doll, 1996).

The disadvantages of research with strictly clinical populations have led many researchers to plea for prospective community-based studies. This kind of research, in which a large risk-group is followed longitudinally in order to determine which subjects will develop an eating disorder, could reveal the possibility of bias. Unfortunately, this research is hard to realize in light of the low incidence of eating disorders. An enormous population may have to be followed in order to find just a few patients. Some prospective studies have nevertheless been performed recently (for a review: see Rathner, 1992). Given the potential for unbiased insight in the etiology of eating disorders, however, it is dissapointing that these studies have yielded so few results. Aside from the findings that the development of eating disorders is linked with earlier dieting and associated with general psychiatric symptomatology, there are few clues to the etiology of eating disorders. Patton and King (1991) noted that 'the crucial question of how often those subjects with a partial syndrome progress to anorexia nervosa has not yet been answered' (p. 289). A few prospective studies have been directed at the development from subclinical to clinical eating disorder. But the subclinical population has been reported to be very heterogenous (Fairburn and Beglin, 1990), and so far it has been nearly impossible to trace persons who changed from a subclinical to a clinical picture (Rathner and Messner, 1993).

In sum, very little is known about the cause and the early course of eating disorders. Because most of our knowledge has been drawn from retrospective studies in selected clinical samples, this information may be biased. Prospective studies are certainly desirable but difficult to conduct, because of the low incidence of eating disorders among the population as a whole. The prospective studies conducted thus far have also yielded little information.

PRINCIPLE 4: THERE SHOULD BE A RECOGNIZABLE LATENT OR VERY EARLY SYMPTOMATIC STAGE.

For a screening program to be effective, there should be early and easy-to-recognize symptoms. A condition with barely or no early signs is simply not suited for early detection. It should be noted that 'recognizability' does not depend on the physical appearance of the early symptoms alone. The availability of valid tests and the individual's willingness to be screened are also crucial factors. The diagnosis of eating disorders is complicated by 'the apparent similarity of the disorder to health' (Frankenburg, Garfinkel and Garner, 1982). As a result, most cases are diagnosed years after the start of the illness (Fairburn and Beglin, 1990; Noordenbos, 1994). According to Vandereycken and Meermann (1984), two mechanisms may be at work here: patient delay and doctor delay.

Patient delay refers to the fact that eating-disordered patients often do not ask for help as a result of their denial of illness (Weeda-Mannak, 1984), shame (Russell, 1992), or the fact that they see the eating disorder as a solution and not a problem (Noordenbos, 1988). The patients are also often supported by their family and friends in their denial (Branch and Eurman, 1980; Crisp, 1979). *Doctor delay* refers to the fact that physicians (or other health care professionals) may simply fail to recognize the illness. This oversight may be caused by the tendency of patients to hide their symptoms; it may also be the result of ignorance on the part of the clinicians (Bryant-Waugh, Lask, Shafran and Fosson, 1992). How this delay can be reduced or avoided will be described elsewhere in this volume (see chapter by Noordenbos).

In sum, there is no clearly recognizable start or pre-stage that can be measured on a large scale and this is especially true for bulimia. This absence may also be strengthened by the patient's tendency to conceal the disorder.

IS THERE A SUITABLE SCREENING PROCEDURE FOR EATING DISORDERS?

PRINCIPLE 5: THE ORGANIZATION OF THE SCREENING PROGRAMS ALLOWS FOR AN IMPORTANT PART OF THE POPULATION TO BE SCREENED.

This is a question of logistics, related to the practicability of the screening. From epidemiological surveys of mental disorders we know that selective non-response of affected individuals is a major problem (Williams and MacDonald, 1986). For screening, this may result in a high false negative rate and thus in less effectiveness. In the discussion of principle 2 an important efficiency problem was highlighted. For the diagnosis of an eating disorder, a clinical interview is necessary but this is not an efficient way in the screening of large risk-groups. A solution can be found in a *two-stage method*, a survey method generally used in epidemiological studies of rare psychiatric disorders (Williams, Tarnapolsky and Hand, 1980): a questionnaire is first administered, and then a clinical interview is undertaken in subjects with an abnormal or 'suspicious' scoring on the questionnaire (for a review: see Hoek, 1993; Rathner, 1992). Thus far, the two-stage method has not often been used for screening purposes. In the following, we will consider four epidemiological two-stage surveys for eating disorders. In these particular studies, some sort of non-response analysis was performed. The organization and the results of these studies will be discussed with special reference to the response rates in both stages of the surveys.

Meadows, Palmer, Newball, and Kenrick (1986) conducted a two-stage survey (a postal survey with selected follow-up interviews) on a complete population of females aged 18 to 22 years registered in two group medical practices. Of the 634 women, 50 did not receive the questionnaire, and 173 did not return the questionnaire. Of the 411 responders, 28 (7 per cent) were found to be 'at risk' as they scored high (30 or more) on the Eating Attitudes Test (EAT; discussed below: principle 6). All of the 28 high scorers received a letter with an appointment for a clinical interview. Six refused to participate, and 7 could not be contacted after considerable effort. No more than 15 females (54 per cent of the high scorers) remained to be interviewed. Of these only 1 fulfilled the DSM-III criteria for bulimia nervosa. She accepted an offer of further assessment and treatment, but quickly dropped out of contact. One case of anorexia nervosa was identified within the initial study population as an indirect effect of the survey: 'She had returned the original mailing but her EAT score was below threshold. Shortly afterwards she consulted her family doctor and a referral was made to one of the researchers. She admitted that she had not completed the mailed questionnaire truthfully because of her mixed feelings about declaring the disorder. At the time of her clinical assessment she produced a high EAT score' (Meadows et al., 1986, p. 355).

In a two-stage survey of 1010 unselected school girls, Johnson-Sabine, Wood, Patton, Mann and Wakeling (1988) performed a non-response analysis in one of the schools involved in the study (see also Patton et al., 1990). Of the 210 girls in this school, 79 per cent returned the EAT. It also proved possible to contact 29 of the 46 girls who did not return the questionnaire for completion. Seventeen girls remained untracable but their teachers' reports were obtained which established that 'seven were habitual absentees, two were being treated for anorexia nervosa, two were thin and had anxiety symptoms and six had refused to cooperate for reasons not obviously related to either eating or body shape' (Johnson-Sabine et al., 1988, p. 618). Most striking is that the two-stage screening program itself did not reveal any cases of anorexia nervosa!

In a study by King (1989) in the waiting room of several general practices, all of the men and women between 16 and 35 years of age were asked to fill out the EAT and some other questionnaires. Of the 748 people contacted, 96 per cent completed the EAT. Of the 76 high scorers, 7 refused an interview. Of the 69 interviewed, no cases of anorexia nervosa and 7 (1 male and 6 female) cases of bulimia nervosa using Russell's (1979) criteria were found; that is 10 per cent of those interviewed. King then performed a non-responders analysis on the 7 refusers: 'Two were untraceable, two appeared to have given false names, and three refused. Practice records on the three who refused interview revealed one who had several entries in the preceding two years for concern about weight, including requests for diets, and two had many entries for psychological problems and concern about weight' (King, 1989, pp. 13–14). Interestingly, not the sensitivity of the questionnaire

(EAT) appears to have caused the false-negative rate in this survey, but the refusal of the high scorers on the questionnaire to undergo an interview.

In their sophisticated two-stage survey, Rathner and Messner (1993) also conducted a third stage in order to evaluate the validity of their study: they investigated the case registers of four hospitals in the area to detect any additional cases of eating disorder that may have been overlooked in the survey. To examine the development from subclinical to clinical eating-disorder, the diagnostic interview occurred one year after the initial screening. The study was conducted in the five German-speaking schools in a bilingual rural town in Southern Tyrol, Italy. Of the 1066 German-speaking female residents between the ages of 11 and 20 years, only 517 received screening at the school. This 52 per cent non-response rate appeared to have several causes. The most important one was that more than 30 per cent of the target population (the adult females in particular) were not enrolled in school. About 20 per cent of the parents did not consent to their daughter's participation, and about 5 per cent of the girls was absent on the day of the screening (there was no selective absenteism as the students did not know on which day the screening would be performed).

On the basis of the scores on several measures (including the EAT and a question with regard to menstruation), a risk group, sub-risk group, and no-risk group were defined. All risk-cases (n=50), a random sample of the sub-risk group (n=25 or 45 per cent), and a small random sample of the no-risk group (n=32 or 8 per cent) were selected for intensive examination one year later. Only two cases of anorexia nervosa were found in the second stage and no cases of bulimia nervosa. Both anorectic patients were found to have met the diagnostic criteria during the screening and both belonged to the original risk group; one was currently in psychotherapy, and the other had never been treated.

In the third stage (hospital case registers), no cases of bulimia nervosa were found and two females (who were part of the target population of 1066) were found to have been hospitalized for anorexia nervosa. One of these patients was also detected during the two-stage screening process, whereas the other belonged to the sub-risk group at screening and developed her anorexia later on (by chance, she was not invited for an interview). Further inquiry with the school personnel nor analysis of the non-responders did reveal other cases of eating disorders.

In summary, the cited epidemiological surveys show that the sensitivity of a two-stage screening program may be seriously damaged by denial, non-attendance, and refusal to do an inter-view. Rathner (1992) presents some interesting recommendations in this light. One is simply not to announce the day of the screening at school in order to prevent selective absenteism. It is also suggested that the sensitivity of the two-stage survey of eating disorders be evaluated retrospectively: 'Cross-validation of the results of interview stages by third party information (relatives, general practioners or hospital records) is a possible corrective measure for denial, limited self-disclosure and social desirability in eating-disordered subjects' (Rathner, 1992, p. 300). Obviously, such a third stage can also help us evaluate the effectiveness and efficiency of a two-stage screening procedure for eating disorders.

PRINCIPLE 6: THERE SHOULD BE A SUITABLE TEST FOR EXAMINATION.

In order to be suitable, a test should fulfil six demands (Holland and Stewart, 1990): simplicity, acceptability, accuracy, cost, preci-sion (or repeatability), and validity. For simplicity, the test should be easy to administer and score. This is especially important when the test is to be used in a large scale program. For acceptability, a test should not be too unpleasant for those screened, otherwise more withdrawal can be expected. For accuracy the test should measure what it is supposed to measure and identify whether or not someone should be treated as a patient (see principle 1). For the screening to be efficient, the cost in money or manpower should not be too high. For precision (or repeatability) a test should give the same result on repeated trials. For the validity of the test, apart from the above mentioned repeatability, two aspects are central: sensitivity, and specificity.

In the screening for eating disorders, the *Eating Attitudes Test* or EAT (Garner and Garfinkel, 1979) was predominantly used. The EAT has been developed as a measure of the degree of anorexia nervosa psychopathology. This American self-report questionnaire consist of 40 items. The total score (all items added together) is seen as a valid measure of disturbed eating (Mann et al., 1983) and an EAT-score above a particular cut-off point is considered a clear indication of an eating disorder. For screening purposes, the shortened 26-item version of the EAT is often used (Garner, Olmsted, Bohr and Garfinkel, 1982).

The simplicity of the EAT, especially the 26-item version, is clear and its acceptability is also satisfactory. The accuracy of the test, however, is less than satisfactory: the test is known not to measure caseness (whether or not the person should be treated as a patient) but rather measures extreme dieting behavior and attitudes that may be found in non-cases as well (Williams, Hand and Tarnapolsky, 1982). The cost of the testing is low. The measures of the validity of the EAT as a screening instrument (specificity, sensitivity, positive-predictive value, and negative-predictive value) will be discussed now in greater detail.

Sensitivity and selectivity are measures of the validity of the test, which is not the same as the possible value of the test as screening instrument. For this purpose, the positive predictive value (PPV) and the negative predictive value (NPV) are more appropriate measures (Williams, 1983). Although the NPV and the PPV are interrelated, they also heavily depend on the base rate of the condition in the screened population. A lucid article on the interrelations between the validity, the base rate and the PPV was written by Williams, Hand, and Tarnapolsky (1982). In one of their scholarly examples they showed how in a population (N=1000) in which 1 per cent was affected by the condition sought, a test with an excellent validity (specificity = .90; sensitivity = .90) results in a PPV of no more than 8.3 per cent. Of the 10 affected individuals in this population, 9 (90 per cent) will be positively and 1 (10 per cent) negatively tested. Of the 990 non-affected individuals, 891 (90 per cent) will be negatively and 99 (10 per cent) positively tested. This means that 99 of the 108 high scorers on the test will wrongly show a positive result. In other words: 10 out of 11 positively screened subjects appear to be false positives! Williams et al. (1982) conclude that a screening test should have a near 100 per cent ideal sensitivity and sensitivity, in case it is used to detect the sparse undetected cases in a large population of non-cases.

As discussed by Beglin and Fairburn (1992b), the specificity of the EAT seems to be satisfactory. However, the fact that this specificity is not perfect has serious consequences for the PPV of the EAT. Given the low prevalence of eating disorders even in well-known risk groups, the PPV of the EAT was found to be low in screening studies: between 20 per cent and 40 per cent (Rathner, 1992). Less is known about the sensitivity of the EAT. The study by Meadows and coworkers (1986) serves as an illustration of the sensitivity to denial. About the NPV of the EAT no information is available. More generally, a picture of the NPV of a screening test can only be achieved when all of the subjects, including the low scorers, are interviewed in the second stage (Beglin and Fairburn, 1992). So far, such studies have not been performed for eating disorders.

In sum, the EAT is only partially suitable for the screening of eating disorders. The low positive-predictive value of the questionnaire may cause problems by creating a high false-postive rate. Unfortunately, the *Eating Disorder Inventory* or EDI (Garner, Olmsted and Polivy, 1983; Garner, 1991) does not seem to be a promising alternative. The problems with the factorial integrity of the EDI in nonclinical populations (Schoemaker, Van Strien and Van der Staak, 1994) and the non-specificity of the scales not directly related to food and eating (Cooper, Cooper, and Fairburn, 1985; Hurley, Palmer and Stretch, 1990; Schoemaker, Verbraak, Breteler and Van der Staak, 1997) seriously raises the question whether the EDI is more suitable as a screening instrument than the EAT. A better alternative might be the *Eating Disorder Examination-Screening version* or EDE-S (Beglin and Fairburn, 1992). This short self-report questionnaire measures such simple data as behavior frequency. The EDE-S revealed less false positives than the EAT (Beglin and Fairburn, 1992) and seems to be a more useful instrument.

PRINCIPLE 7: SCREENING LEADS TO EARLIER TREATMENT.

Screening in itself has no impact on the course of an illness. It is just a means to get treatment started at an earlier time (Crisp, 1988; Holland and Stewart, 1990). Often it is assumed that screening automatically leads to treatment. There are two possible exceptions to this rule.

First, positively screened people may already be in treatment. Redundant screening for eating disorders will only be found in outpatients, however, as inpatients are not attending school and do not receive screening (Rathner and Messner, 1993). Just how many screened cases are already in treatment is not well documented, because this information is rarely reported (Beglin and Fairburn, 1992). In the few studies in which the screen-detected cases were explicitly asked about ongoing treatment, many of the positively-screened cases were found to be in treatment (Beglin and Fairburn, 1992; Johnson-Sabine et al., 1988; Rathner and Messner, 1993). Although this may indeed be viewed as proof of the sensitivity of the screening program, the screening does not lead to earlier treatment.

Secondly, thus-far untreated positively screened people may decide not to comply with treatment. For these non-complying people, screening cannot be considered very effective. Non-compliance is a major problem in the treatment of eating-disordered patients (Vandereycken, 1993). It is generally assumed that the non-compliance and denial of the disorder will vary across the course of the disorder and will be the strongest in the beginning, when the recognizable physical effects are the smallest. Systematic studies along these lines are nevertheless lacking. Should the assumption prove to be true, however, compliance can be expected to be lower for screen-detected cases, because these patients have not sought treatment themselves and may even be avoiding treatment. When the screening would not have been conducted, and these patients would have asked for help themselves several years later, they might have been more motivated for treatment then.

The non-response rates reported in the four epidemiological two-stage surveys discussed above (principle 5) may underestimate the non-response rates that can be expected in a screening program directed at the early treatment of eating disorders (Rathner, 1992). When in a real screening program the subjects are told beforehand that a high score on the screening test will result in the – often unwanted – treatment, the false-negative rate as a result of denial may be quite high.

IS THERE A SUITABLE TREATMENT FOR EATING DISORDERS?

PRINCIPLE 8: THERE SHOULD BE AN ACCEPTED TREATMENT FOR PATIENTS WITH RECOGNIZED DISEASE.

Wilson and Jungner (1968) observed that 'of all the criteria that a screening test should fulfill, the ability to treat the condition adequately, when discovered, is perhaps the most important'. By 'adequate' they mean that research has shown the patient to get better as a result of the treatment. The adequacy of the treatment can be viewed as the sine qua non criterum for the effectiveness of the screening procedure (Smead, 1985a). Moreover, for conditions that can resolve themselves without treatment, screening will be rather inefficient.

The clinical prognosis of eating-disordered patients is almost impossible to predict at present (Russell, 1992). For anorexia nervosa, few controlled comparisons of the effectiveness of different treatments have been undertaken. Roughly, 40 per cent of the clinical anorexia population improves, 30 per cent remains the same, and 30 per cent gets worse (Herzog, Rathner and Vandereycken, 1992). In bulimia nervosa a lot of comparative studies have been carried out on the outcome of different therapies. Compared to anorexia nervosa, the effectiveness of treatment is better documented in bulimic cases. The treatment of eating disorders, however, is only partly effective as relapse is known to occur in many cases (Herzog et al., 1988; Vandereycken and Meermann, 1992).

We don't know in how many cases eating-disordered patients may improve or even recover without professional treatment. Effects occurring 10 to 20 years after treatment may therefore be regarded as a result of the natural course of the disorder and not as a long-term effect of treatment. It is difficult to evaluate the net effectiveness of treatment with the effects of the natural course of the eating disorder partialed out, because very little is known about the natural course of eating disorders (Vandereycken and Meermann, 1992). In the few studies conducted thus far, the outcomes for untreated patients have been found to be no worse than those for treated patients. No firm conclusions can be drawn from these results, however, as the patients were not randomly assigned to treatment and non-treatment: the condition of the treated patients may thus have been more severe to start with (Vandereycken and Meermann, 1992).

Outcome studies to date have been conducted in specialized centers for eating disorders. This means that the sample under study may not be representative for the total eating-disordered population. As discussed above (principle 3), the patients in these centers are negatively selected: they are more severly ill, with a more complex history and longer duration of illness, they may have experienced previous treatment failures, and they often show psychiatric co-morbidity. As a result of this non-representative-ness, the results of these studies may not be a valid reflection of the effectiveness of treatment among patients in general. The outcome of treatment in this severe group may be an underesti-mation of the effectiveness of treatment in a community-based group. Conversely, the natural course of an eating disorder for patients in the community may be better than for patients in a specialized center and thus biases the treatment effects in a positive direction for the community cases. The exact representa-tiveness of treatment outcome studies thus remains unknown.

In sum, an accepted treatment for eating disorders that is effective in all cases does not exist (Garner, 1993; Shaw and Garfinkel, 1990). This conclusion may be regarded as an argument for primary rather than secondary prevention, particularly because the effectiveness of screening has been shown to be totally dependent on the effectiveness of the treatment.

PRINCIPLE 9: THERE MUST BE AN ADVANTAGE TO TREATING THE DISEASE EARLIER THAN AT THE STAGE IT WOULD PRESENT SPONTANEOUSLY.

According to Burr and Elwood (1985), this principle should be met 'for screening to be justified'. This advantage can take several forms: 'In reducing mortality or disability from the disease; in offering less radical treatment than would be necessary when the disease has progressed further; or in relieving a disability for which the patient might never seek help' (p. 375). It goes without saying that this principle is decisive for the evaluation of the effectiveness and efficiency of a screening program (Skuse and Williams, 1984). In conditions for which there is no such advantage, case finding will be as effective as screening.

As it is clearly unethical to experimentally manipulate the time between the onset of the disorder and first admission, there is no direct evidence for the contribution of early intervention. However, many have taken the prognostic value of illness duration in outcome studies of anorexia nervosa as evidence for the assumption that earlier treatment would be more effective than later treatment (Bryant-Waugh et al., 1992; Crisp, 1979; Herzog et al., 1988; Shisslak et al., 1990; Steinhausen, Rauss-Mason and Seidel, 1991). In our own systematic review of the available outcome studies (Schoemaker, 1997), early intervention was not found to improve the effectiveness of treatment for anorexia nervosa. In bulimia nervosa, the duration of illness seems to have little or no prognostic value (Herzog et al., 1988). This does not mean that intervening at an earlier stage cannot improve the outcome of treatment. Rather, we simply cannot predict the outcome of earlier treatment on the basis of the available studies.

PRINCIPLE 10: FACILITIES FOR TREATMENT SHOULD BE AVAILABLE.

This is mainly a question of logistics (Sackett, Haynes and Tugwell, 1985). At the beginning any screening program will lead to an increase of patients applying for treatment. When this increase is not taken into account, there may not be enough facilities to treat the positively screened patients. In that case screening will have no positive effects but most likely a negative one (Smead, 1985a). The word 'available' is particularly important in this principle. In most western countries, there are many facilities for the treatment of eating disorders. In the Netherlands, for instance, despite the increasing number of specialized centers, their availability is limited as most of these centers have waiting lists of several months up to more than one year! The capacity of these centers to handle the extra cases produced by a nation-wide screening program is open to question.

EVALUATION OF SCREENING FOR EATING DISORDERS

In light of the application of the screening principles to the area of eating disorders, we can say that the effectiveness of screening for eating disorders is limited by their low incidence and the fact that the treatment is only partially effective. It is not at all clear whether the outcome of earlier treatment (as a result of earlier recognition) is better. Furthermore, the results of two-stage epidemiological surveys show the capacity of such a screening procedure to bring untreated patients into treatment to be questionable at least. In sum, the benefits of screening for eating disorders seem to be small.

The evaluation of the *efficiency* of screening for eating disorders is difficult because we lack knowledge of both the benefits and the costs. The burden in time and effort for the screened as well as the financial costs may be relatively small. Compared to the benefits for one or two eating-disordered patients who were not yet in treatment, however, these costs may be considerable. Every screening program may also produce iatrogenic effects. Screening for an eating disorder may unwillingly suggest the wrong idea to healthy people. Cases have been reported in which people started their disordered eating behavior (vomiting or the use of laxatives) as a result of doctors' questions about eating disturbances (Chiodo and Latimer, 1983; Herzog, 1982; Garner, 1985; Smead, 1985b). This aspect of screening has not been studied, however. Moreover, very little is known about the effects of a false-positive score in the first stage of a screening procedure on the eating behavior of an otherwise healthy subject. Finally, almost nothing is known about the effects of suggesting treatment or actual treatment in the case of a false positive case, whether this person has a subclinical eating disorder or no eating disorder at all. In sum, there are numerous costs and dangers involved in the screening for eating disorers, but these costs have yet to be studied. At this time, an analysis of the actual costs and benefits is impossible. Because the estimated benefits appear to be relatively small, moreover, the possibility of the costs outweighing the benefits cannot be ruled out beforehand.

Since clearly a suitable screening program and a suitable treatment are not available, at this moment the initiation of large-scale screening programs does not appear to be justified. It should be noted that this conclusion is based on the information available at this time. It cannot be precluded that some form of screening may prove to be effective and efficient at some time in the future. Before this can happen, however, several questions will have to be answered and several problems will have to be solved.

Further research is needed to explore the possibilities for the development of a screening program suited to the detection of eating disorders. Prospective studies are needed to draw valid conclusions about the etiology (Fairburn and Beglin, 1990; Patton and King, 1991). Furthermore, these studies may clarify whether and in how many cases subclinical eating disorders will progress into full clinical pictures. It is impossible to evaluate the effectiveness of screening for eating disorders without taking into account the screenees' own initiative. To be able to make such an evaluation, more studies on help-seeking behavior are necessary. It is important to know why some eating disorder patients ask for treatment while others do not. What are the important factors that may affect this decision? Finally, more research into treatment outcome and compliance during treatment is needed (Garner, 1987), especially for persons who came into treatment as a result of a screening procedure.

The difficulties associated with the screening of eating disorders may imply that *case finding* should be given more effort. The evaluation of case finding is fairly straight forward. Case finding, however, is complicated by patient delay and doctor delay. Because of denial, bodily symptoms such as amenorrhea and measured weight should be attended to (Rathner and Messner, 1993). It may also be useful to interview family members, teachers and/or peers (Vandereycken and Meermann, 1984). As stated earlier, the requirements for case finding are less comprehensive than those for screening. When patients ask for help, there seems to be no reason for not providing what is known to be the best treatment.

REFERENCES

American Psychiatric Association (1994) *Diagnostic and Statistical Manual of Mental Disorders, 4th edition (DSM-IV),* Washington, D.C.: A.P.A.

Beglin, S.J. and Fairburn, C.G. (1992) 'Evaluation of a new instrument for the detection of eating disorders in community samples'. *Psychiatry Research,* 44: 101–201.

Branch, C.H.H. and Eurman, L.J. (1980) 'Social attitudes toward patients with anorexia nervosa'. *American Journal of Psychiatry,,* 137: 631–2.

Bryant-Waugh, R.J., Lask, B.D., Shafran, R.L. and Fosson, A.R. (1992)

'Do doctors recognise eating disorders in children?' *Archives of Disease in Childhood,* 67: 103–5.

Burr, M.L. and Elwood, P.C. (1985) 'Research and development of health promotion services – screening'. In Holland, W.W., Detels, R. and Knox, G. (eds) *Oxford Textbook of Public Health. Volume 3: Investigative methods in public health* (pp. 373–84). Oxford: Oxford University Press.

Chiodo, J. and Latimer, P.R. (1983) 'Vomiting as a learned weight-control technique in bulimia'. *Journal of Behavior Therapy and Experimental Psychiatry,* 14: 131–5.

Cochrane, A.L. and Holland, W.W. (1971) 'Validation of screening procedures'. *British Medical Bulletin,* 27: 3.

Cohen, P. and Cohen, J. (1984) 'The clinician's illusion'. *Archives of General Psychiatry,* 41: 1178–82.

Cooper, Z., Cooper, P. and Fairburn, C. (1985) 'The specificity of the Eating Disorder Inventory'. *British Journal of Clinical Psychology,* 24: 129–30

Crisp, A.H. (1979) 'Early recognition and prevention of anorexia nervosa'. *Developmental Medicine and Child Neurology,* 21: 393–5.

——(1988) 'Some possible approaches to prevention of eating and body weight/shape disorders, with particular reference to anorexia nervosa'. *International Journal of Eating Disorders,* 7: 1–17.

Fairburn, C.G. and Beglin, S.J. (1990) 'Studies of the epidemiology of bulimia nervosa'. *American Journal of Psychiatry,* 147: 401–8.

Fairburn, C.G., Welch, S.L., Norman, P.A., O'Connor, M.E. and Doll, H.E. (1996) 'Bias and bulimia nervosa: How typical are clinic cases?' *American Journal of Psychiatry,* 153: 386–91.

Frankenburg, F., Garfinkel, P.E. and Garner, D.M. (1982) 'Anorexia nervosa: Issues in prevention'. *Journal of Preventive Psychiatry,* 1: 469–83.

Garfinkel, P.E. (1992) 'Classification and diagnosis'. In Halmi, K.A. (ed) *Psychobiology and Treatment of Anorexia Nervosa and Bulimia Nervosa* (pp. 37–60), Washington, DC: American Psychiatric Press.

Garfinkel, P.E. and Garner, D.M. (1982) *Anorexia Nervosa: A Multidimensional Perspective,* New York: Brunner/Mazel.

Garner, D.M. (1991) *Eating Disorder Inventory-2 Manual,* Odessa, Florida: Psychological Assessment Resources.

——(1993) 'The pathogenesis of anorexia nervosa. *Lancet,* 341: 1631–5.

Garner, D.M. and Garfinkel, P.E. (1979) 'The Eating Attitudes Test: An index of symptoms of anorexia nervosa'. *Psychological Medicine,* 9: 273–9.

Garner, D.M., Olmsted, M.P., Bohr, Y. and Garfinkel, P.E. (1982) 'The Eating Attitudes Test: Psychometric features and clinical correlates'. *Psychological Medicine*, 12: 871–8.

Garner, D.M., Olmsted, M.P. and Polivy, J. (1983) 'Development and validation of a multidimensional eating disorder inventory for anorexia nervosa and bulimia'. *International Journal of Eating Disorders*, 2: 15–34.

Gowers, S. Norton, K., Halek, C. and Crisp, A.H. (1994) 'Outcome of outpatients psychotherapy in a random allocation treatment study of anorexia nervosa'. *International Journal of Eating Disorders*, 15: 165–77.

Herzog, D.B., Keller, M.B. and Lavori, P.W. (1988) 'Outcome in anorexia nervosa and bulimia nervosa: A review of the literature'. *Journal of Nervous and Mental Disease*, 176: 131–43.

Herzog, W., Rathner, G. and Vandereycken, W. (1992) 'Long-term course of anorexia nervosa: A review of the literature'. In Herzog, W., Deter, H.-C. and Vandereycken, W. (eds) *The Course of Eating Disorders* (pp. 15–29), Berlin-New York: Springer.

Hoek, H.W. (1993) 'Review of the epidemiological studies of eating disorders'. *International Review of Psychiatry*, 5: 61–74.

Hoek, H.W., Bartelds, A.I.M., Bosveld, J.J.F., van der Graaf, Y., Limpens, V.E.L., Maiwald, M. and Spaaij, C.J.K. (1995) 'The impact of urbanization on the detection rates of eating disorders'. *American Journal of Psychiatry,* 152: 1272–8

Holland, W.W. and Stewart, S. (1990) *Screening in Health Care: Benefit or Bane?* London: Nuffield Provincial Hospitals Trust.

Hurley, J., Palmer, R. and Stretch, D. (1990) 'The specificity of the Eating Disorders Inventory: A reappraisal'. *International Journal of Eating Disorders,* 9: 419–24.

Johnson-Sabine, E., Wood, K., Patton, G., Mann, A. and Wakeling, A. (1988) 'Abnormal eating attitudes in London schoolgirls: A prospective epidemiological study. Factors associated with abnormal reponse on screening questionnaires'. *Psychological Medicine*, 18: 615–22.

Katz, J.L. (1985) 'Some reflections on the nature of the eating disorders: On the need for humility'. *International Journal of Eating Disorders,* 4: 617–26.

King, M.B. (1986) 'Case finding for at risk drinking in general practice: Cost-benefit analysis'. *Psychological Medicine,* 16: 359–63.

King, M.B. (1989) 'Eating disorders in a general practice population. Prevalence, characteristics, and follow-up at 12 to 18 months'. *Psychological Medicine*, Monograph supplement 14.

Mann, A.H., Wakeling, A., Wood, K., Monck, E., Dobbs, R. and Szmukler, G. (1983) 'Screening for abnormal eating attitudes and psychiatric morbidity in an unselected population of 15-year-old schoolgirls'. *Psychological Medicine*, 13: 573–80.

Meadows, G.N., Palmer, R.L., Newball, E.U.M. and Kenrick, J.M.T. (1986) 'Eating attitudes and disorder in young women: A general practice based survey'. *Psychological Medicine*, 16: 351–7.

Newman, S.C., Shrout, P.E. and Bland, R.C. (1990) 'The efficiency of two-phase designs in prevalence surveys of mental disorders'. *Psychological Medicine*, 20: 183–93.

Noordenbos, G. (1988) *Onbegrensd lijnen* [Unlimited slimming], Leiden: DSWO Press.

——(1994) 'Problems and possibilities of the prevention of eating disorders'. *European Eating Disorders Review*, 2: 126–42.

Patton, G.C. (1988) 'The spectrum of eating disorder in adolescence'. *Journal of Psychosomatic Research*, 32: 579–84.

Patton, G.C., Johnson-Sabine, E., Wood, K., Mann, A.H. and Wakeling, A. (1990) 'Abnormal eating attitudes in London schoolgirls – a prospective epidemiological study: Outcome at twelve month follow-up'. *Psychological Medicine*, 20: 383–94.

Patton, G.C. and King, M.B. (1991) 'Epidemiological study of eating disorders: Time for a change of emphasis'. *Psychological Medicine*, 21: 287–91.

Rathner, G. (1992) 'Aspects of the natural history of normal and disordered eating and some methodological considerations'. In Herzog, W., Deter, H.-C. and Vandereycken, W. (eds) *The Course of Eating Disorders* (pp. 198–213), Berlin-New York: Springer.

Rathner, G. and Messner, K. (1993) 'Detection of eating disorders in a small rural town: An epidemiological study'. *Psychological Medicine*, 23: 175–84.

Russell, G.F.M. (1992) 'The prognosis of eating disorders: A clinician's approach'. In Herzog, W., Deter, H.-C. and Vandereycken, W. (eds) *The Course of Eating Disorders* (pp. 198–213), Berlin-New York: Springer.

Sackett, D.L. and Holland, W.W. (1975) 'Controversy in the detection of disease'. *Lancet*, 1: 357–9.

Schoemaker, C.G. (1995) *Screening for Eating Disorders. The Principles and Some Data*, University of Nijmegen, Ph.D. dissertation.

——(1997) 'Does early intervention improve the prognosis in anorexia nervosa? A systematic review of the treatment-outcome literature'. *International Journal of Eating Disorders*, 21: 1–15.

Schoemaker, C., Van Strien, T. and Van der Staak, C. (1994) 'Validation of the Eating Disorders Inventory in a non-clinical population using transformed and untransformed responses'. *International Journal of Eating Disorders*, 15: 387–93.

Schoemaker, C., Verbraak, M., Breteler, R. and Van der Staak, C. (1997) 'The discriminant validity of the Eating Disorder Inventory-2'. *British Journal of Clinical Psychology*, 36: 627–9.

Shaw, B.F. and Garfinkel, P.E. (1990) 'Research problems in the eating disorders'. *International Journal of Eating Disorders*, 9: 545–55.

Shisslak, C.M., Crago, M. and Neal, M.E. (1990) 'Prevention of eating disorders among adolescents'. *American Journal of Health Promotion*, 5: 100–6.

Shisslak, C.M., Crago, M., Neal, M.E. and Swain, B. (1987) 'Primary prevention of eating disorders'. *Journal of Consulting and Clinical Psychology*, 55: 660–7.

Skuse, D. and Williams, P. (1984) 'Screening for psychiatric disorder in general practice'. *Psychological Medicine*, 14: 365–77.

Smead, V.S. (1985a) 'Labeling eating disorders: Weighing costs and benefits'. *Transactional Analysis Journal*, 15: 17–20.

Smead, V.S. (1985b) 'Considerations prior to establishing preventative interventions for eating disorders'. *Ontario Psychologist*, 17: 12–17.

Steinhausen, H.-C., Rauss-Mason, C. and Seidel, R. (1991) 'Follow-up studies of anorexia nervosa: A review of four decades of outcome research'. *Psychological Medicine*, 21: 447–54.

Vandereycken, W. (1993) 'Naughty girls and angry doctors: Eating disorder patients and their therapists'. *International Review of Psychiatry*, 5: 13–18.

Vandereycken, W. and Meermann, R. (1984) *Anorexia Nervosa. A Clinician's Guide to Treatment*, Berlin-New York: Walter de Gruyter.

——(1992) 'The significance of follow-up investigations'. In Herzog, W., Deter, H.-C. and Vandereycken, W. (eds) *The Course of Eating Disorders: Long-term Follow-up Studies of Anorexia and Bulimia Nervosa* (pp. 3–14), Berlin-New York: Springer.

Vandereycken, W. and Vanderlinden, J. (1983). 'Denial of illness and the use of self-reporting measures in anorexia nervosa patients'. *International Journal of Eating Disorders*, 2: 101–7.

Weeda-Mannak, W.L. (1984) *Anorexia Nervosa: Towards an Early Identification*, Hilversum: Benedictus.

Williams, P., Hand, D. and Tarnapolsky, A. (1982) 'The problem of screening for uncommon disease – a comment on the Eating Attitudes Test'. *Psychological Medicine*, 12: 431–4.

Williams, P. and MacDonald, A. (1986) 'The effect of non-response bias on the results of two-stage screening surveys of psychiatric disorder'. *Social Psychiatry,* 21: 182–6.

Williams, P., Tarnapolsky, A. and Hand, D. (1980) 'Case definition and case identification in psychiatric epidemiology: Review and assessment'. *Psychological Medicine,* 10: 101–14.

Wilson, J.M.G. and Jungner, G. (1968) *Principles and Practice of Screening for Disease (Public Health Papers 34),* Geneva: World Health Organization.

CHAPTER NINE

Eating disorders in primary care: Early identification and intervention by general practitioners

Greta Noordenbos

INTRODUCTION

Eating disorders are often of a long duration (Herzog, Deter and Vandereycken, 1992). On average the course can vary from 4 years (Herzog, Rathner and Vandereycken, 1992) to 7.5 years (Noordenbos, 1991), but some patients are ill for more than 20 years (Theander, 1992). Because eating disorders can have severe physical, psychological, social and financial consequences for patients and their families, prevention and early intervention are very important. Although the effectiveness of treatment of patients with eating disorders is improving, treatment results are often frustrating. In general 40 per cent of the patients with eating disorders will recover, 30 per cent improve but do not recover completely, while 30 per cent remain chronically ill, commit suicide or die as a result of their eating disorder (Herzog, Rathner and Vandereycken, 1992; Russell, 1992; Theander, 1992). Although the mortality rate of bulimia nervosa is estimated below 3 per cent (less than for anorexia nervosa), this disorder too is associated with substantial psychological and social dysfunctioning (Yanovski, 1991). To improve the possibilities for recovery of eating disorders, early diagnosis and intervention are very important. General practitioners can play an important role in identifying patients with eating disorders before serious morbidity has developed.

In the first part of this chapter the most important problems in the interaction between patients with anorexia nervosa and their general practitioners will be described. In the second part suggestions will be given with respect to a prevention program for general practitioners in order to improve their ability to identify eating disorders at an early stage, to improve their attitude towards and their communication with these patients, and to increase their possibilities of early intervention in eating disorders.

MAIN PROBLEMS IN THE INTERACTION BETWEEN GENERAL PRACTITIONERS AND EATING DISORDER PATIENTS

The most important problems in the interaction between general practitioners and patients with anorexia and bulimia nervosa are: patient delay (presentation of complaints), doctor delay (diagnosing eating disorders in an early stage), the doctor-patient communication and the negative attitudes of general practitioners towards patients with eating disorders, gender differences between physicians and patients, and the inadequate interventions by general practitioners (including referrals to other specialists).

PATIENT DELAY

Patient delay severely hampers early identification by general practitoners. Research in the Netherlands by de Bloois (1987) and Noordenbos (1991) showed that nearly 90 per cent of the patients with anorexia or bulimia nervosa went to their general practitioner with complaints related to their eating disorder. But the mean period between the start of their eating disorder and the first visit to the physician is nearly four years (Daaleman, 1991). The reason of this 'patient delay' is that in the beginning of an eating disorder the patients do not realize to have a problem. On the contrary, they often feel quite well because their slimming behavior is 'successful' and seems to be the 'solution' for other problems they were faced with (Noordenbos, 1991).

In the beginning phase these patients usually are not willing to see a doctor because they don't look at themselves as being ill or they feel ashamed to reveal their eating and slimming behavior (Yanovski, 1991). In a Dutch sample of 108 patients with anorexia an bulimia nervosa, only 45 per cent took the initiative to see their family physician; 23 per cent mentioned that others advised them to go, while 32 per cent were sent by others who insisted they should visit their general practitioner (Noordenbos, 1992).

For most of the patients with anorexia or bulimia nervosa it is very difficult to tell their doctor directly about their eating behavior (Noordenbos, 1992). They often fear they have to give up their way of slimming, have to be nourished, and hence will become fat. Some are afraid to be sent to a hospital or to be labeled as mentally ill and admitted to a psychiatric hospital. When they finally agree to visit their doctor, it is often for secondary complications of their eating and slimming behavior, such as menstrual irregularities, loss of hair, fatigue, weakness and dizziness, dental problems, abdominal pain and constipation (Yanovski, 1991).

In the first stage of their eating disorder these patients may ask their physician to help them with their slimming behavior. Their main complaint is often constipation for which they request a special diet or laxatives and sometimes even diuretics (Noordenbos, 1991; Yanovski, 1991). Some patients, both anorectics and bulimics, are quite successful in this strategy.

> One patient told her general practitioner that she often had stomach aches and therefore requested a special diet. With this prescribed diet she could legitimate her restricted eating behavior to her family. When she visited her doctor again after a few weeks, she told him that her gastric complaints were still the same. She was then sent to a gastroenterologist who could not find any abnormality in her stomach. (Noordenbos, 1991)

This example shows how difficult it is for general practitioners to make a correct diagnosis. Patients hide their 'real' problems by only mentioning secondary complaints, but many (especially bulimics) hope that their doctor will ask more questions about their eating problems. The following case (Noordenbos, 1991) is a clear example of the strong relation between patient delay and doctor delay.

> Alice did not dare to tell her family physician about her eating behavior. Because everybody worried about her slimming, she finally decided to see her doctor and wanted to know whether her health was in danger or not. But instead of asking direct questions she would tell about her fear of having a tumor in her breast. When the doctor would make any remark about her thinness, she had the intention to tell him

more about her eating behavior. But when he would not notice it at all, she would feel reassured to continue her slimming behavior. And thus happened!

DOCTOR DELAY

Doctor delay is an equally important problem in the early identification of eating disorders. Many general practitioners don't know what the (early) signals of anorexia and bulimia nervosa are. They often miss the diagnosis, especially when the diagnostic criteria for anorexia and bulimia nervosa, as mentioned in the DSM-IV (American Psychiatric Association, 1994), are not clearly met (Button and Whitehouse, 1981). This makes it difficult for them to identify eating disorders at an early stage (Dhondt et al., 1989; Bryant-Waugh et al., 1992; Hoek, 1991; Whitehouse et al., 1992). For general practitioners it is even more difficult to diagnose bulimia nervosa: 'In contrast to anorexia nervosa, a disorder in which the patient's emaciated state is readily apparent, patients with bulimia nervosa are usually of normal weight, and almost appear healthy' (Yanovski, 1991, p. 1231). Clinicians often are confronted with 'subclinical forms' of anorexia and bulimia nervosa, lacking the characteristics of the full-blown clinical picture (King, 1989; Meadows et al., 1986; Szmukler, 1983). Prevalence of partial or subclinical eating disorders among female college and university students has been estimated between 3 and 5 per cent (Clarke and Palmer, 1983). Overlooking the diagnosis will be very likely in case of males, both for anorexia nervosa (Andersen and Mickalide, 1983) and bulimia nervosa (Mitchell and Goff, 1984).

Important signals of (partial) anorexia nervosa are weight loss, amenorrhoea, cold hands, and a persistent overconcern with body weight and shape. Bulimic patients, however, often appear healthy at first sight, because they often have a normal weight, although there can have been great weight fluctuations. Physical examination can reveal some stigmata of bulimia nervosa such as abrasions and scars on the dorsum of the hands (caused by scraping the hands against the teeth during self-induced vomiting), dental erosions and swelling of the salivary glands (Yanovski, 1991).

King (1989) studied four group practices of general practitioners in South London: a screening of 748 patients from 16–35 years old, revealed that only 1.1 per cent of females (6 women) and 0.5

Table 1: One year prevalence rates per 100,000 young females at different levels of care (Hoek, 1993).

Level of morbidity	AN N (%)	BN N (%)
Filter		
1. Estimated in the community	370	1500
Illness behavior		
2. Total in primary care	260 (70)	1050 (70)
Detection behavior		
3. Conspicuous in primary care	160 (43)	170 (11)
Referral to psychiatrist		
4. Total of psychiatric patients	127 (34)	87 (6)
Admission to psychiatric unit		
5. Psychiatric inpatients	30 (8)	? (?)

per cent of males (1 case) were diagnosed as having bulimia nervosa; no case of anorexia nervosa was found. When partial syndromes were included, the prevalence in females raised to 3.9 per cent. A similar study in Cambridge by Whitehouse and colleagues (1992) found a prevalence of anorexia nervosa of 0.2 per cent (1 case), full bulimia nervosa 1.5 per cent (8 cases) and partial bulimia nervosa 5.4 per cent (29 cases). Half of the bulimics, however, had not been identified by the general practitioner and two of these patients had been refered to medical specialists for treatment of secondary complications of their eating disorder. According to Whitehouse et al. (1992), hidden cases of bulimia, or partial syndromes, are relatively common in primary care, but many of these patients remain undetected even when the help of specialists is sought for what are likely to be secondary complications of the eating disorder. Referring to epidemiological research in the Netherlands, Hoek (1993) concluded that less than half of the patients with anorexia nervosa are to be correctly diagnosed by their general practitioner versus only about 10 per cent of the patients with bulimia nervosa (see Table 1).

SHORTCOMINGS IN THE DOCTOR-PATIENT RELATIONSHIP

The communication between the general practitioner and the eating-disordered patients is often inadequate (Noordenbos, 1991;

Vandereycken, 1993). Doctors often fail to ask the rigl.
or they show a distrust of these patients, as is illustrai
following case.

> Britta has had anorexia nervosa for several years. As a medical st.
> she knows that anorexia nervosa can have serious consequences ic
> her health. After a period of doubting whether she would go to her
> family physician, she at last found the courage to do so. She had the
> intention to tell her doctor as honestly as possible about her eating
> behavior. While doing this her voice is trembling and her hands are
> sweating. It is the first time that she seriously talks about her eating
> disorder. The doctor then puts her on the scales: she weighs 43 kg but
> he suspects her weight to be lower. He says he knows that patients
> with anorexia nervosa cannot be trusted; they often lie about their
> weight or have drunk a lot of water. He says she has to try to eat a bit
> more and see him again next week. But Britta feels very angry about
> his distrust and decides never to go back to this doctor. Only later does
> she understand the behavior of her general practitioner, when during
> a course about eating disorders she hears the professor telling exactly
> the same as her family physician did: 'Don't trust people with anorexia
> nervosa'. (Noordenbos, 1991)

A severe problem is the negative attitude of health care professionals towards patients with eating disorders. According to
Vandereycken (1993), anorectic patients challenge the medical
knowledge and the authority of doctors. They not only evoke
mistrust but even hostility because clinicians have great difficulty
in disengaging themselves from an attitude which implies that the
patient's resistance to eat could be controlled with adequate
exercise of will on her part. Physicians have great difficulty in
dealing with the patients' denial of illness and their reluctance to
be treated. 'Anorexics often evoke frustration and outrage in
doctors who regard them as imposters because they do not have a
"genuine illness", deliberately harm themselves, and refuse to cooperate in treatment, just like self-poisoners and addicts do'
(Vandereycken, 1993, p. 13). Hence, physicians tend to see anorectic patients as untrustworthy, obstinate, demanding, bothersome,
manipulative, and likely to polarize people, not only their family,
but also therapists. Feelings of helplessness in the middle of a
power struggle – the battle of control, wherein the doctor tries to
restore his authority – may lead to counteraggressive reactions

disguised as therapeutic measures, ranging from hospitalization to tube feeding (Vandereycken, 1993).

GENDER DIFFERENCES

Communication problems between patients and doctors can also be caused by gender differences between the parties involved. The vast majority of patients with eating disorders is female, whereas the skewed gender distribution of general practitioners is in the opposite direction. Gender differences can inhibit patients in trusting their doctors, while physicians have difficulty in understanding the patients (Dolan and Gitzinger, 1994). For female patients it is often difficult to reveal their eating behavior because they assume that male doctors do not understand why women are so concerned about growing fat (Noordenbos, 1991).

Male patients may also be reluctant to tell their doctors about their eating disorder, because many of them feel ashamed that they have a 'girl's disease'. This stereotyped idea about anorexia and bulimia as 'female' disorders also prevails in the mind of doctors. Hence, one can expect that eating disorders are very often overlooked in males (Andersen and Mickalide, 1983; Bryant-Waugh et al. 1992; Mitchell and Goff, 1984).

> Nick showed all the characteristics of anorexia nervosa, but his family physician thought he had a disturbance in growth hormones, for which he referred the 15-year-old boy to an endocrinologist. After six weeks, when all kinds of tests turned out to be negative, Nick was sent home with the prescription of a diet! It took a few years before he was correctly diagnosed and treated.

Physician bias may also explain why eating disorders are overlooked in non-whites or in lower socioeconomic classes (King, 1989; Striegel-Moore and Smolak, 1996). Research shows that women from non-western cultures tend to adopt the cultural ideal of slenderness when they live in western societies, and hence are equally at risk for developing an eating disorder (Nasser, 1986).

TREATMENT DECISIONS

When the general practitioner has passed the difficult stage of diagnosing anorexia or bulimia nervosa, comes the next step:

What to do now? Should he/she treat this patient or refer her, but to whom? Does the patient need a dietitian, a psychologist, a psychiatrist, or another medical specialist? A Dutch survey in 108 patients with eating disorders showed that 38 per cent of them received medication from their general practitioners: vitamines, laxatives (for constipation), hormones (to induce menses), drugs to stimulate or suppress the appetite. But in many cases patients did not take the prescribed medication (Noordenbos, 1992). Although some form of counseling in patients with a subclinical or partial eating disorder can be helpful, most physicians do not engage themselves due to lack of time. King (1989) showed that the intervention by general practitioners in eating-disordered patients was minimal and in no case did the physician attempt to manage the problem all by him/herself.

The same Dutch survey (Noordenbos, 1992) revealed that of the 93 patients who went with their eating disorder to a general practitioner: 53 per cent were referred to a medical specialist, 19 per cent to a psychiatrist and 10 per cent to a psychologist. The rest was 'treated' by the general practitioner who prescribed a diet (16 per cent) or medication (38 per cent). The retrospective information from this survey applied to the patients' management in the 1980s. A study of 30 general practitioners several years later showed a changing picture in their way of handling eating disorders: they referred patients more often to a community mental health center (31 per cent), to a psychologist (23 per cent) or a psychiatrist (23 per cent), while only 8 per cent was sent to a medical specialist (Aerts, 1992; Dresscher, 1993). Moreover, the prescription of medication was reduced to 23 per cent. The same study showed that 27 per cent completely denied the illness, 46 per cent of the patients minimized the eating disorder and was reluctant to be treated, 19 per cent dropped out, while only 8 per cent had a positive attitude towards treatment. A main goal for the general practitioner might be to help the patients realize the seriousness of their disorder and to motivate them for therapy (Silber and d'Angelo, 1991; Nicolai and Winants, 1994).

POSSIBILITIES OF SECONDARY PREVENTION BY GENERAL PRACTITIONERS

We will focus on two major issues with respect to general practitioners: (1) improving their ability to identify anorexia and bulimia nervosa at an early stage, and (2) changing their attitude and communication with these patients.

SHORTENING PATIENT AND DOCTOR DELAY

Patients should be informed at an earlier stage about the negative consequences of their eating disorder and about the possibilities of treatment. They have to be encouraged to discuss their eating behavior as well as their underlying problems and they have to be assured that they can gain from an adequate treatment. One such possibility of patient education is the use a short brochure about eating disorders available in the waiting room of general practitioners. The Dutch Association of Anorexia and Bulimia Nervosa has distributed such a brochure among general practitioners, entitled 'When the scales are your enemy'.

Patients with eating disorders often start to tell only a part of their real story and expect that the doctor will ask more questions about their eating behavior. General practitioners should realize that for these patients it is often threatening to discuss their eating and slimming behavior. When an eating disorder is presumed, one can start with the following questions (Yanovski, 1991): 'Many young women have concerns about food and weight. Do you have such concerns?' or 'Many young people have trouble with eating too much. Has this been a problem for you?'. If the patient says yes, the physician can ask in a sympathetic and nonjudgmental manner about the following topics:

- eating behavior
- (self-induced) vomiting
- use of laxatives and diuretics
- general physical condition
- attitudes towards body shape and weight
- physical exercises and sports
- self-criticism and lack of self-esteem
- mood disturbances

- perfectionistic behavior and fear of failure
- social contacts with peers
- relationship with parents (boyfriend, spouse)
- menstruation pattern
- possibly negative sexual experiences

Although the patient often is too ashamed to answer these questions, merely asking them gives the patient already the feeling that the physician is informed about the features and background of anorexia and bulimia nervosa (Noordenbos, 1991). The conversation should take place in a non-judgmental atmosphere and without showing distrust, even when the physician senses that the patient is not (yet) willing to reveal 'the whole truth'. In younger patients it is important to include the parents in the assessment, because their information might lead more quickly to the diagnosis especially in denying patients (Vandereycken, Kog and Vanderlinden, 1989).

General practitioners have to be better informed about the early signals of anorexia and bulimia nervosa, the so-called subclinical eating disorders (Button and Whitehouse, 1981) or partial syndromes (King, 1989). The diagnosis should be based mainly on behavioral characteristics of the disorder instead of being the result of an exclusion process. More specialized physical examinations should only be carried out in case of doubt about the diagnosis. All too often patients are subjected to physical examinations which can retard the start of an appropriate treatment (Vandereycken and Meermann, 1984; Whitehouse et al., 1992).

IMPROVING THE DOCTOR-PATIENT RELATIONSHIP

Patients with eating disorders hesitate to disclose their behaviors, thoughts and feelings. General practitioners should view this as part of the problem of having an eating disorder. It is important to compliment the courage of the patient to discuss the eating disorder, even when she only reveals a small part of it. The first contacts are the most difficult, because these patients often 'test' whether the clinician can be trusted. One should avoid a battle over 'who is in control here', which implies that the physician has to accept for a while feeling helpless or manipulated. 'It is precisely when the patient can attribute these feelings to a therapist who can accept and endure these feelings himself, that the patient is first able to achieve personality changes and to experience a greater sense of intrapsychic integration' (Cohler, 1977, p. 386).

The patients' denial of being ill, secretiveness of eating habits and pseudo-happiness are only a camouflage for their own helplessness and lack of basic trust. General practitioners have to understand that the resistance to eat is not a deliberate decision of the patient. Moreover, starvation by itself leads to narrowed consciousness and cognitive dysfunctioning. Only in the process of therapy will the clinician be the witness of growing awareness and recognition by the patients of their real emotional state (Vandereycken, 1993).

Here the gender difference should also be taken into account. 'Whether the therapist is male or female can influence the way in which specific gender-related issues are dealt with in therapy: problems of body experience and sexuality, ambivalence about gender identity, the relationship with their mother, and the need for a role model' (Zunino, Agoos and Davis, 1991). Therefore, feminist therapists claim that women should be treated by a female doctor or therapist (Stockwell and Dolan, 1994). But no research data support this claim; it is more a matter of opinion. When possible, the best might be to leave the choice of a female or male physician/therapist to the patients themselves.

DISCUSSION

General practitioners can play an important role in secondary prevention (early identification and intervention) of eating disorders, but they are hampered by many problems most of which we have described in this chapter. Recent research in the Netherlands shows that general practitioners became more familiar with eating disorders, prescribe less medication, and refer more often to a dietician, a psychologist, a psychiatrist, or an outpatient clinic for eating disorders (Aerts, 1992; Dresscher, 1993). To realize secondary prevention both patient and doctor delay have to be shortened and the treatment of anorectic and bulimic patients has to be improved. However, until now, there are no special prevention program to realize these goals.

A major problem for developing a special prevention program

in primary care is that for physicians eating disorders constitute only a marginal problem; on average they have relative few (new) patients with anorexia or bulimia nervosa (King, 1989; Hoek, 1991, 1993; Whitehouse et al., 1992). Moreover physicians have to make choices in their continuing education programs and it might be expected that they don't give priority to a special course on eating disorders. This does not mean that nothing has been done to improve the diagnosis and intervention by general practitioners. In recent years the following activities have been developed in the Netherlands.

Since 1970, a continuous morbidity registration has been performed in a Dutch network of general practitioners, who together are seeing nearly 150,000 patients a year, that is about 1 per cent of the Dutch population (Barteld et al., 1989). These general practitioners are experienced in registering illnesses and they record every year the data on a few selected disorders. Using this registration system Hoek and coworkers (1995) have studied the registration of anorexia and bulimia nervosa by 58 general practitioners from 1985 to 1989. Annually these doctors received detailed information on eating disorders by means of a circular with information about anorexia and bulimia nervosa and through special meetings convened for this purpose in which they received oral instructions about the detection of eating disorders. In the period concerned, these general practitioners were asked to consider in each patient they saw whether it might possibly be a case of anorexia or bulimia nervosa (according to the DSM-III-R criteria). In case of doubt the researchers asked the physicians for more detailed information or made the decision for them.

In the period 1985–1989, 60 patients received a first diagnosis of anorexia nervosa (an incidence of 8.1. per 100,000 persons/year) and 85 patients a first diagnosis of bulimia nervosa (an incidence of 11.5 per 100,000 persons/year). These results were higher than those found in earlier research. With the forementioned registration system, before 1985 only 28 patients with anorexia nervosa and 31 patients with bulimia nervosa had been detected (Hoek et al., 1995). These findings show that special training of general practitioners can improve their ability to diagnose eating disorders, but the study also confirms the difficulties to detect eating disorders. Although the general practitioners in these study were better informed, they inevitably have missed some cases, because eating disorders are characterized by taboo and denial. In general it was difficult to detect patients with normal-weight bulimia nervosa, although this is the most common condition in a clinical sample (Hoek et al., 1995).

Because of these promising results, it appears to be important to provide all general practitioners with specific information about eating disorders. To reach these goal the following activities in the Netherlands can be mentioned. The Dutch Foundation of Anorexia and Bulimia Nervosa has distributed to all general practitioners a brochure entitled 'When the scales are your enemy'. It informs about the characteristics of anorexia and bulimia nervosa, their physical, psychological and social consequences, and the possibilities of treatment. Patients can find this brochure in the waiting room of their doctor. A Community Center for Mental Health Care and a Center for Women and Health Care have published similar brochures, one for physicians ('To eat or not to eat, that is the question') and one for lay-people ('Do I eat or not'). Both brochures are widely distributed among general practitioners. The Center for Women and Health Care also regularly organises small courses for family physicians about how to diagnose and treat eating disorders. Finally, several articles about eating disorders have appeared in a leading Dutch journal for general practitioners.

All these activities are directed at improving the knowledge, attitude and communication of physicians with respect to patients with eating disorders. However, we are lacking scientific data about the effects of these 'prevention' activities on the diagnostic and therapeutic abilities of general practitioners. Nevertheless, the research by Hoek et al. (1995) shows a promising way for the future: better information may lead to better prevention.

REFERENCES

Aerts, J.J.M. (1992) *Early identification and diagnosis of anorexia and bulimia nervosa by general practitioners* (in Dutch), Dissertation, University of Maastricht.

American Psychiatric Association (1994) *Diagnostic and Statistical Manual of Mental Disorders, 4th edition (DSM-IV)*. Washington, D.C.: Author.

Andersen, A.E. and Mickalide A.D. (1983) 'Anorexia nervosa in the male: An underdiagnosed disorder'. *Psychosomatics*, 24: 1066–75.

Bartelds, A.I.M., Fracheboud, J. and Van der Zee, J. (1989) *The Dutch Sentinel Practice Network: Relevance for Public Health Policy*, Utrecht: Netherlands Institute of Primary Health Care (NIVEL).

Bryant-Waugh, R.J., Lask, B.D., Shafran, R.L. and Fosson, A.R. (1992) 'Do doctors recognise eating disorders in children?' *Archives of Diseases in Childhood*, 67: 103–5.

Button, E.J. and Whitehouse, A. (1981) 'Subclinical anorexia nervosa'. *Psychological Medicine*, 11: 509–16.

Clarke, M.G. and Palmer, R.L. (1983) 'Eating attitudes and neurotic symptoms in university students'. *British Journal of Psychiatry*, 142: 299–304.

Cohler, B.J. (1977) 'The significance of therapists' feelings in the treatment of anorexia nervosa'. In Feinstein, F.A. and Giovacchini, P.L. (eds) *Adolescent Psychiatry: Volume 5* (pp. 352–86). New York: Jason Aronson.

Daaleman, C.J. (1991) *More or less: Research on the prevalence of anorexia nervosa, bulimia nervosa, and obesity* (in Dutch), Warnsveld: RIGG Oost Gelderland.

de Bloois, M. (1987) *Anorexia nervosa from within. How do patients with anorexia nervosa evaluate their treatment?* (in Dutch), Dissertation, University of Leiden.

Dhondt, A.D.F., Volman, H.G., Westerman, R.F., Weeda-Mannak, W.L. and Van der Horst, H.E. (1989) 'Bulimia nervosa: Do general practitioners signal this disorder?' (in Dutch). *Medisch Contact*, 44: 231–3.

Dolan, B. and Gitzinger, I. (eds) (1994) *Why Women? Gender Issues and Eating Disorders*, London: Athlone Press.

Dresscher, C.J.M. (1993) *Early recognition and diagnosis of eating disorders by general practitioners* (in Dutch), Dissertation, University of Leiden.

Herzog, W., Deter, H.C. and Vandereycken, W. (eds) (1992) *The Course of Eating Disorders. Long-Term Follow-up Studies of Anorexia and Bulimia Nervosa*, Berlin-Heidelberg: Springer Verlag.

Herzog, W., Rathner, G. and Vandereycken, W. (1992) 'Long-term course of anorexia nervosa: A review of the literature'. In Herzog, W., Deter, H.C. and Vandereycken, W. (eds) *The Course of Eating Disorders. Long-Term Follow-up Studies of Anorexia and Bulimia Nervosa* (pp. 15–29), Berlin-Heidelberg: Springer Verlag.

Hoek, H.W. (1991) 'The incidence and prevalence of anorexia nervosa and bulimia nevosa in primary care'. *Psychological Medicine*, 21: 455–60.

——(1993) 'Review of the epidemiological studies of eating disorders'. *International Review of Psychiatry*, 5: 61–74.

Hoek, H.W., Bartelds, A.I.M., Bosveld, J.J.F., van der Graaf, J., Limpens, V. Maiwald, M. and Spaaij, C.J.K. (1995) 'Impact of urbanization on detection rates of eating disorders'. *American Journal of Psychiatry*, 152: 1272–8.

King, M.B. (1989) 'Eating disorders in a general practice population. Prevalence, characteristics and follow-up at 12–18 months'. *Psychological Medicine*, Supplement.

Meadows, G.N., Palmer, R.L., Newball, E.U.M. and Kenrick, J.M.T. (1986) 'Eating attitudes and disorders in young women: A general practice based survey'. *Psychological Medicine*, 16: 351–7.

Mitchell, J.E. and Goff, G. (1984) 'Bulimia in male patients'. *Psychosomatics*, 25: 909–13.

Nasser, M. (1986) 'Comparative study of the prevalence of abnormal eating attitudes among Arab females students of both London and Cairo universities'. *Psychological Medicine*, 16: 621–5.

Nicolai, L. and Winants, Y. (1994) 'Early recognition and intervention in eating disorders' (in Dutch). In Noordenbos, G., Jedding, B. and Terheyden, Y. (eds) *Prevention of Eating Disorders* (pp. 86–96), Utrecht: SWP.

Noordenbos, G. (1989) 'Anorexia nervosa and sexual abuse' (in Dutch). *De Psycholoog*, 3: 122–9.

——(1991) *Eating Disorders: Prevention and Therapy* (in Dutch), Lochem: De Tijdstroom.

——(1992) 'Important factors in the process of recovery according to patients with anorexia nervosa'. In Herzog, W., Deter, H.C. and Vandereycken, W. (eds) *The Course of Eating Disorders. Long-Term Follow-up Studies of Anorexia and Bulimia Nervosa* (pp. 304–23), Berlin-Heidelberg: Springer Verlag.

——(1994) 'Problems and possibilities of the prevention of eating disorders'. *European Eating Disorders Review*, 2: 126–42.

Russell, G.F.M. (1992) 'The prognosis of eating disorders: A clinician's approach'. In Herzog, W., Deter, H.C. and Vandereycken, W. (eds) *The Course of Eating Disorders. Long-Term Follow-up Studies of Anorexia and Bulimia Nervosa* (pp. 198–213), Berlin-Heidelberg: Springer Verlag.

Silber, T.J. and D'Angelo, L.J. (1991) 'The role of the primary care physician in the diagnosis and management of anorexia nervosa'. *Psychosomatics*, 32: 221–5.

Szmukler, G.I. (1983) 'Weight and food preoccupation in a population of

English schoolgirls'. In Bergman, J.D. (ed.), *Understanding Anorexia Nervosa and Bulimia: Fourth Ross Conference on Medical Research* (pp. 21–8), Columbus (Ohio): Ross Laboratories.

Stockwell, R. and Dolan, B. (1994) 'Women therapists for women clients?' In Dolan, B. and Gitzinger, I. (eds) *Why Women? Gender Issues and Eating Disorders*, London: Athlone Press.

Striegel-Moore, R. and Smolak, L. (1996) 'The role of race in the development of eating disorders'. In Smolak, L., Levine, M.P. and Striegel-Moore, R. (eds) *The Developmental Psychopathology of Eating Disorders* (pp. 259–84), Mahwah (NJ): Lawrence Erlbaum Associates.

Theander, S. (1992) 'Chronicity in anorexia nervosa: Results from a Swedish long-term study'. In Herzog, W., Deter, H.C. and Vandereycken, W. (eds) *The Course of Eating Disorders. Long-Term Follow-up Studies of Anorexia and Bulimia Nervosa* (pp. 217–27), Berlin-Heidelberg: Springer Verlag.

Vandereycken, W. (1993) 'Naughty girls and angry doctors: Eating disorder patients and their therapists'. *International Review of Psychiatry*, 5: 13–18.

Vandereycken, W., Kog, E. and Vanderlinden, J. (1989) *The Family Approach to Eating Disorders: Assessment and Treatment*, London: PMA Publications.

Vandereycken, W. and Meermann, R. (1984) *Anorexia Nervosa: A Clinican's Guide to Treatment,* Berlin-New York: Walter de Gruyter.

Weeda-Mannak, W.L. (1981) 'The importance of early detection of anorexia nervosa' (in Dutch) *Tijdschrift voor Psychiatrie*, 23: 5–12.

——(1984) *Anorexia Nervosa: Towards an Early Identification*, Hilversum: Benedictus.

Whitehouse, A.M., Cooper, P.J., Vize, C.V., Hill, C. and Vogel, L. (1992) 'Prevalence of eating disorders in three Cambridge general practices: Hidden and conspicuous morbidity'. *British Journal of General Practice*, 42, 57–60.

Yanovski, S.Z. (1991) 'Bulimia nervosa: The role of the family physician'. *American Academy of Family Physicians*, 44: 1231–8.

Zunino, N., Agoos, E. and Davis, W.N. (1991) 'The impact of therapist gender on the treatment of bulimic women'. *International Journal of Eating Disorders*, 10: 253–63.

Index

[abbreviations: ED = eating disorder]